T0369059

UNIVERSAL TRUTH

Thinking outside the Box: Book II

UNIVERSAL TRUTH

Thinking outside the Box: Book II

DR. PETER C. ROGERS, D.D., PH.D

authorHOUSE®

AuthorHouse™
1663 Liberty Drive
Bloomington, IN 47403
www.authorhouse.com
Phone: 1-800-839-8640

First published by AuthorHouse   09/14/2011

ISBN: 978-1-4567-9560-3 (sc)
ISBN: 978-1-4567-9559-7 (ebk)

Library of Congress Control Number: 2011915091

Printed in the United States of America

Any people depicted in stock imagery provided by Thinkstock are models, and such images are being used for illustrative purposes only.
Certain stock imagery © Thinkstock.

This book is printed on acid-free paper.

Table of Contents

Special Thanks

I would like to thank my beautiful wife Elsa Rogers for her undying love and support; my mother Diane Alexander for never criticizing my views on spirituality and for loving me in spite of them; my grandfather Orrin Murray Jr. for his companionship, his time and his razor—sharp criticism; my grandmother Louise Murray for her unwavering faith in the God of her understanding; my step-daughter Kimsandra Williams for being one of my greatest teachers in the area of patience and acceptance; my Higher Self for keeping me on course and for knowing the plan long before I chose to experience it; the fellowship of Narcotics Anonymous for a new way of life; the Universe for the instruction; planet Earth for the classroom; and everyone who supports me and the higher consciousness movement; the Enlightened Ones; the Ascended Masters; the Spirit Guides; all the great writers, teachers and illuminated beings here on this planet during our time of ascension. And finally, I would like to thank my publisher my agent and my publicist . . . all of whom have not yet materialized in my life.

"Truth is the imperative condition of all well-being. To be sure, to know the truth and to stand confidently on it is a satisfaction beside which no other is comparable. Truth is the underlying verity, the condition precedent to every successful business and social relation. The fruit of this knowledge is, as it were, a gift of the gods. It is the truth that makes men free. Not only free from every lack and limitation, but free from sorrow, worry and care."

—*Charles F. Haanel*

Introduction

"Believe not because some old manuscripts are produced, believe not because it is your national belief, believe not because you have been made to believe from your childhood, but reason truth out, and after you have analyzed it, then if you find it will do good to one and all, believe it, live up to it and help others to live up to it."

—Buddha

I'm often asked what exactly is Metaphysics and how did I come to be a student of this branch of Science and Philosophy? I know in trying to answer this question, it would require both time and understanding as there are many schools of thought on what this actually deals with. So let's take a closer look at Metaphysics as well as Truth in order to determine the foundation for this book. Hopefully together we can arrive at an understanding that resonates in the core of our being with a resounding; *YES . . . We hold these truths to be self-evident*!

If we look at Metaphysical Truth from a rudimentary level, it basically deals with the invisible world of phenomenon. However, if we were to actually delve further into this branch of science we would find that Metaphysics deals with so much more than just phenomenon. It deals with everything in the manifested Universe as well as things unseen. It's a transcendental knowledge. In fact, it's the origin, or should I say, the reason for everything. Now don't come unglued, let me explain. It would appear by this statement that Metaphysics is the source or cause of all things in the manifested world because we know that everything in the visible world was derived from the source of all creation which we know to be God, the Universe or the Creator. It really doesn't matter which label you associate with it because it's all the same principle. Having said this then; the study of Metaphysics deals with the origin of all things.

In past times, Metaphysics was referred to as the First Philosophy by Aristotle and before the development of modern science it was addressed as Natural Philosophy. But, by the turn of the eighteenth century, it had begun to be addressed as a science to make the distinction from philosophy. Therefore, Metaphysics is a branch of science that investigates certain principles of reality and yet transcends that of any particular science. It is the philosophical inquiry into the nature of existence and it deals with the nature of being. As such, it touches upon branches of study that include both "Cosmology" (which is the study of the Cosmos or Universe) as well as "Ontology" (which is concerned with the nature and relations of being).

Cosmology is the branch of Metaphysics that deals with the Universe as the totality of all phenomena in space and time which addresses questions about the Cosmos that are beyond the scope of physical science. It is primarily concerned with such things as; the origin of the Universe, first cause, and the reason for existence. While Ontology deals with the philosophical study of the nature of not only being but also existence and reality in general. It further postulates the claim of certain existences that may or may not be held by the majority. Ontology investigates not only what types of existences there are in the world but also what relation these things have on one another in particular the effects that you and I have on each other as well as our environs.

Simply put, Metaphysics goes beyond the confines of ordinary logic or reason and touches upon the unmanifested world of reality. In dealing with reality, we must therefore be referring to truth. But "truth is relative" you say, therefore how can one reality be constant for everyone? And the answer is—it's not. Truth comes in many shapes and sizes and is therefore localized in the individual. It extends outward onto the planet by the honoring of every person's truth as a manifestation of the One Truth. But what holds true for one may not hold true for all. This is why there are countless belief systems, philosophies and understandings. For example; there is the belief in correspondence which says that truth should actually correspond with the state of affairs. Or the coherence theory which says that truth has to have a proper fit within the whole system. Or the constructive theory which holds that truth is constructed by the social processes and is historically and culturally specific. And finally, the consensus theory which supposes that truth is whatever is agreed upon. But one thing does hold true for all and this is that we must all seek our own understanding of truth and honor that which we hold to be true for ourselves while at the same time honoring the truth of others. This allows each of us to coexist within our philosophies without needing to change each others beliefs.

Herein you will find various truths, some of which you may be familiar with and some of which you may not. Be that as it may, as a seeker of truth, you should always be willing to expand upon your foundation by opening up to greater and greater knowledge. The Universe is forever revealing itself in the form of wisdom to those that are willing to accept it regardless of how unusual it may appear. Often times we become hindered in this acceptance by the rigidity in our beliefs. We condition ourselves only for certain truths while truth is eternal and will forever evolve into greater forms of itself. In The Emerald Tablets of Thoth it reads, "The infinite jewel of truth can never be fully read for truth brings forth extensions of itself and as one truth is mastered other truths appear."

Universal laws are static and immutable much like truth itself and while truth appears to be constantly shifting and changing like the wind re-shaping itself into newer and fresher versions for different eras, it remains constant for the most part. Only the open-minded and the fluid thinkers can grasp the ever-changing nature of truth. Whatever the case, a change in the status quo is long over-due. It is time for us to break free of the out-dated, systematic approach to our existence and seek to formulate new ways of viewing the world in which we live. A new and updated paradigm is necessary if we are to grow spiritually. But we must first open our minds and realize that the change we seek to experience in the world has to first come from within. *We* have to be the change that we desire to see in others and as Peter Joseph states in the addendum to the movie *Zeitgeist*, "In the end, the most relevant change must occur first inside of you. The real revolution is the revolution of consciousness, and each one of us first needs to eliminate the divisionary, materialistic noise we have been conditioned to think is true while discovering, amplifying and aligning with the signal coming from our true empirical oneness—it is up to you."

Chapter One

Ancient Truth

Ancient Truth

"All through the ages has knowledge existed, never been changed, though buried in darkness, never been lost, though forgotten by man."

—*The Emerald Tablets*

In ancient times, truth was a thing to be cherished. It was coveted and pursued. Many of the truths of ancient times have served as a doorway in which for modern man to crossover into a limitless understanding of being. This form of seeking often led to a heightened sense of awareness among the adepts. Prior to one becoming enlightened, he or she would undergo ceremonial initiations as rights of passage into the everlasting state of consciousness. Before the "initiate" could partake of this godly state, they would undergo various processes enabling them to overcome fear and other debilitating emotions. They would come face-to-face with their deepest fears and ultimately rise above them. They came to understand some of the greatest mysteries of the stars the planets and the processes of life and death. Among some of these ancient bearers of truth were *Thoth/Hermes* and his female counterpart *Ma'at* of which we will discuss in greater detail in the forthcoming chapters.

In discussing ancient truth, we will also be looking at some of the age old practices of *Sacred Geometry,* as well as integral figures of history such as *Ra, Isis, Osiris, Horus* and some of *The Original Trinities.* We will also seek to understand the ancient truth behind *Alchemy* and the process of mental forces and the transmutation of one kind of mental vibration into others as opposed to the changing of one kind of metal into another. Many of these ancient truths have since been crystallized into creeds which was never the intent. Unfortunately, many of the teachers of these truths ultimately became priests whereby these mystic teachings became co-mingled with theology giving way to various religious superstitions, cults and creeds that have systematically led us away from the true and divine presence in the Universe. Accordingly, this has been the case with the Gnostics and the early Christians having been lost under the rule of Constantine who squelched their original teachings and philosophies with theology thus formulating the Christian Church which is still to this very day trying to find its way back to its ancient origins in mystic truth.

Throughout these pages you will learn of truths that are heretofore not known by many and yet understood by only the few. Truth, real truth is not known by the masses for if it were, there would be no hierarchy. For this reason, truth is concealed away from the world by the select few for fear of us becoming *"like the gods."* Consequently, many of us today wouldn't recognize truth even if it were to walk up to us and introduce itself. For some, truth seems stranger than fiction and for this reason; we close ourselves off from it at every opportunity. It is only when we are ready to welcome in a new understanding that certain truths will become apparent to us. In the Kybalion it reads:

> "So that according to the teachings, the passage of this book to those ready for the instruction will attract the attention of such as are prepared to receive the teaching. And likewise, when the pupil is ready to receive the truth, then will this book come to him, or her. Such is The Law. The Hermetic Principle of Cause and Effect, in its aspect of The Law of Attraction, will bring lips and ear together pupil and book in company. So mote it be!"

If you are reading this book, consider yourself ready for these truths for were it not so, you wouldn't have attracted it into your awareness. Nothing comes to us until we are ready to receive it. When the student is ready, the teacher always appears and one of the greatest teachers of ancient times was none-other-than Thoth of Egypt, the Atlantean who later manifested in the form of the Greek god Hermes.

Hermetic Wisdom

"When the ears of the student are ready to hear, then cometh the lips to fill them with wisdom."

—*The Kybalion*

Long ago, there existed one with untold wisdom of things not yet known by most. He was the Atlantean priest-king Thoth who later incarnated into the being known as *Hermes Trismegistus* (thrice great), known by the ancient Egyptians as "The Great Great" and "Master of Masters" and the "God of Wisdom" in ancient Greece. He was an immortal who conquered death, passing only when he willed and even then, not through death. He ruled ancient Egypt for roughly 14,000 years between 50,000 BCE and 36,000 BCE and he was considered to be the "Scribe of the gods." It is believed that all the fundamental and basic esoteric teachings of every race can be traced back to Hermetic Teachings. Hermes was the father of the Occult Wisdom; the founder of Astrology; and the discoverer of Alchemy. The original truths taught by Hermes have been preserved in tact and passed along to the few who are ready to comprehend and master them. However, there are still many who are not ready for such truths or who would even recognize them if they were presented to them. Hermes left many of his teachings in what is called *The Emerald Tablets* which has various characters engraved upon them in the Atlantean language. These characters are attuned only to thought waves which releases the associated mental vibration in the mind of the readers. However, he is widely known for *The Seven Hermetic Principles* upon which the entire Hermetic philosophy is based. They are:

> ➢ *The Principle of Mentalism*
> ➢ *The Principle of Correspondence*
> ➢ *The Principle of Vibration*
> ➢ *The Principle of Polarity*
> ➢ *The Principle of Rhythm*
> ➢ *The Principle of Cause and Effect*

> *The Principle of Gender*

Following is a detailed explanation of each of these Hermetic principles.

The Principle of Mentalism

"The All is Mind; the Universe is mental."

—The Kybalion

The Universe is mental and therefore all is Mind. All creation flows from the Cosmic Mind of the all encompassing source. Within this Mind, you and I live and move and have our being and nothing exists outside of this awareness. Mind is everything. There is nothing in creation that did not come from the all pervading Mind we call the Universal Intelligence. We refer to this as "Spirit" or "Essence" because essentially it is the living Mind of all. There is only the one Mind, all else is merely a derivative of it. We each share in this one Mind and although it may seem as if we each possess our own individual mind in which to think, in reality we are all entangled in this massive intelligence which adheres to our ability to utilize this Great Mind.

We are connected to this Universal Mind and are therefore able to partake of its creative properties by way of our thought process. The Universal Mind can create in no other way except mentally. So too can we, only our creation is in no way comparable to the vastness of Infinite Mind. While the two are definitely similar in kind, they are infinitely different in degree much like the drop of water is similar to the ocean it is by far not the ocean in its entirety. Therefore the Universe and all therein is simply a mental creation of the All.

Through the Principle of Mentalism or the art of Mental Chemistry, we can utilize what is referred to as Mental Transmutation whereby mind may be transmuted from state to state; degree to degree; condition to condition; pole to pole; and vibration to vibration in order to change the very world in which we exist. And since the Universal Mind is mental in nature, this process is therefore the art of changing conditions of the Universe along the lines of matter, force and mind. Understanding this then, enables us to not only change mental conditions but since all is subjected to mind, then we become masters at controlling material conditions through the very process of Mentalism and Mental Transmutation.

The Principle of Correspondence

"As above, so below; as below, so above."

—*The Kybalion*

The Principle of Correspondence basically states that there is a harmony which exists between things that are seen and the unseen. In other words, anything done on one level has an immediate effect on all levels; *As above, so below; as below, so above.* This means that that which is below (meaning the slowed down vibration of matter in the material form) directly corresponds to that which is above, (meaning the higher vibrations of the spiritual realms) all of which is for the purpose of fulfilling the one great cause.

Subsequently, what happens on one level simultaneously happens on all levels. The spiritual level has a direct impact on the mental level and the mental level in turn has a direct influence on the physical level. The Universe being the spiritual, acts as the macrocosm or the bigger aspect of the whole while you and I and all of creation serve as the microcosm or the smaller aspect. In truth, since we are all connected to the spiritual internally, then by reason, the entire Universe or the macrocosm resides right within our being. All that is without originates from within. *As within, so without; as without, so within.* It stands to reason then, that by understanding one, you inherently come to know the other.

There is a constant correspondence or agreement between the Universal and the various forms of phenomena on different planes. This is made possible because everything within the Universe emanates from the same source. Metaphysically, there are numerous planes of existence beyond that of the physical world. Understanding the principle of correspondence allows us to know how things function on the multiple planes of existence. Within each plane, lies several degrees of awareness or existence, each of which acts in accordance with spiritual laws. These levels or degrees are simply various forms of vibration which determines the plane in which something is to exist. Not only are there different rates of vibration that distinguish the difference between planes but also different rates of motion. The degree or the rate of vibrations is what constitutes the degrees of measurement or the plane in which something exists; the higher the degree or rate of vibration, the higher the plane which ultimately determines the quality of manifestation occupying that particular plane. So we know that when one is affected, all is affected in like manner. This principle applies to all levels on all planes of the spiritual, mental and physical realms—it is Universal Law and nothing escapes its reach. The Principle of Correspondence manifests in all and for all as there is a correspondence, harmony and agreement between all planes on all levels. *As above, so below; as below, so above.*

The Principle of Vibration

"Nothing rests; everything moves; everything vibrates."
—The Kybalion

The Principle of Vibration basically states that the only difference between certain manifestations of Matter, Energy, Mind and even Spirit is the rate in which they are vibrating; the higher the vibration, the higher the plane. Accordingly, there are millions upon millions of varying rates and degrees of vibration ranging from the highest level of vibration of the One, down to the mineral world where matter is considered to be inanimate. The rate at which the Divine resonates is so extremely high that it is literally in a state of rest. This is analogous to seeing an object moving so fast that it appears to be standing still;

somewhat similar to the wheel on a car moving at high speeds but appears to be fixed. Through the process of Mental Transmutation, we are able to mentally change the rate of our own vibration which will in turn allow us to resonate on a higher frequency. And since we know that everything has a frequency or rate of vibration, what is needed is to simply fix our mind on the desired condition in which we would like to achieve and the transmutation will occur. One thing we must always be aware of when seeking to raise our vibration is our associations. If we constantly surround ourselves with people that are emitting lower or negative frequencies, chances are through the process of inductance, the stronger vibration will subdue the lesser causing our efforts to become thwarted. This is not to say their will is much stronger than ours but rather the frequency in which we like to maintain is lessened to a degree whenever we are in the presence of negative people. This is due to the contention between energies. As such, we can become drained whenever we are not functioning at our peak levels and at times it can become very difficult to remain resilient against lower vibrations. By the same token, we too have the ability to raise the vibration of others through our resonance. Our strong rate of vibration can often help others to feel uplifted or invigorated simply by being in our presence. By having an understanding of this law, we can learn to not only control our own mental vibrations but also that of others.

The Principle of Polarity

"Everything is dual; everything has poles; everything has its pair of opposites; like and unlike are the same; opposites are identical in nature, but different in degree, extremes meet; all truths are but half-truths; all paradoxes may be reconciled."
—*The Kybalion*

The Principle of Polarity basically states that everything is dual and that all manifested things have two sides; two aspects; or two poles with multiple degrees between the two extremes. Nothing is definitive or absolute and there are two poles or opposite aspects to all. In reality, opposites are really two extremes of the same thing having a range of difference between them. If we think in terms of hot and cold, we know they are basically varying degrees or temperatures of the same thing manifesting as either hot or cold based upon their rate of vibration. The same holds true for everything else we consider to be opposites such as; *light* and *darkness, large* and *small, hard* and *soft, black* and *white, sharp* and *dull, high* and *low, positive* and *negative, love* and *hate,* etc. etc., you get the picture. All are simply varying degrees of the same thing which can easily be transmuted by simply changing the vibration from one to the other, causing hate to become love and vice versa. As such; good and evil are essentially one in the same which can also be transmuted by altering the vibration of either.

This means everything "*is*" and "*is not*" at the same time and that all truths are but half-truths because here again, there are two sides to everything. Consequently, good and bad (terms I don't like to use) are not absolutes but rather different ends of the same scale. We refer to one as being good and that which is on the opposite end of the scale as being bad. But in reality, a thing is less good than the thing further along on the scale, but the same thing is ultimately "more good" according to the thing further down the scale and so on. The only difference being that of degree. The same holds true for the polarity of human beings who are both masculine and feminine in nature with the masculine being the positive pole and the feminine being the negative pole, each of which serves to bring balance and harmony to the whole being. When the poles are out of balance the equilibrium of the body is shaken and inharmony and disease can set in. This understanding of polarity within the whole being is crucial to having a balanced and well rounded existence allowing both the mental and the spiritual aspects to co-exist without one becoming the antithesis to the other. Perfect balancing of the polarities eliminates sickness and disease. Understanding the principle of polarity allows us to become less regimented in our outlook on life because we're beginning to understand that there are no absolutes and nothing is all good or all bad and there really is no such thing as good and evil but rather two extremes of the same thing vibrating at opposite ends of the scale which are merely being viewed differently.

The Principle of Rhythm

"Everything flows, out and in; everything has its tides; all things rise and fall; the pendulum-swing manifests in everything; the measure of the swing to the right is the measure of the swing to the left; rhythm compensates."

—The Kybalion

The Principle of Rhythm embraces the reality that everything is constantly in motion and nothing is ever truly at rest. In everything, there is a manifested measure of motion. There is a constant measure of motion in which everything is operating according to a certain rhythmic law of compensation. This allows for there to be a compensating swing from one pole to the other by way of the Universal pendulum. This swing is analogous to action and reaction, the ebb and flow of tides, rising and falling and it is felt and experienced by universes, suns, worlds, men, animals, mind, energy and all forms of matter. The Principle of Rhythm is very closely related to the Principle of Polarity although in dealing with this principle, we will find that there is a constant rhythm that manifests between the two poles.

We see this principle manifested daily in the rise and fall of the Sun, with the in-breathe and out-breathe of our bodies, through the change of seasons and even in the mental fluctuation and succession of moods, feelings and other changes within our very selves. Periods of joy can be followed by periods of sadness, while enthusiasm is followed by depression and courage is followed by fear. Coincidently, the measure of the swing to the right is the measure of the swing to the left; rhythm compensates. Therefore, the swing in one direction determines the swing in the opposite direction or to the opposite pole—the one balances, or counterbalances, the other. In other words sometimes the most joyful moments can be followed by some of the most sorrowful ones and what makes you laugh can also make you cry.

This principle is all pervading and it operates on all planes at all times and it can never be destroyed. It is the reason for the destruction of worlds; the rise and fall of nations; and the life history of all things. Universes are created; reach their extreme low point of materiality; and then begin their upward swing. Massive suns come into existence and then suddenly they begin the process of retrogression becoming dwarfs once again. Everything from vast galaxies to the smallest of matter must go through this rhythmic process of coming into being and then no longer existing. They are born, grow and die; only to be reborn again. There is a constant flow or cycle of birth and death and the pendulum is forever swinging.

While there is no escaping the principle of rhythm, our will is superior to the conscious manifestation of this principle. We may escape its effects through the law of Neutralization which allows us to rise up to a higher plane of the Ego transmuting our level of consciousness. Since there are two planes of consciousness, the lower and the higher, we can avoid the swing of the rhythmic pendulum by transmuting to the higher plane because the principle of rhythm only manifest on the lower plane. In other words, the swing of the pendulum still happens on the unconscious plane but the consciousness was not affected. This is considered self-mastery where we refuse to allow our moods or negative vibrations to affect us. Once we understand that the principle of rhythm is forever at work causing everything to ebb and flow, in and out, backwards and forwards, we can train ourselves to rise above the constant effects of this law using yet another law and while the pendulum ever swings, we may escape being carried along with it through our awareness of the law of neutralization and our strong resolve.

The Principle of Cause and Effect

"Every Cause has its Effect; every Effect has its Cause; everything happens according to Law; Chance is but a name for Law not recognized; there are many planes of causation, but nothing escapes the Law."—The Kybalion

The Principle of Cause and Effect states that every thing happens according to a series of events that eventually lead up to certain outcomes based upon a succession of causes. In other words, all things happen according to a law which states that nothing happens by chance and that chance is merely an expression pertaining to causes not yet known or understood. As such; the Universe is governed by these immutable laws of which nothing is exempt. I explain this principle in much greater detail in *Ultimate Truth: Book I.* Suffice to say; there is nothing that happens in our Universe without an initiating cause whether it is a thought, an event or a predetermined action. For every action, there is an equal reaction. Every occurrence has its cause. There is a cause for every effect and an effect for every cause.

In truth, nothing happens by chance because chance is merely a situation perceived as having no definite cause but in reality the cause is not yet known. But rest assured, there is always something to instigate every occurrence whether the cause is known or unknown. Careful examination will always show that nothing happens by chance otherwise it would be operating outside of the law and there is nothing within the Universe that can operate outside of its laws. If this were the case, it would be independent of the laws of the Universe rendering it superior to the original cause which is the All. Realistically, there is no accounting for anything within the Universe to be outside of or independent of its laws.

There is a relation existing between everything that has gone before, and everything that follows no matter how far back one has to trace the cause. There is always a "cause" and every event has its "be-cause." In fact, many things exist today because of a chain of events. This includes the formation of the stars, the planets, the Sun and the whole manifested Universe. Similar to the principle of rhythm, we can learn to rise above the ordinary plane of cause and effect by mentally rising to a higher plane. This allows us to become the cause in most cases rather than merely being subjected to effects.

The majority of people today are unaware of these truths. As such, they are always being subjected to the effects of the environment, stronger desires and the will of others that are aware of how to use these laws in their favor. They are carried about haphazardly like pawns on the chessboard of life. But we are able to be the "cause" by simply rising above the unconscious state to a higher plane where we then become the master of moods, characters, qualities, powers and environments. We become the mover instead of the pawn. We help in the game of life rather than being played by it. We utilize this law rather than being its tool. We are all susceptible to the ramifications of cause and effect but this doesn't mean that we can't obey these laws from a different vantage point as one knowing rather than one not knowing. We can obey these laws from a higher plane while mastering our situation and the situations around us on the lower planes. Since there is no denying the law of cause and effect, it would be in our best interest to know and understand how to become the cause thus enabling us to always be aware of the outcome or the effect.

The Principle of Gender

"Gender is in everything; everything has its Masculine and Feminine Principles; Gender manifests on all planes."
—*The Kybalion*

The Principle of Gender basically states that everything has both masculine and feminine qualities much like the *yin* and *yang* concept that I discuss in greater detail in *Ultimate Truth: Book I*. Simply put, all things have dual aspects to include an out-going or aggressive, active principle as well as an in-going or passive, silent principle. This principle is not referring to gender as in sex but rather gender as in masculine and feminine qualities. While it may be expressed on the physical plane in the form of male and female or gender, it also manifests on the mental and spiritual planes as well. However, gender is active in all phases of phenomena on each and every plane of existence. All things in the manifested Universe exist because of this principle and nothing can exist without these two faculties.

Everything and everyone has both aspects of gender within their makeup; within the male there also exists aspects of the female and within the female there are also aspects of the male. Each of these aspects is constantly seeking to strike a balance. Any upset in this balance will result in disharmony and or disease. The male or masculine aspect of humanity is considered to be the positive force and it is this characteristic that allows us to be actively involved in the processes of life through our out-ward expression. Its characteristics are that of warmth, dryness and light. On the other hand, the characteristics of the female or feminine aspects are considered to be the negative force and are that of being passive, dark or cold. This is not to say that the masculine energy is good in the sense of the word positive and the feminine is bad in the literal sense of the word negative. On the contrary, in fact, the so-called negative is truly the cause for the production of new forms and there is nothing negative or weak about it. The feminine principle is always the one doing the active creative work on all levels of reproduction although it cannot operate without the existence of the masculine which directs the energy toward the feminine principle during the process of creation. Therefore, gender is always in constant operation when it comes to energy and force.

A balance is struck between these two seemingly opposing forces in order to establish a cohesive unit. On the mental plane, the masculine principle corresponds to the so-called objective mind or the conscious mind which is the active aspect of thought while the feminine principle corresponds to the so-called subjective mind or sub-conscious mind. This dual aspect is present in the mind of every individual where the masculine is represented by the "I" or the aspect of being and the feminine is represented by the "Me" or the aspect of becoming. As such; the feminine is always poised to receive impressions as the sub-conscious mind while the tendency of the masculine is to express. One expresses while the other is impressed. Since the feminine is poised to receive, it has a much wider field of operation than does the masculine. The feminine is responsible for the creation of new thoughts, concepts and ideas which include the work of the imagination, while the masculine is focused on the work of the will. But without the will, the feminine would only generate mental images rather than being able to produce mental creations. Creation requires both the use of imagination as well as focused thought or will.

Under normal circumstances, both the masculine and feminine in our minds coordinate and act harmoniously. However, in most cases the average person is too lazy to display a strong enough will and they allow others with a more willful mind to do their thinking for them. Many of us are weak thinkers allowing those with stronger wills or minds to impose their thoughts upon us. Typically, this is seen in people who are magnetic. These are the people that are able to utilize the masculine principle to impress their ideas upon other people. It is through the awareness of mental gender that we are able to become willful people thus allowing our thoughts to be impressed upon the feeble thinkers. However, this is not about exerting our will onto others but rather understanding how thought works according to the law of gender. The masculine is the aspect of being while the feminine is the aspect of becoming. Therefore, the masculine projects thought or energy toward the feminine aspect of others which in turn takes the seed-thought and impresses it upon itself. In this way, we can learn to be more impressionable not only upon humanity but upon the Universe as well simply by understanding the principle of mental gender.

True Alchemy

Alchemy is a philosophy, and a spiritual way of life which seeks to achieve ultimate wisdom and immortality by the adherent. In ancient times, Egyptians held the reputation of being skillful workers in metals, and, according to Greek writers, they were familiar with the process of transmutation by learning how to separate gold and silver from the native matrix. The result was said to possess amazing powers associated with the underworld god Osiris who was credited with having magical properties. This is the scenario which gave way to the belief that magical powers existed in fluxes and alloys. There is very little doubt however, that Egyptian custom was the groundwork upon which the art of Alchemy was built. This is evident by the fact that Alchemy was first accredited to Hermes and all of his works. It has been practiced in Hermetic schools and philosophical systems spanning at least 4,000 years.

Essentially, Alchemy was known as the Art of Transmutation and the intended purpose was the transmutation of common metals into gold or silver. However, on a more esoteric level, it was actually practiced in hopes of creating a *"panacea,"* or a universal remedy that would cure all diseases and prolong life indefinitely. Although this was not the only use for this discipline, it was the one most widely accepted or documented.

In Hermeticism, the transmutation of lead into gold is actually a metaphor for the transmutation of the physical body. In looking at Alchemy as a spiritual discipline, the metaphysical aspects were actually the true basis of the art. Organic and inorganic chemical substances, physical states, and molecular material processes were all simply metaphors for spiritual entities, spiritual states, and, ultimately, transformations. Theoretically speaking, the transmutation of metals can also be thought of as a symbol of the change of the self to a state of higher consciousness and the discovery of the elixir as an extension of eternal life. However; the exact meaning of Alchemical Formulas and their true spiritual philosophies were concealed due to their conflict with the Christian Church and the threat of heresy. Even though the bible itself can be considered to be alchemical in nature if we look at the book of Exodus, where Moses grinds up the golden calf and gives it to the children of Israel to drink. Also, it was believed that the knowledge Moses received from the Egyptian priests, reflected what many thought to be an ancient, pure wisdom that had been corrupted over time but could be rediscovered.

As an art of ancient origins, the practice of Alchemy carried many connotations. For some, it was interpreted as an inquiry into man's relationship with the cosmos and the will of the Creator. This form of understanding was marked by a devotion and philosophy that could supposedly transform man into a perfect being. While on the other hand, there are those that would practice the art merely for the purpose of changing base metals into gold. But, in reality the transmutation of common metals into gold and the universal *"panacea"* ultimately symbolized an evolution from an imperfect, diseased, corruptible, and temporary state towards a more perfect, healthy, incorruptible, and everlasting state that would be indicated by mans progress from ignorance to enlightenment and spiritual truth.

Subsequently, Alchemy is both a symbolic practice, as well as the technical research into the nature of matter, and an imaginary exercise on the spirit of matter and its overall potential for change. While some Alchemists were driven by technological traditions, others were inspired by a more spiritual approach; this was based in large part on the discovery of some ancient texts presumably belonging to the Egyptian Hermes. This particular school of thought came to be known as *Renaissance Hermeticism*, whereby the celestial bodies were often observed through the intervention of a cosmic spirit or the link between God and physical matter. Their belief hypothesized that celestial qualities permeate everything in existence, and these Alchemists sought to extract such powers solely for the purpose of making useful medicines.

It was the Renaissance physician and Alchemist Paracelsus who set out to describe the physical Universe and the processes that maintained the life of the body in essentially alchemical terms. He stated that all of nature stemmed from an initial separation of light from dark, Earth from water, and so on, and the body operated by means of an Inner Alchemist, called the *"archeus."* This was a system which separated that which was pure from that which was not. In a work called *De Natura Rerum* (On the nature of things) Paracelsus notes, "Transmutation is when a thing loses its form or shape and is transformed so that it no longer displays at all its initial form and substance . . . . When a metal becomes glass or stone . . . when wood becomes charcoal . . . (or) . . . when cloth becomes paper . . . all of that is the transmutation of natural things." Based on this analogy, practically everyone in those times was engaged in Alchemy in some form or another. Paracelsus continues by saying, "Nature brings nothing to light which is completed in itself, rather, human beings have to do the completing and this completing is what is called Alchemy." The art of separation became the basis for natural philosophy and medicine; thus distinguishing between what Paracelsus called *"alchemia transmutatoria"* and *"alchemia medica."* Both of these types of Alchemy involved looking for a powerful agent that was capable of perfecting or healing. Paracelsus subscribed to the belief in the Greek concept of the four elements, but he also introduced the idea that the cosmos was formed from three spiritual substances which he called: the *"tria prima"* of Mercury, Sulfur and Salt. These are not the simple substances we recognize today, but rather broader principles that give every object both its inner essence and outward form. According to Paracelsus, Mercury represented the transformative agent of fusibility and volatility; Sulfur represented the binding agent between substance and transformation or flammability; while Salt represented the solidifying/substantiating agent of fixity and non-combustibility. The *"tria prima"* also defined our physical make-up where Sulfur embodied the soul or the emotions and desires; Salt represented the body; and Mercury symbolized the spirit or imagination, moral judgment, and the higher mental faculties. By understanding the chemical nature of the *"tria prima,"* a physician could then discover the means of curing disease which was the highly sought after *"panacea."*

That elusive agent was referenced by many names, including *"elixir of life," "grand magisterium,"* or *"Philosophers' Stone,"* which was thought to have its genesis in certain forms of matter. The Philosopher's Stone was the combination of both the male and female seed that forms gold. The composition of which was so veiled by symbolism as to make their precise identification extremely elusive and impossible to find by the untrained practitioner. The Philosopher's Stone was thought to be able to intensify one's power in Alchemy and grant the user immortality. It is believed that the only thing the Alchemist could still be subjected to was burning or drowning which were the two greater elements that were implemented into the creation of the Stone.

In Alchemy, nature is divided into four aspects: the dry, the moist, the warm and the cold, and all things in existence are derived from some aspect of these four parts. It is an original energy that was separated in space-time into distinct physical elements which were separated into four directions. It is perceived as transmutable through shared qualities or associations all of which could one day be reunited into a unified whole. Alchemy also considers nature to be divisible into two primary components; the male and the female and that nature is the divine breath, the central fire, invisible yet ever active. As such; the Alchemist has to be ever patient in following nature in its alchemical performance. They must also understand that like attracts like, and know how to obtain the nature of metals, which was produced by the four elements through the will of the Universal Intelligence and the imagination of nature. But we have to be very careful when utilizing such terms as they can easily be misinterpreted by someone that is not trained in the way of the Alchemist thus taking these to be literal references as opposed to the metaphysical nature offered by spirituality.

In more recent times, psychologist Carl Jung began to see Alchemy as a form of psychology dedicated to the achievement of individuation. He understood the psyche, the unconscious, and depth analysis to be a truly alchemical process, and the proverbial stone as a transformation in consciousness, which served as both the means and the goal of individuation. In this regard, Jung saw Alchemy as being comparable to that of Yoga in the East, and believed it to be more sufficient to the Western mind than Eastern religions and philosophies. At this point, he set out to prove the inner meaning of alchemical work as a spiritual path.

Another enthusiast of Alchemy was Isaac Newton who suggested that the largest particles of every sort of matter, was composed of very subtle particles surrounded by larger unpredictable particles which piled up like rings or shells around an unstable nucleus. He held that every single substance was composed of particles equivalent to tiny universes. It was Newton's belief that transmutation occurred when the larger particles of a substance were reduced to smaller particles and then rearranged. Newton was very fond of ancient texts, especially those relating to the works of Hermes, and he collected bits and pieces of alchemical wisdom in the form of transcriptions, extracts, and collations of ancient, medieval, and contemporary alchemical authorities. Newton believed in the presence of spiritual agents in nature concluding that metals could both grow and decay as part of the cycle of creation in which the return to chaos would then give rise to newer substances. It is believed that Isaac Newton devoted considerably more of his writing to the study of Alchemy than he did to either optics or physics, for which he is famous.

The practice of Alchemy somehow changes the mind and spirit of the Alchemist. Understandably, this causes a transmutation in consciousness. The art of transmutation is nothing more than finding the Philosopher's Stone within the inner workings of spirit and thus seeking to change the molecular structure of thought energy. We are all Alchemist in the sense that each and everyday of our lives we seek to change that in which we're displeased into something more appealing. We rearrange some things here-and-there just as if we were engaged in a chemical process. We use the elixir of thought vibration to literally rearrange the chemical structure within our bodies. This elixir of positive vibrations permeates every cell of our being thus bringing about a transfiguration. What was once lacking in value such as lead now becomes gold and much like the Sheppard boy in the famous story written by Paulo Coelho in *The Alchemist*, we are each seeking to find our hidden treasure by pursuing our own personal legend.

Throughout our journey, we will come to find that Alchemy in its truest sense is nothing more than coming into our own personal greatness. We will find that the language of the Alchemist is about learning to communicate with the Soul of the World through signs, omens and by simply listening to our hearts desires because it is in that yearning that we become nearer to our true power. In doing so, we come to know our own soul which is actually the Soul of God. Throughout our transformation, we will gradually start to notice that all things change and they are continuously changing or being transformed into something different and perhaps even better than they were prior. Symbolically, gold has evolved beyond any other metals thus far making it the example of our own evolutionary goals as spiritual beings. It's no secret that if we subject metal to extreme temperatures that it's just a matter of time before it begins to free itself of any impurities leaving only the purest nature of itself. So too is it with you and I. Therefore, ridding ourselves of any impurities starts to become our own "Master Work" where we are able to discover for ourselves what the true elixir of life is thus transforming us into the true Philosophers' Stone.

In centuries past, the Alchemist would spend countless years in their laboratories studying the effects of how fire could purify metals. Unbeknownst to them, they were actually purifying themselves through this very same practice. Discovering how to purify metals had actually led to them purifying themselves. This also holds true for each of us. Literally speaking, there is no magic potion or special elixir that will bring about perfect health or eternality. We are actually the Philosophers' Stone by virtue of our oneness with the Divine. We don't have to seek out any special formulas or secret concoctions in order to have all we desire in life. Everything we could ever possibly need or want has already been provided for us on this journey, we just have to pay attention and listen to our heart for it knows all things because it is one with the same hand that created all. So, wherever our hearts are, that's where our secret treasure lies. There's a story of a man who wanted to find God, so he set out to find God on the highest mountain top but God was not there. He then looked in the deepest valley hoping to find God there, but still God was not there. Finally, in desperation he cried out asking where he could find God and the Universe responded by saying that God could not be found in all of these places but rather God could be found in the heart where man would never think to look. If it's transformation we're seeking, we should always be aware that in each and every small detail of our search, God is in the details, not the devil. In this regard, we are already Alchemists because we understand that we have to come in contact with the Soul of the world if we are ever to find our secret treasure and step into our own true greatness. As Alchemists we must come to realize that what we see with our eyes is only the physical aspect of God and the practice of Alchemy being a metaphysical process will transform the material plane through the progression of spiritual perfection. Everything ultimately seeks to become something better by pursuing its own personal legend and as we strive to become better versions of ourselves, we will notice that everything around us will also improve. Herein lies the Art of Transformation and the true process of Alchemy.

Ra: The Solar Deity

People have worshipped the Sun for thousands of years. The single most important, symbolic, and venerated symbol among the Egyptians was that of the Sun. The Sun itself was revered as a god under the name Ra (pronounced Ray). He was the Sun god in all its magnificence, and he was the creator of the Universe, and the first king of Egypt. All other gods originated from him and so they were him. Many of the primary gods of Egypt were associated with the Sun in some phase of its journey through the sky or its journey through the underworld at night.

Religion in ancient times was very similar to that of recent times. In fact, the Jesus figure is an adaptation from Ancient Egyptian Sun worship in the form of Ra the Sun god who was considered to be the creator of all things. Constantine the Great of Rome merged the solar gods of the Romans under the Catholic Christian Pope and to this very day, people are still worshipping the Sun without realizing it in the form of the Sun/Son of God. Each time we end our prayers with Amen, we should know this is one of the monikers given to *Ra* as *"Amen-Ra"* so we are actually paying homage to the Sun-god unconsciously. In the pyramid chambers the dead Pharaoh is called the "Son of Ra." From the Fifth Dynasty the title, "Son of Ra" was adopted by the Pharaohs. Ra was God, so they became "Sons of God"—Ramses means "Born of Ra" and therefore "Son of Ra."

As the story goes; the eye of Ra, is the mythological symbol for the Sun and it is believed that at some point, Shu and Tefnut, who were his twin children, became separated from him. He therefore sent his eye to find them. While his eye was searching, he replaced it with another one. When his eye returned with Shu and Tefnut, he wept with joy, and thus his tears created humankind. However, his eye was enraged at having been replaced so he placed it on his forehead so that it could rule the world where it later became associated with the Sun while the second eye became associated with the moon.

The Sun-god Ra was indicative of many things to the Egyptians. They saw meaning in different aspects of the Sun as it appeared in many different forms and with many different titles. They referred to him as the "King of gods," the "Creator of the Universe," the "Author of All Things," "Time Conductor" and "Direct Master of the Sun, Sky and Underworld." He was believed to have appeared by detaching himself from the primordial chaos and so he was the giver of life. He is often depicted as holding an ankh which was the symbol of eternity and life. This symbol represented not only the reliability but the wisdom of the Universe as well. To the Egyptians, the Universe was a balanced and constant place, one in which they could predict events with astonishing regularity and there was nothing that represented this rationality and regularity quite as powerfully as the daily course of the Sun. For it was the Sun-god Ra that passed through the upper world during the day bringing life and light with it, and during the night, he passed through the Underworld, bringing renewal and life to the dead souls. Ra personified the Sun as a vital force and he was the ultimate judge of the Universe. He was worshiped in Egypt as the Creator and Supreme God where he had his religious center at Heliopolis which was *The City of the Sun.* Coincidently, the holy bible is derived from the words holy which is an adaptation of *"helio"* which means Sun and *"biblio"* which means book; therefore the holy bible is simply the "Sun Book." As you read on, you will come to understand exactly where many of the religions of today were derived from.

Ma'at the Goddess of Justice

In Egyptian Mythology, the goddess Ma'at which was depicted as a woman wearing an ostrich feather on her head literally ruled everything. She was the daughter of Ra and she embodied Truth, Justice, Harmony and Balance. According to mythology, Ma'at was with Ra on his celestial barque when he first emerged from the primeval waters along with his company of gods and goddesses. When Ra emerged in his "Barque" for the first time and creation came into being, he was standing on the pedestal of Ma'at. Thus the Creator, Ra, lives by Ma'at and has established creation on Ma'at which represents the very order which constitutes creation. Therefore, it is said that Ra created the Universe by putting Ma'at in the place of chaos. So creation itself is Ma'at. Creation without order is chaos. Ma'at is a profound teaching in reference to the nature of creation and the manner in which human conduct should be cultivated. It refers to a deep understanding of divinity and the manner in which virtuous qualities can be developed in the human heart so as to come closer to the Divine.

Ma'at is also known as the "Eye of Ra," "Lady of Heaven," "Queen of the Earth," "Mistress of the Underworld" and the "Lady of the gods and goddesses." She has a dual form or *Maati* and in her capacity of God, she is *Shes-Ma'at* which means "ceaseless-*ness*" and regularity of the course of the Sun (i.e. the Universe). In the form of *Ma'ati*, she represents the south and the north which symbolize Upper and Lower Egypt as well as the higher and lower self. Ma'at is the personification of justice and righteousness upon which God has created the Universe and she is also the essence of God and creation. Therefore, it is Ma'at who judges the soul when it arrives in the judgment hall of Ma'at. Sometimes she becomes the scales upon which the heart of the initiate is judged. She judges the heart or unconscious mind of the initiate in an attempt to determine what extent the heart has lived in accordance with truth, correctness, reality, genuineness, uprightness, righteousness, justice, steadfastness and the unalterable nature of creation.

Ma'at is also a philosophy, a spiritual symbol as well as a cosmic energy or force which pervades the entire Universe. The Egyptians believed that the Universe was an ordered and rational place that always functioned with certainty and consistency. They understood how the Universe operated and all phenomena could be explained by an appeal to this understanding. The Universe itself was virtually maintained by the goddess Ma'at. As such; the cycles of the Universe remained forever constant where purity was rewarded and wrong deeds were punished. In fact, the Universe was said to be in perfect balance both morally and physically. The Egyptian word for this balance was truth or Ma'at which became the cornerstone of ancient Egyptian culture.

The Greeks called the underlying order of the Universe, *logos*, meaning, order, or pattern. The early Christians adopted the logos in order to explain the moral order of the Universe; the first line of the Gospel of John is, "In the beginning was the logos, and the logos was with God." But the concept for the Greeks and the Christians was more or less the same as Ma'at. The Egyptians believed that the Ma'at of the Universe was a god that benevolently ruled all aspects—human, material, and divine—of the Universe; the Christians would likewise make the underlying rationality of the Universe into God: And the logos was God.

In ancient Egypt, the judges and all those connected with the judicial system were initiated into the teachings of Ma'at. Thus, those who would discharge the laws and regulations of society were well trained in the ethical and spiritual-mystical values of life, fairness, justice and the responsibility to serve society in order to promote harmony and the possibility for spiritual development in an atmosphere of freedom and peace. For only when there is justice and fairness in society can there be an abiding harmony and peace. Harmony and peace are necessary for the pursuit of true happiness and inner fulfillment in life. Ma'at encompasses the teachings of Karma and Reincarnation or the destiny of every individual based on past actions, thoughts and feelings. Understanding these principles, leads us into becoming free of the cycle of reincarnation and human suffering and to discover supreme bliss and immortality.

The principle of Ma'at was formed to meet the complex needs of the developing Egyptian state having diverse peoples with conflicting interests. The development of these rules was to avert chaos which later became the basis of Egyptian law. From an early period, the king would describe himself as the "Lord of Ma'at" who decreed with his mouth the Ma'at he conceived in his heart. The importance of Ma'at developed to the point that it embraced all aspects of existence, including the basic equilibrium of the Universe, the relationship between essential parts, the cycle of the seasons, heavenly movements, religious observations, fair dealings, honesty and truthfulness in social interactions. The Ancient Egyptians had a deep conviction of an underlying holiness and unity within the Universe. They believed that cosmic harmony was achieved by correct public and ritual life and any disturbance in cosmic harmony could have consequences for the individual as well as the state. To them, Ma'at bound all things together in an indestructible unity: the Universe, the natural world, the state, and the individual were all seen as parts of the wider order generated by Ma'at. Upon closer review, we can see that the underlying concepts of Taoism and Confucianism resemble the principles of Ma'at. Many of these concepts were classified into laws, and many of them were discussed by ancient Egyptian philosophers and officials who referred to the spiritual text known as the *Book of the Dead*.

Isis of the Nile

In ancient Egypt, all religion and civilization began with the womb of the goddess Isis. She was the ancestral mother of a world-wide dynasty of godly kings through her divine bloodline. Divine kings of the pagan world ruled by divine right and they were considered to be descendants of the gods. But Isis was considered to be the most powerful of all the gods and goddesses of the ancient world; for she was "The One Who Is All," and the "Lady of Ten Thousand Names."

Isis was the Mother and Goddess of Earth during ancient times. Osiris which was her brother became her lover and cohort. When they married, he became the first King of the Earth. This infuriated their brother Seth who set out to murder Osiris in an attempt to overtake the throne. As the legend goes, Seth duped his brother into stepping into a beautifully enamored box made of cedar, ebony and ivory which only he could fit into. Upon entering the box, Seth quickly sealed the box making it a coffin for Osiris and he launched it into the Nile where it was carried to another country. Traditionally, in order for a god to properly transition from one life to the next, they would have to undergo a proper ceremonial burial. But because of the way in which Osiris was murdered, Isis knew that her beloved would not make the transition without a proper burial. She then set out to find the corpse of her lover whereby she could perform the appropriate rituals enabling him to pass through the underworld. Once she found the body of Osiris, she returned to Egypt and hid the body in the swamps on the delta of the Nile River until she could provide the proper burial. Accordingly, Seth was out hunting whereupon he found the box containing Osiris's body. Seth was enraged by this and commenced to kill Osiris once and for all by hacking his body into fourteen pieces and tossing them into the river to be eaten by the crocodiles. Still wanting to provide Osiris with the proper burial, Isis set out to find the pieces in order to re-unite his soul. It was believed that in order for the soul to be intact, the corpse had to be complete. The preservation of the body was regarded as essential for eternal life. Without a body there could be no survival after death. In addition to the body, the Egyptians acknowledged the existence of a "*BA*" and a "*KA*." While the "*BA*" was the soul, and pictured as a bird with a human head, the "*KA*" acted as a kind of guardian double of the body which was born with it and stayed on as a companion in the world of the dead. Therefore, Isis searched and searched and each time she found a missing piece, she would unite it with the corpse in order to re-form his body. Accordingly, she was successful at locating all of the missing pieces with the exception of the fourteenth piece which happened to be his penis. Through magic and the help of the Goddess Nut, she was able to fashion a penis out of gold and wax and perform a ritual that brought her husband back to life. Isis then copulated with the resurrected Osiris allowing her to give birth to a son named Horus which formed the beginning of the royal bloodline of divine kings.

Upon closer examination, we learn that Osiris went on to become the god of the heavens and the judge of the dead that is spoken of in the bible. While Horus or Heru went on to become the father of Pharaohs and the progenitor of the bloodline of divine kings. "*Haroah=Heru. Pharaoh=PHeru.*" While Isis went on to become the original "Eve" or great Mother Goddess. The very word Genesis contains the name Isis. "*Genesis = genes-of-Isis.*" We can even find origins of Isis in the name "*Jesus = Jisis*" if we understand that a lot of the vowels were interchangeable and spellings varied dependent upon certain phonetics. The Christian figure Jesus was fashioned after Isis and her teachings of love rather than that of Jehovah who was a wrathful, jealous god. Both the names "Isis" and "Jesus" come from the same root meaning salvation or savior. In fact the Savior was considered to be female at times. Even the resurrection of Jesus is a distinct reproduction of the resurrection of Osiris. Jesus is purported as being the Alpha and Omega the Beginning and the End, but this is also a reproduction from Isis's temple in Sais, Egypt where the inscription "*I am all that has been, that is and that will be*," is carved.

So while the story of Isis is allegorical in nature, it is a true tale of Ancient Egypt that was taught to the children who had no written education. Rather than taking this story literally, we have to understand what is being conveyed. On the website; Isis Resurrected it says:

"Isis didn't resurrect the corpse of a man who had been murdered and chopped into pieces. The resurrection of Osiris was a religious renaissance. Isis resurrected an ancient fragmented and defunct religion. Via her womb, she reinvigorated the royal bloodline of a deified ancestor. That ancestor was the ancient ancestral patriarch god El. By one path or another, El was the ancestral father god of numerous civilizations. Our word royal (real) is composed of Ra, the sun god plus El, the legendary founder of the first civilizations. The name *Israel* means 'Isis Royal,' the royal line of Isis. The name Israel is a compound of Isis, the mother goddess + Ra, the sun god + El, the ancient father god. El was the ancestral father god of ancient Syrian, Canaanite and Hebrew nations prior to the biblical Yahweh. El-issa (El+*Isis*) was a wife of Ba'al. El-issa, in Hebrew means the wife/female of El. Ba'al and Elissa were the gods of Israel up until about 600 BCE."

There is still a much deeper aspect to the Isis legend. But what is the significance to this legend and what is the esoteric meaning behind it? Well for starters, it was the beginning of the real "*Trinity*" of which we will discuss in later chapters, but it was also the beginning of many of the beliefs held by religious factions throughout the world today. Some early Christians are even known to have called themselves "*Pastophori*" meaning the shepherds or servants of Isis. It is also believed that this is how the word "*Pastor*" originated. Today, we can even see where the Mother figure of Isis is still depicted in the Christian faith as an iconic figure in the form of Mother Mary. In fact the original image of mother and child portrayed with Isis nursing the infant Horus inspired the style of religious art and the Madonna and child, for centuries. This is the result of early Christian exposure to Egyptian art. Dating back some 3,500 years long prior to the Christian immaculate conception on the walls of the Temple at Luxor can be seen images depicting the birth and adoration of Horus with Thoth (Not an Angel) announcing to the Virgin Isis (not Mary) that she will conceive Horus with Kneph (Not the Holy Ghost) impregnating her and that this infant would be attended by three kings bearing gifts. To further support this, there are pictures of the baby Horus being held by the virgin mother Isis the original Madonna and Child, in the burial chambers in Rome. Gerald Massey says in his book *Gnostic and Historic Christianity*:

> "It was the Gnostic art that reproduced the Isis, (Mary) and Horus, (Jesus) of Egypt as the Virgin and child-Christ of Rome . . . You poor idiotai, said the Gnostics to the early Christians, you have mistaken the mysteries of old for modern history, and accepted literally all that was only meant mystically."

Historian Will Durant says:

> "Early Christians sometimes worshipped before the statues of Isis suckling the infant Horus, seeing in them another form of the ancient and noble myth by which woman (i.e., the female principle), creating all things, becomes at last the Mother of God."

In a survey of twenty leading Egyptologists by Christian scholar Dr. W. Ward Gasque, he discovered that all who responded recognized ". . . that the image of the baby Horus and Isis has influenced the Christian iconography of Madonna and Child." After the Christian religion gained popularity and started dispersing into Europe and then throughout Rome, the Christians converted an Isis shrine in Egypt into one for Mary and in other ways ". . . deliberately took images from the pagan world." In the *Christ Conspiracy: The Greatest Story Ever Sold*, Acharya S. says; "Mary, like many other Christian 'saints' are not historical personages but are, in fact, the gods of other cultures usurped and demoted in order to unify the Holy Roman Empire." It's apparent then that much of what the religions of today hold to be factual are nothing more than allegorical, mythological plagiarisms and blatant reproductions of ancient cultures.

Isis came to be known as one of the greatest lights of the ages and her inception came right near the dawn of writing. Her legend begins in the era just before the dawn of writing and ends in the historical era of modern civilizations. She existed about 6,000 years ago in an Upper Nile or East African kingdom amongst a race of *Homo sapiens* who had one eyebrow with no gap in the middle. The original Isis was a mutant. She was the first of her kind. She was the first twice-wise *Homo sapiens sapiens*. Her twice-wise genus has since become the genotype of all humankind. She is the ancestral mother of *Homo sapiens sapiens*, twice-wise humans with two eyebrows. *Homo sapiens sapiens*, humans who are twice-wise, now includes the entire human population of planet Earth which makes us all descendants of the Mother Goddess Isis.

The name *Homo sapiens sapiens* is not a scientific term. It began as a term to designate descendants of Isis who were twice-wise. (Humans who are twice-wise) are descendants of Isis. *Homo sapiens sapiens* now includes all of the people on this planet. She had a high rounded forehead and a parted eyebrow. Her parted eyebrow was an Asian characteristic which meant she had Asian ancestry somewhere in her background. Supposedly, the people of her bloodline were attempting to improve human civilization by breeding a line of more intelligent humans from an original genius female. This is how she came to be referred to her as the original "Eve" and the model for the biblical Eve. Her womb, her works and her teachings were the foundations of the first historical civilizations. There were earlier civilizations, but they didn't have written histories. The genesis of Isis was a major force responsible for the spread of writing over the ancient world and for the creation of modern writing systems that are still in use today.

As the Mother Goddess, Isis is the ancestral mother of all people with two eyebrows. Monotheism was able to destroy her temples and erase her legend from the living memory of humankind, but they couldn't erase her sign. Today, we are all wearing the mark of Isis in the middle of our foreheads. We are all *Homo sapiens sapiens*, twice wise children of Isis with two eyebrows.

In Rome the noble fathers were of the Isis bloodline which classified them as descendants of the gods and worthy of kingship. At the time, the monotheists were seeking to usurp political power by doing away with pagan worship by eliminating the Isis bloodline as the only means to political power. As such; the worship of Isis was annihilated and all those who followed her were brutally suppressed. Monotheist then instituted a two-thousand-year crusade to annihilate all traces of the Mother Goddess, primarily because she was a woman but mostly for political gain. Subsequently, Jewish people rewrote their history all the way back to their origins eliminating any traces of the goddess Isis. And for fifteen-hundred-years, anyone found to be in possession of any pagan artifacts was to have it immediately destroyed by the village priest. Since then, Isis and her works have been plagiarized and their true origin forgotten or written off as mere mythology. But she will forever be remembered by those of us that are aware of these ancient truths for we know that we are all but children of the great Mother Goddess Isis and we are all ancestors of divine royalty.

God Osiris

Osiris was the son of the Earth god Geb and the sky goddess Nut, husband to Isis and father to Horus. He was considered to be the oldest god on record and the only deity ever referred to simply as god. Osiris was Egypt's greatest king who ruled through kindness and persuasion and it was his teachings that helped civilize Egypt and other neighboring people. Osiris was considered to be the most important god in terms of religious practice because he was the god of the living and the dead. His key function as the god of the dead was to judge the soul of the deceased. If that soul were found to be pure and just, it would be admitted into the realms of bliss. However; if it were found to be weighted with unjust deeds or crime, it was thrown to Amenti, a horrid god with the face of a crocodile, the front of a leopard, and the back of a rhinoceros, who would consume the soul in its frightening jaws.

Subsequently, Osiris became known as the god that every soul had to answer to after death, accounting for all aspects of the life lived on Earth. Belief in Osiris applied to everyone, from the King down to the lowest member of society. He was a god of fertility; all the principal Egyptian gods (including the pharaohs who were God Incarnate) were creator gods, that is, they gave life to the world. Evidently, the Doctrine of Incarnation had long since been evolved and established by Osirian worshippers 5,000 to 10,000 years before the advent of Christianity. Since Osiris gave life to the living and the dead, the pharaoh was generally regarded as the Incarnation of Osiris—in fact, the very name of the god, *Us-Yri*, means "Occupier of the Throne." Osiris was admired and highly worshipped up until the 18th dynasty at which time Egyptian religion became suppressed by the Christian era. It is believed that the worship of Osiris continued right up until the 6th century CE on the island of Philae in the Upper Nile because the Theodosian decree to destroy all pagan temples had not been enforced there.

Based on the previous explanation of Set killing Osiris followed by his resurrection from Isis, it's interesting to note the significance of this story and the vast amount of similarities that are shared by the Christian tale of the Jesus figure. There are many parallels between the Osiris resurrection and those found in Christianity. For example; many Egyptians believed Osiris was of divine origin and that he suffered a horrendous death of suffering and mutilation at the hands of his brother Set which later became the epitome of evil and who has today become an amalgamation of "*Sat-an.*" Subsequently, after a great battle between good and evil, Osiris overcame these struggles henceforth conquering death and becoming the king of the underworld and judge of the dead. Being the first person to die, he ultimately became lord of the dead. As a result, all Egyptians felt they too might be able to conquer death and they labeled Osiris as a risen "Savior" and confidently hoped to rise, as he arose, from the grave.

Over time, Osiris came to represent many things for the Egyptians. He represented someone who died and was then reborn and he also represented the cycle of death and rebirth which the Egyptians saw as the dominant principle and promise of the Universe. He was the god of fertility and he brought life, in the form of agriculture, to all living humans. As King, Osiris created life for the living in the administration of the state and as the lord of the dead, he represented the moral order of the Universe, judging each soul by its life and rewarding or punishing that soul with a rigorous justice. Anthropologist and historian Nigel Davies says, "The agony of Osiris was a sacrifice with a universal message. As the one who died to save the many, and who rose from the dead, he was the first of a long line that has deeply affected man's view of this world and the next." He further states that the passion and sacrifice of Jesus Christ is linked conceptually to Osirian and other traditions in the Ancient world. The Passion and Resurrection of Osiris contain patterns that made their way into Christianity:

> "That the Passion as it was distinctly called and Resurrection of Osiris were yearly and openly celebrated by the worshippers of the Alexandrian gods with alternate demonstrations of grief and joy, the classical poets have put beyond doubt."

The resemblance to Christ is unmistakable, as:

> "Osiris was to his worshippers 'the god-man, the first of those who rose from the dead,' whose death and resurrection were therefore supposed to be in some way beneficial to mankind."

So, the "Passion and Resurrection" of Christ are symbolical and not actual but representing an image and not the death and resurrection of a real person. The archetypical death and resurrection of the god provides a spiritual example for his followers:

> "Osiris was regarded as the principal cause of human resurrection, and he was capable of giving life after death because he had attained to it. He was entitled 'Eternity and Everlastingness,' and it was Osiris that made men and women born again."

This is depicted in thousands of tombs throughout the Nile valley: "Osiris died and rose again from the dead, so all men hoped to arise like him from death to life eternal." These important religious and spiritual concepts were popular in Egypt from very early times, long before the purported advent of Christ.

During the birth of Osiris, a voice proclaimed, *"The ruler of all the Earth is born."* As can be seen, this exalted, divine status is entirely unoriginal with the Christian savior, as it long pre-dates Christ's purported advent. This idea bears an eerily striking resemblance to that of Jesus and much like the prototypes for the Virgin Mary and child were found in the figures of Isis and Horus, so too was the prototype for Jesus found in the god Osiris. It was Osiris that was the prototype for early Egyptian Christians to model the Christ figure after. Davies concludes by saying, "Whilst Christianity rejected anything 'pagan' it did so only at a superficial level and early Christianity was 'deeply indebted' to Ancient Egypt."

The Christ Conspiracy: The Greatest Story Ever Sold, clearly spells out how the figure we know as Jesus came into being. There are far too many similarities or coincidences as you would say when it comes to Jesus of Nazareth and how he came to be worshipped. But it is not surprising that Genesis and other biblical texts, concepts and stories are largely Egyptian in origin, especially since Israel and Egypt are in such proximity.

Accordingly, Osiris contributed several aspects to the Jesus character to include:

➤ Being born of a virgin on December 25th, and placed in a manger.
➤ He was a traveling teacher that performed miracles.
➤ He rode in a triumphal procession on an Ass.
➤ He was a sacred king killed and sacrificed for fecundity and purification.
➤ He rose from the dead.
➤ He was the god of the vine that turned water into wine.
➤ He was called "King of Kings" and "God of Gods."
➤ He was considered the "Only Begotten Son," "Savior," "Redeemer," "Sin Bearer," "Anointed One," and the "Alpha and Omega."
➤ He was identified with the Ram or Lamb.
➤ His sacrificial titles of "Dendrites" or "Young Man of the Tree" suggest he was hung on a tree or crucified.
➤ And, according to biblical scholar Bruce M. Metzger, Osiris died on the 17th of the month of Athyr and is resurrected three days later on the 19th.

There are also many sayings attributed to both Osiris and Jesus that have striking similarities. Two of which are; when Osiris exclaims:

> "I have welcomed the chief spirits in the service of the Lord of things! I am the Lord of the fields when they are white ready to harvest."

While Christ says:

> "Behold, I say unto you, Lift up your eyes and look on the fields that are white already unto the harvest."

The Egyptian ritual says:

> "He is thine, O Osiris! A well, or flow, comes out of thy mouth to him!"

Christ says:

> "I am the Father, inundating when there is thirst, guarding the water. Behold me at it."

So, one must continually ask, why so many similarities? Could it be that the story of Jesus is in fact a forgery based upon earlier figures all arising from the original god Osiris? If so, then everything we hold to be factual in terms of Christianity is based upon a lie dressed up as modern day truth.

It's pretty evident that Osiris was in fact the prototype for Christ. Purportedly, in the 1st century BCE, the Jews worshipped Dionysus who was represented by the symbol (HIS) or (IES), which later became "*Iesus*" or "*Jesus*." Coincidently, the (IHS) is still used to this very day in Catholic observances and traditional symbols. The letters (IHS) are read by Christians as (Jes), whereby the Roman Christian priesthood later added the term (us). In 1970, Karl Anderson wrote a book entitled, *Astrology of The Old Testament* where he writes:

> "The Romans at that time were the worst of pagans or idolaters; but knowingly well the power of state religion, strove to make from their original 'Sun' worship a religion which should embody Trinity; and so from the story of Buddha and Osiris, Isis and Horus, and the zodiacal signs,

clothed the stories in new garments, and personified the Sun into a 'living' man, and the moon into a virgin mother, and the cross as the life-saving symbol, and then forced the slaves of Rome by sword and wild beast, by inquisition and torture and *auto-da-fe*, to acknowledge as truth that which their souls abhorred; forcing them to teach this to their children established that abomination, the confessional, making spies and traitors in every household till, sinking deeper and deeper in despair and forced ignorance, generation after generation dared no longer even to think their soul was their own and given by God, but were led to believe that God the Father damned them from the beginning and delivered them over to the devil, to be saved (no matter how abominable their crimes) by this man called the Son of God . . . In fact, the whole story is incomprehensible; and as no one could explain it, the priests when questioned at once forbid such sacrilege as questions; and 'It is a mystery' sufficed to stay all inquisitive minds."

Joseph Wheless attest to this in his book *Forgery in Christianity* written in 1990 by saying:

"The ultimate merger and total identity of Paganism with 'the new Paganism called Christianity' was finally established by law and Imperial policy of 'One State and One Religion,' to which conformity was enforced by laws of confiscation and death; all the other religions of the Empire were fused by fire and sword into a bastard Christianity."

My point here is to show how Christianity is a plagiarism which was savagely foisted upon hapless believers and how Osiris was the god in antiquity that later became known as the "Jesus Christ" figure that many of us ardently worship today without question. In knowing the real truth, my prayer is that we will begin to develop a better understanding of the things we consider to be true. A huge part of becoming aware and spiritually empowered is by first knowing the truth of what it is we believe. It's really unfortunate that many of us today are not privy to this type of wisdom simply because we have not yet taken the time to seek out the true meaning behind our beliefs. As a light-worker, my goal is to spread truth and light which will help enlighten us so that we will be able to make more educated choices about what it is we believe which will ultimately cater to our spiritual awakening. Many of us have already arrived at a point of realization where these words resonate as an already known truth within. Unfortunately, there are those of us that are still wading in the mired truths of Christianity and that's okay because at some point, they too will ask that one question which will eventually lead them on a quest to greater understanding. For those of us that have already asked the sacred question to know more of the truth, this is what is being presented.

Horus of Lower Egypt

Horus carried the epithet "He who is above" and he was considered to be the first known national god of Lower Egypt. He was married to Hathor, the "goddess of love" and while in this form, he was sometimes given the title *"Kemwer,"* meaning (the great black one). Since Horus was said to be the sky, he was considered to also contain the Sun and Moon. It was said that the Sun was his right eye and the Moon was his left eye and together they traversed the sky when he, a falcon, flew across it. Horus is linked with the eye of time (Hours). He is also part of the ancient mystery school teachings sometimes referred to as the "Right Eye of Horus" mystery school which holds the truth about reality. These teachings were allegedly programmed by Isis and Osiris—left behind with their priests in Egypt to be passed down through the millennia until the time was right for consciousness to awaken. Many believe these are the same souls who were the priests in Atlantis. Essentially, the "Eye of Horus" and the "Eye of Ra" or God, are one-in-the-same. Thus he became known as *"Harmerty"* or "Horus of two eyes." Later, the reason the Moon was not as bright as the Sun was explained by a tale, known as the "Contestings of Horus and Set," originating as a metaphor for the conquest of Upper Egypt by Lower Egypt in about 3000 BCE. In this tale, it was said that Set, the patron of Upper Egypt, and Horus, the patron of Lower Egypt, battled for Egypt brutally, with neither side victorious, until eventually the gods sided with Horus.

In Egyptian Mythology, Horus and his father Osiris are commonly interchangeable hence the phrase; "*I and my father are one.*" This is why there are so many similarities with regards to both Horus and Osiris. Since Horus, as the son of Osiris, was only in existence after Osiris's death, and because Horus, in his earlier guise, was the husband of Isis, the difference between Horus and Osiris gets blurred at times. And so, after a few centuries, it came to be said that Horus was the resurrected form of Osiris. Although Osiris has always been Horus' father and Horus is not both Horus and Osiris. Nevertheless, gods were often known to reincarnate in the form of other gods as in Thoth/Hermes. It is even believed that all of the Pharaohs were Horus in human form. The Egyptian pharaohs were considered to be "*the word of God become flesh*" or incarnations of the Egyptian Logos/God, Horus. By making this claim they were able to consent to a divine right to rule and they considered themselves not only answerable to God alone but to actually have become God in the flesh. Even the theory of "The Divine Right of Kings" in Europe is a later version of the Horus scenario.

If you were to actually study the mythologies of ancient Egypt, you would have no trouble in realizing that they are all fashioned after a common outline dating right up to our current religions. You would see that they are basically symbolic of how there is always the principle of polarity at work and how duality is present on all levels, especially in the pantheons of creational forces linked to one another. This is often depicted by the pattern of creation and destruction that often gets repeated throughout the cycles of time thus shaping the human experience. Many of the gods and goddesses fall into this category of duality where there is both "good and bad"—"light and dark" as well as struggling for balance and the return to full awareness. There is always the god who comes from the sky which is usually a representation of light or a higher vibrational frequency and of course there are those that come from a lower vibrational frequency which represents darkness or unconsciousness.

When we look at how Jesus actually originated, we can see there are many striking similarities between both Horus and Jesus. This makes it increasingly obvious how ancient Egypt was usurped of its gods with the inception of Christianity. According to a former professor of Theology, even the Christian usage of the term "Christ" was derived from Egypt. He argues that the application of the term Christ to Jesus developed from the Egyptian term *"Karast"* (covered in embalming oil) to describe Horus. Christ in classical Greek usage could mean covered in oil, and is a literal translation of Messiah "The anointed one." The word utilized in its original classic Greek and Jewish contexts refers to the office, or status of the person but not to their actually having oil on their body. Horus was anointed by Anubis, who was regarded as the main anointer; this anointing made Horus into *"Horus Karast,"* or *"Horus The Anointed One,"* an epithet which is written in Egyptian documents as HR KRST; The embalmed/anointed Horus. By comparison, the baptizing of Jesus made him into Jesus Christ or *"Jesus The Anointed One"* by being baptized by John.

It becomes all the more obvious how certain elements of the Jesus story were merely embellishments which were derivatives from that of Horus. The relation between the story of Jesus and the story of Horus with regards to the "Virgin Birth" is the fact that Horus's story is the original "Immaculate Conception," while that of Jesus is the "Immaculate Deception." Inscribed about 3,500 years ago, on the walls of the Temple at Luxor were images of the Annunciation, Immaculate Conception, Birth and Adoration of Horus, with Thoth announcing to Isis that she will conceive Horus, and with the infant being attended by three kings, or magi, bearing gifts. Also in comparison is the fact that Horus raised at least one man, Osiris, from the dead. Jesus raised Lazarus or (El Azarus/El Osiris). However, aspects of Jesus' raising Lazarus from the dead are also borrowed from the Egyptian myth of the resurrection of Osiris by Horus. Like Jesus, Horus was born at the "House of bread," an historic capital of Egypt which translates to mean Bethlehem, the same city of Jesus' birth. The city was also named Annu in Egyptian, translated into Hebrew is Beth-any, or house of Any/Anu. The Jewish Bethany is where Lazarus was supposedly raised from the dead. The Egyptian Bethany (City or House of Annu) is where Osiris was raised from the dead. Coincidence?—hardly! In fact, in *The Christ Conspiracy: The Greatest Story Ever Sold* we learn of Horus that:

> He was born of the virgin Isis-Meri on December 25ᵗʰ in a cave/manger with his birth being announced by a star in the East and attended by three wise men.
> His Earthly father was named "Seb" (Joseph).
> He was of royal decent.
> He was a child teacher in the Temple at age 12, and at 30, he was baptized and disappeared for 18 years.
> He was baptized in the river Eridanus or Iarutana (Jordan) by "Anup the Baptizer" (John the Baptist) who was later decapitated.
> He had 12 disciples, two of whom were his "witnesses" and were named "Anup" and "Aan" (the two Johns).
> He performed miracles, exorcised demons and raised El Azarus (El Osiris) from the dead.
> He walked on water.
> His personal epithet as "Iusa," the "Ever-becoming Son" of "Ptah," the "Father."
> He was called the "Holy Child."
> He delivered a "Sermon on the Mount" and his followers recounted the "Sayings of Iusa."
> He was transfigured on the Mount.
> He was crucified between two thieves, buried for three days in a tomb, and resurrected.
> He was also the "Way, the Truth, the Light," "Messiah," "God's Anointed Son," the "Son of Man," the "Good Shepherd," the "Lamb of God," the "Logos," "Word Made Flesh," and the "Word of Truth."
> He was "The Fisher" and was associated with the Fish (Ichthys), Lamb and Lion.
> He came to fulfill the Law.
> He was called the "KRST," or "Anointed One."
> He was supposed to reign for one thousand years.

Apparently, the story of Jesus is practically identical on countless aspects to that of Horus. In fact; these similarities are strikingly similar to Jesus which hadn't originated until thousands of years later. These findings have been concealed and remain hidden away from society as an elaborate scheme to dupe the masses into believing in the Christ

Conspiracy. Practically every concept or belief in Christianity can be traced back to many cultures long prior to what is known today as Christianity. Graham says; "This knowledge has been hidden from the masses for many centuries for the purpose of enriching and empowering the ruling elite. Its conspiring priest-kings have ruled Empires in full knowledge of it since time immemorial and have 'lorded' it over the heads of the serfs."

In ancient times, Horus was often depicted as the "Sun God." In the Sun Book or Holy Bible which is an amalgamation of *The Book of the Dead*, *The Pyramid Texts* and *The Books of Thoth*, the story of the Son of God, is actually a transfiguration of the original Sun of God, whereby stories were told that were based upon the movements of the Sun through the heavenly bodies. In the late 1700's Thomas Faine said: "The Christian religion is a parody on the worship of the Sun, in which they put a man called 'Christ' in the place of the Sun, and pay him the adoration originally payed to the Sun." Subsequently, Jesus Christ and his 12 disciples were in reality celestial depictions of the Sun and its movements through the heavens and its 12 constellations. Therefore, the 12 disciples of Jesus are merely symbolic for the zodiacal signs and are not literal depictions of people who were actually alive during that time. Consequently, the historical Jesus figure is nothing more than a fictitious and astrological hybrid that was created and nurtured solely for the purpose of political gain and control. In terms of the "Three Wise Men" or "Three Kings," they were actually the three stars in Orion's belt "whose rising announced the coming of "*Sothis*," the "Star of Horus" which is Sirius, the brightest star in the sky." When looking at the similarities between both Horus and Jesus' supposed ages or times in which they carried out certain events, it becomes obvious that like Horus, Jesus has no history between the ages of 12 and 30, and *The Christ Conspiracy: The Greatest Story Ever Sold* again says; "The mythos alone will account for the chasm which is wide and deep enough to engulf a supposed history of 18 years." And there are other commonalities such as the story of Horus/Jesus being in the Temple which is analogous to that of the Sun at midday hence; 12 noon or its highest point; thus being the "Temple of the Most High." And even the fable of Jesus being baptized and beginning his ministry at 30 is a shadow of the original story of Horus or the Sun moving into a new constellation at 30 degrees. The stories of good triumphing over evil or light over darkness, summer over winter and day over night as depicted by Jesus and Satan is symbolic of the story of Horus prevailing over the evil Set. Even the so-called sufferings and death, and resurrection of both Jesus and Horus are celebrated each year on the Vernal Equinox which is actually Easter. And finally, it was Horus that was carried off by *"Set"* (the Egyptian name for *"Satan"*) to the summit of Mount Hetep just as Jesus was supposed to have been carried by Satan to an exceedingly high mountain and tempted. Practically everything we hold to be true about the Jesus story is actually an elaborate rehashing of the story of Horus. Gerald Massey author of *The Historical Jesus and the Mythical Christ*, concludes by saying: "The Christ is a popular lay-figure that never lived, and a lay-figure of Pagan origin; a lay-figure that was once the Ram and afterwards the Fish; a lay-figure that in human form was the portrait and image of a dozen different gods" . . . to include Horus!

The Original Trinity

The English word Trinity is derived from the Latin *"Trinitas,"* meaning "the number three, a triad." This abstract noun is formed from the adjective *"Trinus"* (three each, threefold, triple), as the word *"Unitas"* is the abstract noun formed from *"Unus"* (one). The doctrine of the Trinity states that God is a triad or a group of three consisting of God the Father, Jesus the Son and the Holy Spirit or comforter as the Godhead where the members of the Trinity are said to be co-equal and co-eternal, one in essence, nature, power, action, and will. The *Oxford Dictionary of the Christian Church* even goes so far as to describe the Trinity as "The central dogma of Christian theology." This belief held by Trinitarians states that God is sub-divided into three and yet Jesus would often refer to God the Father as distinct from himself, as well as The Holy Spirit as being distinct from either God the Father or Jesus himself.

The whole foundation of the Trinity is somewhat confusing and contradictory in that throughout Jesus' purported teachings he is ascribed to be God himself. It becomes complicated in trying to understand how Jesus came (from) God and yet how he is still considered to [be] God. This same ideology can be felt in The Gospel of John where it says: *"In the beginning was the Word, and the Word was with God, and the Word was God. He was with God in the beginning. Through him all things were made; without him nothing was made that has been made."* The Gospel of John further clarifies that "The Word" refers to Jesus the Christ. However, this appears to be an outwardly impossible contradiction, that Jesus could be both "with God" and "was God" at the same time since the beginning of creation. John further exaggerates this claim by portraying Jesus the Christ as the creator of the Universe, by stating that . . . *"without him nothing was made that has been made."* This belief is in stark contrast to the belief in monotheism where there is only one deity and one person or being as in the case of Deuteronomy 6:4 *"Hear, O Israel: the Lord our God is one Lord."* In truth, the term "Trinity" wasn't coined until 100 years after the theoretical death of Christ. Therefore; the dogma of the Trinity did not come from Jesus. So, while the majority of Christians consider the concept of the Trinity to be essential to their beliefs, several historians and bible scholars argue that the Trinity of Christianity found its origins in pagan polytheism and Greek Philosophy rather than the supposed monotheism of the Jews.

At the First Council of Nicaea which took place around 325 CE, it becomes apparent how this concept originated. In *The Origin of the Trinity: from Paganism to Constantine* Cher-El Hagensick writes; "On one side were persecutions; on the other the seduction of philosophy. To remain faithful to the belief of Jesus Christ meant hardship and ridicule. It was only for the simple poor and the rich in faith. It was a hard time to convert to Christianity from the relatively safer paganism. In the desire to grow, the Church compromised truth, which resulted in confusion as pagans became Christians and intermingled beliefs and traditions."

It was at this Nicaean council that the doctrine of the Trinity was established whereby it would later become orthodoxy and then adopted as the Nicene Creed, which described Jesus the Christ as

"God of God, Light of Light, very God of very God, begotten, not made, being of one substance with the Father." Saint Athanasius, who was a participant in the Council stated; "The bishops were forced to use this terminology, which is not found in Scripture, because the Biblical phrases they would have preferred to use were claimed by the Arians to be capable of being interpreted in what the bishops considered to be a heretical sense. They therefore 'commandeered' the non-scriptural term *homoousios* (of one substance) in order to safeguard the essential relation of the Son to the Father that had been denied by Arius."

There was a great deal of debate throughout this period on how to articulate the issue of the Trinity but the most significant developments took place in the 4th century, with a group of men known as the Church Fathers who affirmed the teachings of the Apostles, but yet their focus was still on their pastoral duties to the Church under the persecution of the Roman Empire. This prevented them from being able to create doctrinal treatises or theological expositions. That is until the rise of Constantine when the persecution of the Church was abated which then created an environment conducive to open dialogue. According to Hagensick, the evolution of the Trinity is apparent in the Apostles' Creed, Nicene Creed, and the Athanasian Creed stating while each of the creeds became wordier and more convoluted, the simple, pure faith of the Apostolic Church slowly became lost. Consequently, as these creeds became more specific and less scriptural, the adherence to them became stricter, and the penalty for disbelief even harsher.

Since the Council of Nicaea, various passages from both the Christian and Hebrew scriptures have been cited as supporting the Trinity doctrine while other passages are cited as opposing it. Many scholars dispute the authenticity of the Trinity and feel it is the result of an earlier belief. Since we know Christianity converts cultures from within, the doctrinal formulas as they have developed bear the marks of the ages through which the Church has passed. But where exactly did the idea of a "triune" god develop and how did it become a part of the Christian belief? Well, it's no secret that much of what Christianity holds to be authentic is in reality a synthesis of earlier beliefs very cleverly morphed into another form of religion. All the stories and depictions are fabrications of earlier writings by the

Ancient Egyptians, Babylonians, Hindus, Sumerians, the Greeks and other earlier civilizations. When Christianity was being formulated, the Priests took writings from earlier beliefs and adopted them into their own and upon doing this; they destroyed the previous records of antiquity in order to squelch any former beliefs. Therefore, many of the characters in the bible are merely depictions of earlier figures. In the documentary *Zeitgeist* written and produced in 2007, Peter Joseph says, "Christianity, along with all other theistic belief systems empowers those who know the truth, but use the myth to manipulate and control societies. It reduces human responsibility to the effect that 'God' controls everything, and in turn awful crimes can be justified in the name of Divine Pursuit. The religious myth is the most powerful device ever created, and serves as the psychological soil upon which other myths can flourish."

In looking at some of the more original stories of the Trinity which predate Christianity by thousands of years, it can easily be seen how Christianity could have adopted this ideology. In fact; Dr. Gordon Laing, retired Dean of the Humanities Department at the University of Chicago, agrees by stating; "The worship of the Egyptian 'triad' Isis, Osiris, and the child Horus probably accustomed the early church theologians to the idea of a 'triune' God, and was influential in the formulation of the doctrine of the Trinity as set forth in the Nicaean and Athanasian creeds." To illustrate this, there are three scenes painted on the north wall of the burial chamber of Tutankhamun. The first scene shows Aye dressed in the priestly leopard skin, performing the ritual of "*the opening of the mouth*," to resurrect the dead king. The second scene shows Tutankhamun entering the heavenly realm of the gods, being greeted by the sky goddess, Nut. The third scene shows Tutankhamun the god-king, in his three forms: as Osiris, the father; as Horus, the son; and as Ka, the (holy) spirit. The manner in which the three embrace one another, as well as their identical profiles, emphasizes how they are three-in-one and one-in-three—the original, Egyptian Trinity.

The Encyclopedia of Religions declares that as Christianity came in contact with the triune gods of Egypt and the Near East, it developed a trinity of its own. But this was not the only Trinity that early Christians were exposed to says Hagensick, but rather how Christians slowly passed from Babylon through Greece and went on to Rome bringing with them their Trinity of Tinia, Uni, and Menerva. Even the names of the Roman Trinity: Jupiter, Juno, and Minerva, reflect the ancestry. It is a known fact that Christianity was not ashamed to borrow its themes from pagan culture. They didn't destroy paganism; they simply adopted it.

Some other prototypes which helped shape the Christian version of the Trinity include the Trinity of the ancient Sumerians where Anu was the primary god of heaven, the "Father," and the "King of the Gods"; Enlil, was the "Wind-god" the god of the Earth, and a creator god; while Enki was the god of waters and the "Lord of wisdom." Then of course there is the ancient Egyptian Trinity in the form of Amun who was actually three gods in one where Re was his face, Ptah was his body, and Amun was his hidden identity. Another earlier version of the Trinity comes from one of the oldest religions in the form of Hinduism. At the center of this religion is the belief in a Triune system of gods: "Brahma the Creator," "Vishnu the Preserver," and "Shiva the Destroyer." This is considered to be one of the oldest forms of the holy Trinity on Earth and the Christian version of Father, Son and Holy Ghost came in the shadows of this system among other patterns of a three-in-one god prototype. But considering there were races of beings on this planet as early as 500 million years ago, I'm almost certain there were other forms of a "triune" system in existence long before any human practice. Be that as it may, the common theme of pagan worship was a system based upon triune gods dating back to ancient Sumerian's Anu, Enlil, and Enki and Egypt's dual trinities of Amun-Re-Ptah and Isis, Osiris, and Horus to Rome's Jupiter, Juno, Minerva and the whole concept of paganism which revolved around the magic number "three." Metaphysically speaking, the Trinity is nothing more than the human being personified in a three-fold nature as the soul, body, and spirit where Spirit is associated with the "I AM," Soul is known as the "I Am consciousness" and the Body is its physical manifestation.

Chapter Two

Scientific Truth

Scientific Truth

"All truth is safe and nothing else is safe; and he who keeps the truth, or withholds it from men, from motives of expediency, is either a coward or a criminal, or both."

—*Unknown*

The word "Scientific" comes from the Medieval Latin root "*Scientificus*" meaning "producing knowledge" through the methods and principles of science which basically means "to know." According to Webster's definition: *"science in and of itself is; knowledge or a system of knowledge covering 'general truths' or the operation of 'general laws' especially as obtained and tested through scientific method."* In other words, science leaves very little to chance through its methodical approach to understanding and discovering properties which help make our existence all the more fathomable.

For years, science has sought to explain the age old questions of "Why are we here?" and "How did we get here." In recent times, science and religion, or should I say science and spirituality have slowly begun to agree with one another. Science and spirituality are now beginning to merge and support one another as opposed to being in conflict. Science is now proving many of the things that mystics and ancient civilizations have known for thousands if not millions of years. Through evolution, we are entering an age where many of the beliefs we hold about who and what we are as energetic beings are slowly being confirmed by science and modern technology. We are finally beginning to marry science with spirituality by understanding how as spiritual beings we are so much more than just physical beings but rather complex systems of energy and vibrations that can be measured and felt within the confines of a holographic Universe.

Today, through scientific studies, thoughts can be measured and determined to have a resonance or frequency just as any other form of vibration. Knowing this has a tremendous impact on the world in which we live because now we can understand how each and every occurrence comes into our being or our field of awareness.

By learning about and understanding such things as *Schumann's Resonance, The Mer-ka-ba Field, The Christ Consciousness Grid, Inner-Technology, The Genetic Code, Sacred Geometry, Star Tetrahedron, Flower of Life, The Photon Belt, Zero Point, Polar Shifts,* and *Resonance and Vibrations* (all of which I will address in greater detail in the upcoming chapters) we will become better acquainted with this phenomenal world in which we live. We will come to see how every individual on this planet plays a very intricate and necessary part in the overall scheme of consciousness and planetary awareness. As we become more familiar with our place within the consciousness grid, we will begin to see just how important our contribution really is to humanity. With each and every tiny awakening in consciousness, the shift in awareness also begins to increase. As each person starts to understand more-and-more just how truly important they are, the vibration they are emitting will slowly begin to raise the overall planetary vibration.

What is being presented here in this chapter is not just sound truth or general truth but rather scientific truth which is both sound and general in its application. It is a matter of fact and truth that cannot be refuted or contradicted for it has stood the test of time and experience and it has shown itself to be worthy of its weight in gold. There is nothing fictitious or speculative about this knowledge as it has proven itself time-and-time again in every arena of life since time immemorial. All that is needed to understand these principles is your willingness to believe. But I am not asking you to simply believe in something without providing proof as religion would have you do but rather believe after having been shown the evidence of this knowledge so that you can learn how to align yourself with such teachings thereby becoming a true student of wisdom. All the knowledgeable mystics throughout the ages in the form of Ptah, Thoth, Hermes, Socrates, Aristotle, Plato and countless others have all subscribed to these truths and have thus handed down this knowledge for the select few.

The Mystic teachings and cryptic sciences have long since been a mystery to the unlearned. But today, these truths are being presented to us and the only thing that separates the wise from the unenlightened and the erudite from the unlearned is our willingness to know the truth and a perpetual desire to seek the truth at all cost.

It is this yearning for truth which has allowed the fearful to become fearless and the cowardly to become courageous. For time has proven throughout the ages that whosoever possesses knowledge holds within their grasp an understanding of the mysteries of the Universe. It is in this knowing that we will come to understand the nature of our being and the very purpose for our existence.

Inner Technology

"Any sufficiently advanced technology is indistinguishable from magic."

—*Arthur C. Clarke*

We are so much more than mere flesh and blood. In fact; we are an elaborate system of electromagnetic pulses and impulses which are so intricate and dynamic that it's hard to comprehend just how magnificent we truly are. The Human DNA consist of 120 billion miles of encoded data which is 100 trillion times more information than any computer science could ever come up with. In our physical form, we are a sophisticated system of circuitry and mechanisms that make up our human body, but on a much more intricate level, we are an energetic system that communicates with the world around us by way of vibrations, frequencies and tones which are designed to orchestrate our manifested reality. In essence, we are magical masterpieces designed in the image and likeness of pure Love and Divine Intelligence. Everything we could ever want or need is already a part of our unique make-up. We are a miraculous phenomenon of "Inner Technology" which has existed inside of us since our inception. The key however, is to know and understand exactly how to go about cultivating this wondrous internal system.

Believe it or not, once upon a time, we actually had twelve DNA strands as opposed to the two we now have. At some point in our evolution, for whatever reason, these strands were tampered with decoded and dispersed throughout the body until some far-off time in the future when we could be fully recoded with the wholeness and fullness of our divine selves. This decoding of our DNA is critical if you truly understand the ramifications it entails. In order to fully comprehend what has been lost here, let's look at the primary function of our DNA. *Deoxyribonucleic Acid* (DNA) is a nucleic acid that contains the genetic instructions used in the development and functioning of all known living organisms and it serves as a crucial storage house for genetic information. Essentially it is the blueprint to our very existence and it contains the instructions needed to build other components of cells called genes. A gene is a unit of heredity and is a region of DNA that influences a particular characteristic in an organism known as traits. Therefore; DNA contains the genetic information which allows all modern living things to function, grow and reproduce. Without the full capacity of our genetic make-up, it's safe to say that our potential has been reduced. Essentially, we are only functioning with about ten percent of our full capabilities and the other ninety percent has been decoded and dispersed throughout the body in the form of what science has termed "junk" DNA. While science has yet to figure out how to utilize these other strands, we know the Universe doesn't make "junk" and these missing parts of our genetic make-up are definitely necessary if we are to function at full capacity. In her book *The Mission Remembered* Jelaila Starr says; "The twelve primary DNA strands are the DNA blueprints for the original twelve species that occupy this Universe." This being the case, we are the progeny of a much higher form of intelligence with far greater potential to that of simply being human.

Essentially, we were multidimensional beings, simultaneously existing on multiple planets, in numerous dimensions, galaxies and Universes. However, our ability to fully experience this reality, not to mention interact with our celestial lineage is greatly hindered by the fact that our DNA needs restoring. In the book *Maya Cosmogenesis* written by John Major Jenkins he emphasizes this by saying:

> "The ancient Mayan civilization understood the universal principles that create and sustain the world. These 'first principles' underlie the physical laws that modern science has partially mastered and used to create technological miracles, but the first principles of Mayan sacred science embraced a much larger Universe in which human beings

were seen to be 'multidimensional' and 'capable of traveling beyond time and space,' beyond the confines that limit modern science with its 'laws' that are valid only in the physical three-dimensional plane. But human beings, with our capacity for supra-sensory spiritual vision, are more than three-dimensional. And that somewhere among the ruins, perhaps, lies an Inner technology of personal transformation that our civilization lost long ago."

He postulates how we can only hope to create a cultural context in which human beings might once again cultivate this kind of Inner Technology.

In my first book *Ultimate Truth: Book I*, I write about the Nibiruans and how it is believed they took part in our evolution as well as our proverbial "downfall" through genetic manipulation and DNA restructuring. Apparently, *homo-sapiens* are an upgraded version from a lower primate by including a very advanced technology in the form of one additional endocrine gland and ten additional DNA strands. This inclusion gave us seven endocrine glands and twelve DNA strands which enabled us to become much more technologically advanced with the ability to communicate with our parentage in all twelve dimensions. Being that we were still a very new race of beings with very little discernment, we were also very naïve spiritually. As a result of what was beginning to happen with these new found abilities and our misuse of them, it is believed that the Nibiruans disconnected ten of our twelve DNA strands and scattered them throughout our bodies thus deactivating the ability to be multidimensional beings. In time, we simply forgot about them and it's hard to miss what we never knew we had. The Nibiruans would wait for us to develop spiritually in order to fully appreciate and understand our inner technological development at which time we could become advanced enough to fully handle the power of our twelve DNA strands. When this occurs, the Inner Technology would reactivate thus reassembling the additional ten strands enabling us to remember a time when we once had these capabilities and begin to embrace our celestial heritage.

There are no sufficient words to fully explain just how valuable we really are. The diminutive and intricate details of our inner-workings are so awe inspiring that at times it's hard to even fathom just how dynamic we actually are. The human body has often been compared to the most advanced computer with memory so vast it can't even be measured. In nano-technology there is a computer the size of a drop of water that operates from a single molecule of DNA which does not require any external power source. With over 50 to 75 trillion cells in our body, just imagine the overwhelming capacity we possess. We are highly sophisticated bio-computers fully loaded and upgraded with the most advanced software. This bio-system, much like the world-wide-web is hardwired to the universal source of all possibilities and through our Inner Technology, we are able to exist in a quantum field of awareness where everything is connected on an energetic level. This informational matrix holds all thoughts, emotions and states of being, either historic or potential, in holographic energetic form, at the subatomic level of reality. This "Matrix" so to speak, enables us to create and manifest simply by concentrating our focus and intention on a desired outcome. Quantum scientists tell us that we, as observers, create reality from this seething field of unlimited energetic potential through our perception and focused intention. However, we have to work on our Inner Technology in order to establish a conscious communication with the mainframe.

The memory we possess in our DNA comes from a long lineage of Earthly as well as Celestial parentage not to mention the fact that Earth's entire history is encoded within each of our cells. Our human DNA is a biological internet far superior to that of anything man could ever imagine. Science has even determined that just as we use the internet, our DNA can not only feed suitable data into the network, but it can also retrieve data from the network, and establish contact with other participants within that very same network. Researchers believe once we are able to regain group consciousness through our Inner Technology, we could reclaim our god-like power to create, alter and shape things to suit our desired reality. Undoubtedly, we are slowly and collectively moving toward such a reality. Once we are able to synchronize our thinking and begin to focus our thoughts in a collective effort, it is just a matter of time before we can influence the world in which we live. As a group conscious, we would not experience environmental issues or shortages of any kind but rather by utilizing our mental capabilities as a unified consciousness, we would have control of the resources of our planet as a normal outcome.

It is through this Inner Technology that we are empowered to restore our bodies and our lives by invoking conscious intention into the field of all possibilities. What exactly is this field of all possibilities and how does it pertain to us? I'll tell you how. Because we are galactic beings with far more capabilities than we've been led to believe and we've been functioning here in this physical incarnation on limited capabilities because our access to the infinite field has been hindered. This hindrance has come in the form of emotional and genetic blockages that have yet to be cleared and healed. Upon this clearing, an activation or should I say a re-activation will take place thus allowing us to function as the multidimensional beings that we were intended to be.

The Genetic Code

We hold within our genetic coding, everything in which we will ever need to find our way back to our divine selves. The genetic information that is passed on from parent to offspring is carried by the DNA of a cell or the genes in the DNA code for specific proteins that determine appearance, different facets of personality, health etc. In order for these genes to produce the protein, they must first be transcribed from DNA to RNA in a process known as transcription. Thus, transcription is defined as the transfer of genetic information from the DNA to the RNA. Translation is the process in which genetic information, carried by messenger RNA (mRNA), directs the synthesis of proteins from amino acids, whereby the primary structure of the protein is determined by the nucleotide sequence in the (mRNA). Although the genetic code is not a code in the literal sense, however a fundamental understanding of the genetic code is essential to understanding the molecular basis of our DNA.

All living things share the same genetic code, a fact that represents strong evidence for evolution. Unraveling the genetic code was one of the great scientific achievements of the twentieth century, and it opened the way to genetic engineering. Despite the variations that exist, the genetic codes used by all known forms of life are very similar. Since there are many possible genetic codes that are thought to have similar utility to the one used by Earth life, the theory of evolution suggests that the genetic code was established very early in the history of life. The fact that there is a standard genetic code, with very few variations, that is used by all species, suggests an argument that life had only one common ancestor. So, it is argued, if creatures now living are not descended from a common ancestor, then the same genetic code must have originated twice. Since the code is arbitrary, this could not be a result of convergent evolution, but would also have to involve a massive coincidence. The more probable explanation, then, is common descent from a single common ancestor. The minor variations in the genetic code from species to species do not particularly invalidate this argument so long as it is possible for such variations to evolve. For the massive similarities that remain after we have acknowledged the existence of these minor variations are still too great to be reasonably accounted for by mere coincidence alone.

Through genetic manipulation, we have been reduced to only ten percent of our full potential in an effort to allow our spiritual development to finally catch up to our galactic heritage. What do I mean by this? Well, in a word, we are not just our "human" selves but rather intricately developed beings with potentialities from all over the Universe. We were fashioned in the image and likeness of divine and celestial beings and the very same coding and intelligence which courses through their genes also courses through ours as their progeny. As human beings we are not just physical beings but rather we are wondrous specimens possessing the vestiges of higher forms of beings. Jelaila Starr, author of *We Are The Nibiruans: Return of the Twelfth Planet*, explains how many of these higher incarnate beings have never been able to communicate with our dimension because there were no channels with a frequency high enough in which to connect on. But now, as more and more conscious beings begin to raise the frequency by way of genetic recoding, soon we will be able to re-establish contact with these higher beings receiving their messages of love and support.

Recent information has revealed the higher purpose of our DNA which supports the idea of a multidimensional consciousness as our natural state. As multidimensional beings, our physic ability becomes reawakened and we develop a second neural network at the etheric level. This second neural network is what allows us to live in multiple dimensions simultaneously. We can hear, see and communicate with others in these dimensions. DNA recoding, reconnecting and activation, reunites our ten "unplugged" DNA strands back into our endocrine glands and reconnects us with our higher dimensional selves. Our endocrine glands, especially the hypothalamus and pineal, will awaken from their atrophied state and begin to function as they were intended. This will give our bodies the rejuvenation and spirituality necessary for multidimensional access. Through this process, our crown chakra crystals will become activated allowing us to receive and interpret communications from other realms.

When our planet was first formed, it was seeded by other races of beings of which we are their progeny. As such, we have within our DNA the ability to reconnect with our divine parentage through what is called Genetic recoding. This procedure enables us to communicate and interact with all the various levels of existence that we were unaware of heretofore. This method will allow us to function at full potential by utilizing all twelve DNA strands and one hundred percent of our brain's capacity. Can you even begin to imagine the ramifications of such a wondrous thing? Of course not, it's too farfetched especially if someone is coming from a limited per view. But let's suggest here, just for a minute the effects this would have on us a race of beings on planet Earth during this time.

Let's start by first looking at how we can begin the process of accessing this untapped aspect of our being. Bill Harris of the Centerpointe Research Institute says new research suggests how sound, mind, and emotion all affect our personal software or genetic coding which is found in each of our 70 trillion cells. Just to give you and idea of the vastness of our genetic makeup, if we were to somehow unwind this genetic string of information, it would span an amazing 120 billion miles. Our genetic code is the center which controls the production of all the chemicals in our body including the hormones that affect aging and longevity. Through certain modalities, we can actually access our DNA causing it to renew and restore itself. Because our genetic code is the interface between the physical world and the world of energy, thought and consciousness, it would behoove us to begin a practice which will enable our genetic code to re-activate its missing components if we are to ascend into a higher version of ourselves. But why is this so important to us now as opposed to any other time. Well, today, we are living in an unprecedented time of spiritual evolution and according to Starr, we are remodeling our bodies, changing them from carbon-based forms to more silicon-based forms or as some call it, crystalline-based forms. The dimension to which we are headed is less dense than our present one so our bodies must adapt in order for us to get there. At present, the Schumann Resonance of our planet which is the Earth's vibrational tone, is at a dramatic high of about 11.6 or more cycles per second, up from 8.6 18 years ago in 1992, and up from the earlier somewhat consistent frequency of 7.8 cycles per second. As energetic beings, our energy patterns affects the Earth, as well as changes in the Earth's energy patterns affect us. As Earth's energies continue to evolve to higher frequency ratios, our human energy acts in response to these higher frequencies and we become increasingly stimulated by the faster cycles causing us to feel a sense of urgency in our spiritual development. At this rate, we are certainly headed for much higher octaves, ones of unconditional love but we must first address our inner workings if we are to enjoy the benefits of such a wondrous event. We must recode our DNA if we are to ascend.

Imagine a world where everyone is on one accord, a world where love is the order of the day. In fact, imagine a galaxy where all of the various races are one family co-existing together in harmony. Such a vision becomes more attainable as we let go of our fears and come to terms with the fact that there is so much for us to know and understand as spiritual beings. Once we begin to unveil the truth of who and what we truly are as galactic beings, understanding that we possess within our being the very keys to our divine selves, we will finally start to seek out the ways and means to begin expanding upon our divinity. This is a wonderful opportunity because the increased Earth energies are now giving us the necessary framework and support in order to utilize the dormant ninety percent of our brains for which science has not found a purpose. This transition will allow us to have the best of both worlds—the joy of our physical bodies, and the psychic gifts of being wholly conscious of our multidimensional place in the Universe. By being wholly conscious I mean being able to receive communication from incarnate beings in the various dimensions beyond our own.

One of the ways in which to do this is through what Starr calls (DNA Recoding or the RRA Process), which we will discuss here in greater detail. According to Starr, There are nine levels in the DNA Recoding process and each requires emotional clearing at the level that activates the thymus to change the coding sequence of our DNA. This process entails switching on the forty-four DNA codes that were previously switched off. The entire process takes place on the etheric level or in the light body where the ten strands of "junk" DNA along with our two connected strands are realigned above the crown chakra. Because our DNA is holographic, it can be simultaneously realigned, reconnected and activated. This process will enable the "junk" DNA strands to simultaneously realign themselves at the crown, thus reconnecting them into the twelve crown chakra crystals. This reactivation will cause the life force energy to flow through them once again. Starr believes that once our twelve DNA strands are plugged back into our twelve Crown Chakra Crystals, then our Genetic Engineer's and Recoding Guide's (which are higher dimensional beings assigned to assist us with this process) jobs are nearly complete. They will continue to watch over us and monitor our twelve-strand reconnection until we reach the frequency needed to fully activate this reconnection. Here Starr outlines how the activation of the twelve strands actually occurs:

➤ Activation of the Crown Chakra Crystals. You should experience a tingling sensation at the top of your head or Crown Chakra.
➤ Activation of the Merkaba antenna. The Merkaba antenna is used to receive messages from other dimensions.
➤ Activation of the Hypothalamus. This is the universal translator which translates all messages into your chosen language. Messages are received as frequency thought-forms. Many are complete with emotions, pictures and language. Some have only one or two of these. The Hypothalamus also

provides us with the identity of the sender. Starr says we will eventually learn to identify the senders of these messages. Once the hypothalamus is activated the recoding process is complete. Proof of this recoding can be seen in visual (aura photos), because emotionally, we are no longer holding negative emotions in the body, and physically we will feel more in control of our power and we will begin to receive these messages daily.

➢ While this may sound like something from a science fiction movie, the reality is it's actually true. In dealing with things of this nature, truth can sometimes seem stranger than fiction. However, as we re-establish the twelve DNA strands, we will ultimately reactivate the pineal and hypothalamus enabling us to experience a multidimensional state of awareness that will reunite us with our divine essence on all levels of existence.

The key to our multidimensional state of conscious lies solely in our ability to impress upon and modify our elaborate genetic coding.

Merkaba

As spirit beings, we are not mere flesh and blood but rather complex systems of light, energy and information which surrounds our physical body. The word *"Merkaba"* is an Egyptian term that means *Mer* = Light, *Ka* = Spirit, *Ba* = Body. Esoterically speaking, *Mer* refers to a specific kind of light which was known during Egyptian times shortly after the reorganization from many gods toward the worship of the one God of all creation. It is viewed as two counter-rotating fields of light spinning in the same space and it is believed that these fields can be affected by performing certain breathing techniques. In terms of the *Ka*, this refers to the individual spirit of a person, with *Ba* representing the spirit's interpretation of its particular reality. However in this case *Ba* is usually defined as the body or physical reality. Although in other realities where spirits don't have bodies, **Ba** simply refers to their interpretation of reality in the realm in which they exist. The Merkaba field exists not only within our cells, but also as a unified force field around our bodies. When we begin to consciously affect this field, we are ultimately affecting the particles that form the basis of our very make-up. Therefore, anything we do to alter the Merkaba will have a direct effect on the DNA structure. Our light-bodies originated immediately upon conception within the first eight cells of our physical body. This light-body later formed the Merkaba or the Time-space vehicle so-to-speak. It is known as the "Star-Tetrahedron" which is pictured below and is based on the idea of Platonic solids of which will be discussed in the coming chapters.

Fig 1

Much of the work I've studied on the Merkaba is credited to Drunvalo Melchizedek. Here he provides an explanation which helps us understand the intricate details of our energy flow and how it pertains to this field that exists in and around the body. He says:

"In order to explain what the Merkaba is, we must first generally explain the flow of energy and energy fields that surround the body. The first definition refers to the Prana or Chi which is the Life force. This unseen energy exists everywhere in the Universe in great quantities. Prana enters the body through the top of the head (this is the reason there is a hole in the skull of unborn embryos). The major Prana flow runs through the center of the body looking like a tube. From there it flows into eight main centers known as "*Chakras.*" This is an Indian Sanskrit word meaning "turning wheel," due to the look of these complex energy flows. According to the early Egyptians there are thirteen chakras as they relate to different energy centers. From the Chakras there are branched energetic lines (meridians) that reach every cell of the body. There is a Prana field that surrounds the body as a result of the meridians and the Prana flow. Then there is the field of the aura. The auric field is an egg shaped energy field that surrounds the body and changes its color according to ones thoughts, feelings and emotions. Beyond the auric field there are hundreds of electromagnetic fields. These fields have precise geometrical shapes. Each one of them is made up of three identical fields with the same size and shape. The Prana field is the star tetrahedron, a three dimensional Star of David. We can rotate two of the three star tetrahedron fields in opposite directions by using the ancient Prana breathing technique, thus creating a huge 17 meter energy field—the light body, or the Merkaba which assists in spiritual growth by connecting with the higher self."

The Merkaba, also spelled "*Merkabah,*" is also considered to be the divine light vehicle used by Ascended Masters to connect with and reach those in tune with higher realms. It is actually the spirit-body surrounded by counter-rotating fields of light or wheels within wheels, spirals of energy much like that of the DNA which transports the spirit-body from one dimension to another. Essentially, the Merkaba can be used as a tool to help us reach our highest potential because it enables one to experience an expanded state of awareness by reconnecting them with higher potentials of consciousness, ultimately restoring access and memory of the infinite possibilities within every being. All of this plays a huge part in becoming more spiritual because Merkaba and DNA are what bring the God Essence into manifest experience. As our Merkaba builds and DNA activates, we literally become more able to embody the God Essence within our bio-energetic systems. As such; we can actually generate more of this essence into our biological form and our ability to understand and know ourselves as God increases and essentially our ability to love increases as well. When we concentrate on developing Merkaba, we are repositioning the rotation within the body and its bio-rhythms. This allows us to release certain blocks which enable us to explore more dimensions of space and time. By building the Merkaba adequately to the point where these blockages no longer occur, we will experience a release from all dimensions. And then, we can return to a state of one-ness with the God-Essence. This process is known as "Ascension" and it results in having a deeper contact with the Higher Self and a more strengthened aspect of life.

According to some of the work done by Drunvalo, the Merkaba is in fact, a crystalline energy field that is comprised of specific sacred geometries that align the mind, body, and heart together. It is created from sacred geometry which extends around the body for a distance up to 55 feet. These geometric energy fields normally spin around the body at close to the speed of light, but for most people they have slowed down or stopped spinning entirely due to a lack of attention and use. He asserts that we can activate a non-visible saucer shaped energy field around the human body which is anchored at the base of the spine through various gestures, and mudras (hand movements) along with specific "*prana*" breathing techniques. He further suggests that these geometric energy fields can be turned in a particular way causing reactivation and proper alignment. Coincidentally, a fully activated Merkaba looks just like the structure of a galaxy or a UFO and it is through this vehicle that a person is able to transcend time, space and dimensionality all of which caters to the ascension into higher realms of existence.

Spiritually speaking, the Merkaba is the interdimensional vehicle which consists of two equally sized, interlocked "*tetrahedra*" of light with a common center, where one "*tetrahedron*" points up while the other points down similar to that of a three dimensional Star of David. Again once activated, this saucer shaped field is capable of carrying the consciousness directly into higher dimensions. In an interview with Alton of the Alpha Omega order of Melchizedek, he describes the Merkaba as the hologram of Love which is the sacred geometric pattern that gave birth to the entire Universe. It is comprised of a band width or frequency of 13:20:33 which is the vibration of pure unadulterated Love. This particular tone actually coincides with non-limitation where the 13 chakras in the body become harmonized. It is believed that the ancient Mayan civilizations used the frequency of 13 and 20 for their calendar of time thus awakening the God Consciousness within, enabling them to access the center of the Universe and thereby becoming one with it. They referred to this state as having "Omni" perspective which helped them to become non-judgmental thus becoming truly empowered and galactically aligned. All of this plays an intricate part in the ascension process because by understanding how to create a new physical form having higher consciousness, a person can then begin the process of merging back into their own God Essence. This is not to say that anyone has ever separated from their oneness but rather through the Merkaba, we can all begin the process of transitioning back into our light-bodies thus eliminating time and space creating a time continuum which is actually the true state of being. We are already in unity consciousness and we have always been. However, we have not allowed ourselves to expand in consciousness where we once again recognize this. Once we begin the work of raising our vibration to the pattern of unconditional love, this higher vibration will allow for a much stronger Merkaba field.

In his book *Awakening to Zero Point*, Gregg Braden says that the Merkaba provides the blueprint for a radiant field of energy that extends through and beyond the physical boundaries of the body. He says that an awareness of this field provides a tool toward the access of creation, the God force or the energy of our Creator, directly and consistently. He also asserts that within each individual and through certain life experiences that these fields tend toward a dynamic phase of rotation at specific speeds and ratios. Under normal circumstances, the Merkaba rotates around the body at 186,000 miles per second, assuming a saucer-like shape where the extremes of polarity begin to neutralize one another. This is what is known as "Unity-Consciousness." However, due to certain conditions; this is not the case for many of us. In fact, for most people, this field is hardly rotating if at all. Seeing as how this field is the vehicle of ascension, without it performing at optimal levels, the ascension process then becomes very difficult if not impossible. Be that as it may, each individual is equally equipped at birth with the means in which to access the Merkaba field directly. Although this is typically a process whereby the individual is totally unaware, it usually comes in the form of lifes experiences. Many, if not all of the experiences we attract into our awareness are simply opportunities in which to feel and experience differently. These experiences further cater to our awakening because the Merkaba field is activated by the vibrations emitted through the emotions by way of our thoughts and feelings. Each of us is affecting this field without even knowing it. And, according to Braden, "Consciously vibrating differently—regulating the body vibration through thought and feeling—is where we may discover our greatest power." Subsequently, it is this Merkaba field that facilitates unconditional love within each conscious being thus constituting the healing not only in ourselves but others as well. It gives us the ability to manifest any kind of reality we desire and it can be adjusted to do just about anything, with the only limitation being that of our own thoughts.

Star Tetrahedron

As spiritual beings, we have numerous energetic fields surrounding our physical bodies. These energetic fields have various geometric shapes associated with what is called "Sacred Geometry" of which we will discuss in the upcoming chapter. Suffice it to say, these geometric shapes are the basis of all creation. These energetic fields are the consciousness that surrounds the body and as we become more aware of this field, we can learn to develop into more enlightened beings.

This consciousness consists of various dimensions and degrees with the field furthest from our body being the most powerful because it is connected with the highest dimensional level of the Universe, while the Star Tetrahedron field is the one closest to our body and the primary field most people are aware of. According to Drunvalo, there are numerous geometrical patterns numbering in the hundreds of thousands but many of them are not appropriate for us at this time in our awareness stating that knowledge of these other patterns would only do us more harm than good if we are not yet ready to embrace their meaning. He compares this analogy to a parent allowing a three year old to drive a Mack truck. Subsequently, this happens to be the field related to the lower dimensional levels of the Universe, and as we become more aware of this energetic system, we can learn to adjust the positioning of our "Merkaba" thereby raising our consciousness. This vast field of energy is connected to multidimensional realities with the Star Tetrahedron representing the 3rd dimensional level as well as the gateway to other dimensions. With this field being the closet to the body, it is considered to be much easier to activate and once activated, the consciousness begins to expand allowing for experiences with higher dimensions. By further activating the higher spiritual energy fields around the body, we can learn to expand the consciousness even further into other multidimensional experiences. Here is a detailed explanation taken from recent commentary on how this process actually works:

> "In order to create manifest reality fields, God-Source down steps a portion of Unified Consciousness through specific energetic forms. At the beginning of this sequence, the divine blue-print is embedded within a geometrical structure called the Kathara grid. The conscious primal currents of God-Source are then arranged, according to the order set in the Kathara grid building up through various constructs to create dimensionalized reality. Merkaba fields are one of these constructs in the manifestation sequence. These Merkaba are electromagnetic spiralling fields which can be considered as the primal lungs and circulatory systems of Creation, breathing primal currents from God-Source into (via the electric, clockwise rotating, male Merkaba) and out of (via the magnetic, counter-clockwise rotating, female Merkaba) manifestation with harmonious precision. All things in manifestation are expanding out and returning back to Source repeatedly and continually. The rate at which this expansion and contraction (or phasing) occurs can vary and this phase rate is one of the ways the experience of dimensionalized form is created. Dimensions are differentiated from one another by the phase rate and also by the angle at which

particles spin. The particles within each dimension spin at a specific angle and have a specific phase rate. Merkaba fields, through their own specific rates and angles of spin, communicates the phasing rates and angular rotation of particle spin to the forms that exist within them. This keeps manifest forms in dimensionalized phase lock. The phase lock communicated by the Merkaba is intentional. Without Merkaba, we would not have dimensional existence. Just as Merkaba fields are tools by which individuations of Source are kept in dimensional phase lock, they are also the tools by which phase lock is released and individual expressions of Source return to Unified At-One-Ment. It is worth reminding ourselves of the intrinsic, primal order of manifestation that is repeated throughout all structures expressing from and within God-Source. The Divine template that is set by the Kathara grid is repeated over and over from the smallest to the largest of forms. The same can be said for Merkaba fields. The spirals of electro-magnetic energy called Merkaba exist around and within all forms."

There was a time in our history when this knowledge was known by people throughout the world ranging from Ancient Egypt, to Israel, India and Tibet. It was taught in various mystery schools where special spiritual techniques were used in order to purify one's self allowing for an expansion in consciousness. This expansion would enable a person to experience a multidimensional state of being where they could rapidly increase their spiritual evolution and ultimately reach the level of pure unconditional love. Unfortunately, these powerful Star Tetrahedron spiritual energy field activation techniques were only made available to those in the schools who were ready to handle these powerful energies. Therefore, they were only given to select initiates in mystery schools who had attained high levels of consciousness. This has always been the way of spiritual evolution throughout our existence, where only the very few who are ready are able to come into such knowledge. Purportedly, when the overall level of human consciousness reached the level of the "Harmonic Convergence" in 1987, it haled a new era of spiritual development. It was a "New Age" which marked the planetary alignment. The timing of this event correlated with the Mayan calendar where specific dates marked the planetary alignment with the Sun, Moon and six out of eight planets. In his book, *The Mayan Factor: Path beyond Technology*, Jose Argüelles suggest that this date marked the end of twenty-two cycles of 52 years each, or 1,144 years in all. The twenty-two cycles were divided into thirteen "heaven" cycles, which began in 843 CE and ended in 1519, when the nine "hell" cycles began, ending 468 years later in 1987.

In recent times, Drunvalo Melchizedek has probably been the most instrumental in helping people to activate their Star Tetrahedron into a Merkaba through his *Flower of Life* workshops. His work along with the spiritual efforts practiced by mass numbers of awakened people has helped to raise the level of consciousness that is being achieved on a global level. This heightened state of awareness was reached during the mid 1990s and has continued to expand due to the work of people like Drunvalo and a man named Alton who also taught some of the advanced Merkaba activation techniques. They taught the activation of 9 spiritual energy fields into 4 Merkabas. However, today sacred Merkaba techniques are activating 29 spiritual energy fields into all 12 Merkabas throughout the Universe and it is believed that these sacred Merkaba techniques are the most powerful spiritual techniques on the planet. These techniques rapidly expand the consciousness which helps to increase the rate of spiritual evolution. By learning to master these techniques, a person can cleanse their emotional and mental energy fields allowing the consciousness to expand to such an extent, that they are able to travel through consciousness and experience the wonders of higher dimensions. This is so very important because any genuine individual healing that is created within the "Self" creates a reciprocal healing affect within the planet and any planetary healing we undertake directly has a self-healing effect. If we continue to utilize techniques that activate Merkaba and re-align the Merkaba within our divine blue print, we can directly activate the DNA according to its original template. All the systems that are built on the chemical lens of the DNA are brought back into integrity, energetic pollutions are transmuted and karma is cleared. And because our individual template is intrinsically connected to the planetary, Universal and Cosmic template, we are reminded that our distortions as well as our cleansing, also affects the very cosmos we are a part of.

Sacred Geometry

Sacred Geometry is considered to be the blueprint of creation and thus the origin of all form. It is an ancient science that explores and explains the energy patterns that create and unify all things and reveals the exact way the energy of creation organizes itself. Ronald Holt, Director of the *Flower of Life* research says that when we relate Great Spirit, Consciousness, or "God" and the opening of the heart to geometry, we are creating Sacred Geometry. He says it is the expression of geometry related to the evolution of consciousness, mind, body, and spirit in geometric terms and that true Sacred Geometry is not just static angular forms but rather organic and living where it is in constant evolution (transcendence) or devolution (materialization), ascending or descending from one form to another.

Everything from DNA, snow flakes, pine cones, flower petals, diamond crystals, the branching of trees, a nautilus shell, the stars we spin around, the galaxy we spiral within, the air we breathe, and all life forms as we know them, materializes from Sacred Geometry. Apparently, there are five perfect 3-dimensional forms depicted here which are; the *Tetrahedron, Hexahedron, Octahedron, Dodecahedron,* and *Icosahedron* collectively known as the "Platonic Solids" which form the foundation of everything in the physical world.

Tetrahedron
Four triangular faces, four vertices, and six edges.

Cube
Six square faces, eight vertices, and twelve edges.

Octahedron
Eight triangular faces, six vertices, and twelve edges.

Dodecahedron
Twelve pentagonal faces, twenty vertices, and thirty edges.

Icosahedron
Twenty triangular faces, twelve vertices, and thirty edges.

The faces of Platonic Solids are congruent regular polygons, with the same number of faces meeting at each vertex; thus, all its edges are congruent, as are its vertices and angles. The name of each figure is derived from its number of faces: respectively 4, 6, 8, 12, and 20. In the 1980s, a professor at the University of Chicago named Robert Moon, demonstrated how the "Periodic Table of Elements" (which constitutes everything in the physical world) is based on these same five geometric forms. Literally on every scale, every natural pattern of growth or movement adheres to the rules of one or more of these geometric shapes.

Since time immemorial, the ancients knew these patterns were codes that were somehow symbolic of the inner realm and how understanding these Sacred Geometric figures was essential to understanding the mysteries of our soul and the laws and wisdom of the Universe. They consciously understood how Sacred Geometry could take on a much deeper level of significance when grounded in the experience of self-awareness. As such, Sacred Geometry has played a significant role involving consciousness and the profound mysteries of awareness. Through it, we can discover the balance and harmony existing in any and all situations even the circumstances of our everyday life. By truly understanding the inner-connectedness of all things through these geometric patterns, we can begin to see the unity and wholeness in geometry which can help eliminate our false sense of separateness from nature and from those around us. This explains why most shapes associated with spirituality are pyramids and hemispheres such as the domes that are the basis of religious buildings, mosques, churches and synagogues. These particular shapes are energy emitters which produce a type of penetrating signal that acts as a radio wave that carries sound vibrations.

The understanding of Sacred Geometry as an underlying part of existence is nothing new. In fact, it can even be seen imbedded in many of the ancient monuments that still exist today such as The Great Pyramid at Giza. The height of this pyramid is in Phi ratio to its base. Conversely, it is a known truth that the geometry in the great pyramid is far more accurate than any structure in existence today. However, one of the most important aspects of Sacred Geometry is the "Golden Mean Spiral," derived by using the "Golden Ratio." The Golden Mean was used in the design of sacred buildings in ancient architecture to produce spiritual energy that facilitated connectivity with spiritual realms through prayer. As a part of this Universal construct, reality is very structured, and life is even more structured. This is illustrated in all natural occurrences in the form of geometry. This cosmic structuring of physical matter is the very basis of reality; hence we live in a coherent world governed by unseen laws. These laws are always manifested in the physical world and The Golden Mean is what governs this aspect of reality.

In his book *Nothing in This Book Is True, But It's Exactly How Things Are,* Bob Frissell describes Sacred Geometry by saying, "It is the morphogenic structure behind reality itself, underlying even mathematics and that it is actually geometric shapes that generates all the laws of physics." Subsequently, there can be nothing on any level which does not possess some form of geometry within it because the atoms themselves are merely spheres with electrons circling them. This circling process creates what is called an "Electron Cloud" which resembles a circle. In crystallization, different sized atoms align in a straight edge, a *Triangle*, a *Tetrahedron*, a *Cube*, an *Octahedron*, an *Icosahedron* or a *Dodecahedron*. And since the body is made up of these very particles, we are in fact nothing but geometric images and shapes through-and-through. As such, all physical laws are embedded in the body's intricate geometric structure. This minute world of images and geometric shapes forms the very field around the body as the Merkaba in the form of the Star Tetrahedron which is the very same image that surrounds everything in creation.

There is unity among creation, for without it the Universe would be chaotic. Everything is connected by way of a sacred geometric system which unites all things unto itself. Nothing is outside of this unified field. There is only unity. Anything outside of this understanding is delusional at best. Nothing can be separated from the whole; therefore we are complete in our composition as divine reflections of this great oneness. Seek to understand this sacred system of geometry for in doing so; one will have come into the greatest secret man has ever known which is "unity of being." Through an expanded understanding, we will come to see how we are not merely "*A being*" but rather "*being*" itself. We are the key to wisdom and greater understanding because hidden within the genetic blueprint lies the secret to all creation in the form of Sacred Geometry.

Flower of Life

Thoth who was considered to be one of the wisest beings to ever grace this planet said that "All levels of consciousness in the Universe are integrated by a single image in Sacred Geometry." He described this image as being the key to time, space, dimensions and consciousness itself. This image is known as the *Flower of Life* and there are many spiritual beliefs associated with it. For example; depictions of the five Platonic Solids are found within the symbol of Metatron's Cube, which may be derived from this pattern. As earlier discussed, these Platonic Solids are geometrical forms which are said to act as a template from which all life springs. In his book *Serpent of Light: Beyond 2012*, Drunvalo Melchizedek describes the Flower of Life by saying "It is the creation pattern for the entire

Universe and everything in it, including all living creatures." He says it's even the creation pattern for aspects of the Universe that are not considered things or matter, such as emotions and feelings. At the Flower of Life website it says this symbol contains both ancient and religious values that describe the fundamental forms of space and time. In this sense, it serves as a visual expression of the common thread that weaves through all mankind. The Flower of Life symbol was sacred throughout various cultures of antiquity because it contained all of the building blocks of the Universe. While this topic is very scientific in nature, this chapter will serve only as an attempt to provide you with a more simplified understanding of this symbol and how it pertains to life as we know it. For a more detailed understanding of the Flower of Life symbol, feel free to visit www. floweroflife.org or pick up one of Drunvalo Melchizedeks books on the subject.

Since Platonic Solids are the foundational patterns in which life is expressed, the Flower of Life symbol serves as a multifaceted template with countless applications that provide glimpses into the oneness and the unity of being for all things. It is by far the clearest expression of God and it is through this symbol that one is able to unify mind, heart and spirit thus transforming the world. The Flower of Life symbol illustrates how all things emanate from the same source and it demonstrates how everything is intimately and permanently tied together. This realization has an overwhelming affect on the person who is able to grasp its wisdom because although a person may agree with this notion, it is not until they actually embrace it that they are able to fully comprehend it. So, in order to provide a better understanding, let's look at this ancient symbol from a systematic approach.

The *"Vesica Piscis"* is a symbol made from two circles of the same radius, intersecting in such a way that the centre of each circle lies on the circumference of the other. It has been called a symbol of the "fusion" of opposites and a "passageway" through the world's apparent polarity. Its design is one of the simplest forms of Sacred Geometry. It has been depicted around the world at sacred sites, most notably at the Chalice Well in Glastonbury, England, and has been the subject of mystical speculation throughout history. One of the earliest known occurrences of the *"Vesica Piscis,"* and perhaps the first, was among the Pythagoreans, who considered it a holy figure. The symbol is formed from the almond shaped area in the overlap between the circles, together with the upper arcs as far as the edges of a rectangle whose sides coincide with the widest points of the almond. The resulting figure resembles that of a stylized fish in the middle, and a flattened Greek alpha. *"Vesica Piscis"* literally means the *"flesh of the fish."* This figure is depicted here:

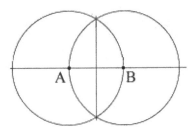

Fig. 2 Vesica Piscis

In Christianity, this figure is known to be the basis for the *"Ichthys"* fish which is used as a depiction of Jesus the Christ who ushered in the age of the fish or Piscis. According to some religious beliefs, the *"Vesica Piscis"* represents the second stage in the creation of the "Seed of Life," in that it was constructed by the "Creator" through the creation of a second spherical Octahedron joined with the first. It is believed; the Creator's consciousness began inside the first sphere and journeyed outside the surface of that sphere to create the second. In fact, God is said to have created light through the creation of the second sphere (or Vesica Piscis). *"Let there be light"* which is a relevant excerpt from the Old Testament. Another notable example of that which may be derived from the Flower of Life is the "Tree of Life*"* which has been an important symbol of Sacred Geometry for many people from various religious backgrounds. Particularly, the teachings of the *"Kabbalah"* have dealt intricately with the "Tree of Life."

The pattern of the *"Vesica Piscis"* is said to be a geometric formula which represents the electromagnetic spectrum of light according to the book, *The Ancient Secret of The Flower of Life* written by Drunvalo Melchizedek. The Flower of Life is the accepted name for this geometrical figure which is composed of multiple evenly-spaced, overlapping circles which are arranged to form a flower-like pattern with a six-fold symmetry like a hexagon. The center of each circle is on the circumference of six surrounding circles of the same diameter as seen here in the "Seed of Life:"

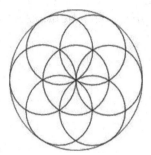

Fig. 3. Seed of Life

According to Drunvalo Melchizedek, in the Judeo-Christian tradition, the stages which construct the "Seed of Life" are said to represent the seven days of Creation, in which God created life; Genesis 2:2-3, Exodus 23:12, 31:16-17, Isaiah 56:6-8. Within these stages, among other things, are the symbols of the "*Vesica Piscis*" and "Borromean rings" which represent the "Holy Trinity" as depicted here:

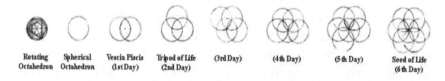

Rotating Octahedron	Spherical Octahedron	Vescia Piscis (1st Day)	Tripod of Life (2nd Day)	(3rd Day)	(4th Day)	(5th Day)	Seed of Life (6th Day)

The circle is considered to be a representation of infinity. Therefore, if we are at the circumference of a circle then there is no end or beginning and it is from this origin that larger infinities must follow. If we were to intersect the two circles, it would form the Vesica Pisces which is the second stage of the creation of the "Seed of Life." Next is the third stage which is the intersection of three circles which is called the tripod. Based on certain religious beliefs, the first step in building the "Seed of Life" was the creation of the Octahedron by the divine Creator. The next step was for the

Creator to spin the shape on its axes forming a sphere. (See diagram above). The Creator's consciousness is the only thing that exists in the membrane of the sphere itself. It should be noted that the "first step" so to speak, is not to be confused with the "first day," the latter being in reference to the seven days of creation. Subsequently, this pattern of creation happens to be identical to the cellular structure of the third embryonic division where the first cell divides into two cells, then to four cells then to eight. This is the creation method used by the body and all of the energy systems including the ones used to create the Spirit-Light-Body or the "Merkaba." All life begins with the imploding-splitting-combining-creation of new cells, (spheres), through a specific Sacred Geometrical sequence called the *Fibonacci* sequence, whereby each number adds to itself the last number to create the next number in the sequence: (0 1 1 2 3 5 8 13 21 . . .). All life begins and creates itself in this manner and through the representation of the *"Seed of Life," "The Tree of Life,"* and the *"Flower of Life"* which contains informational patterns and systems with each one explaining different aspects of reality. Through this system, we are able to access everything ranging from the body to the far reaching galaxies.

Fig. 4 Flower of Life

The Flower of Life, as seen above, is by far the most important of all symbols in Sacred Geometry because it contains the entire design for all creation. Sacred Geometry is the mystical yet universal language which allows access to ancient knowledge contained within the cellular memory. It can enable us to interpret the wisdom of beings far more intelligent than we now are and it can also allow communication between other worlds and dimensions. But most importantly, by understanding Sacred Geometry and the Flower of Life wisdom, humanity is able to gain a more scientific understanding which allows us to consciously shape our future and accelerate the ascension process.

The Flower of Life can be found in all major religions of the world. It contains the very "patterns of creation" as they emerged from the "Great Void." Everything is manifested from the Creator's thoughts and after the creation of the Seed of Life; the same motion is continued, ultimately creating the sacred Flower of Life. A more in depth study of this symbol will provide you with deep spiritual meaning and a greater form of enlightenment. There are various groups around the world that coordinate workshops where they teach certain methods and interpretations of the Flower of Life and by studying the nature of these sacred forms of geometry and their relationship to each other, we are better able to gain insight into the scientific, philosophical, psychological, aesthetic and mystical laws of the Universe because in contemplating them, we are actually contemplating the genesis of all creation.

Christ Consciousness Grid

In Plato's *Timaeus*, he refers to the Christ Consciousness Grid as *"The ideal body of the cosmos,"* describing it as the synthesis of the platonic solids. It is referred to as the Christ Consciousness Grid because it serves as an individual characteristic of the collective consciousness. It is the unity of being which carries the potential of the Christ principle. Within this grid all the necessary information is imprinted to experience the Christ Consciousness.

Since the formation of our planet, Sacred Geometry has served as the foundational structure and building blocks to which all things in creation emanate. In an article published in the Ezine *Spirit of Ma'at Earth Energies*, Vol. 3, July 2003, Ronald L. Holt, Director of The Flower of Life Research describes the Christ Consciousness Grid by saying "It is an actualized geometric and energetic expression of the principles of creation that serves as the bridge between our planet's physical and energetic manifestations." In talking about this grid, he says it was born at the moment of the "Big-Bang" or even prior to that when the void was actually preparing for the birth of the Universe. He goes on to explain how the Christ Conscious Grid is actually fractal and holographic in nature which spans all of creation including its many dimensional levels. He says this grid and others like it are not just on Earth, but correspond to the entire physical Universe and that the Universe cannot exist without these grids. They are needed to ensure the appropriate distribution of life-force energy and to provide the templates needed for material creation. Not only that, but they are a physical expression of the sacred code of creation itself. These grids, according to Holt are not inanimate objects but rather they are the blueprint to consciousness itself being expressed in harmonic form. This very science has been the precursor to every form and every manifestation in physical reality because the grid serves as the blueprint around which the smallest and most minute particles formulate. Unfortunately, this information is not known by the average person. However, it's a known fact that government agencies have been aware of this information for quite some time.

While this grid is considered to be feminine in character, it is actually bipolar in nature because it combines both the feminine and masculine energies which integrate emotions and information into light and love. Both work harmoniously with each other to integrate the diversity of life. It is linked to the collective unconscious as an emotional reflection of the entire planet which serves as the matrix that supports our planetary awareness. It is the *"magnetosphere"* which maintains our gravitational field around the Sun. While this may seem like a new concept to some, the ancients were aware of this spiritual grid in times of antiquity. Although it wasn't until recently that we have become reacquainted with this understanding through various forms of channeling and open communications from higher life forms.

Based on what we know, this grid is shaped similar to a doughnut or "toroid" and its size and form can vary based upon solar radiation. It is connected to the magnetic axis of the Earth and therefore, it is associated with the emotional state of the planet and all therein. Because of certain changes within the Sun like solar explosions and other internal variations, we have begun to experience a very erratic shift contributing to the extreme changes and polarization within our environment.

There are basically two forces at work within the Earth's grid forming a lattice of lines that are termed "ley lines" where energy is created at the vortices that in turn coincide with so-called power spots. These ley lines are the supposed footprint on the Christ Consciousness Grid of the Earth. First there is the "telluric force" which is responsible for the adjustments of the Earth's crust. It releases energy through the geological faults, the subterranean water currents and magma. Basically, the telluric force serves as the Earth's circulatory system which is its vital force. The other force is the "geo-pathogenic" lines that form a pattern with the telluric force. These patterns are being created by the accumulation of disharmonic energies within the Christ Consciousness Grid. The wars, constant bloodshed, slaughter, death and pain are the earmarks of this energetic pattern which will ultimately cause the same patterns to occur in those same places time and time again.

Our planet is sheathed in these grids or webs of geometric shapes and figures so to speak which caters to the proper delivery and grouping of energy and variations of frequencies needed to sustain the planet's rhythmic pattern. This grid is sometimes referred to as the "Unity Consciousness Grid" and it serves to keep everything intrinsically connected via Sacred Geometric figures or the five platonic solids. The Christ Consciousness Grid is the electromagnetic force field that surrounds our planet reflecting and amplifying our levels of consciousness and awareness. Drunvalo Melchizedek asserts that there are virtually millions of these patterns that appear from space as a glow of light around the Earth and that every living thing has a grid of energy surrounding it in order for it to exist. This grid coincides with every part of our being because it is holographic and fractal in nature as well. This includes all of our vital organs, cells, and even our DNA. So, the Christ Consciousness Grid surrounding the Earth has its fractal counterparts fully within the body, spirit, and consciousness. There, nestled in the pureness of being lies this Christ Conscious awareness of only Love and interconnectedness to all of creation.

Drunvalo Melchizedek believes that without this unified grid of Christ Consciousness, humanity would be doomed to the material world and we would never be able to ascend into the higher levels of consciousness. Fortunately for us, Earth's grid serves as some what of a spiritual telecommunications system which when properly aligned allows us to connect with higher consciousness. This connection then enables us to increase our ability to serve as conduits of pure and divine energy. As spiritual beings which are holographic in nature, we are vastly more capable of connecting with the source of our being through an awareness of this Christ Consciousness Grid. Accordingly, this is the "fabric" or grid that holds the holographic recollection of immense interconnectedness that generates higher consciousness for anyone seeking it. It serves as a constant reminder of our true nature and it encourages us to always seek the highest level of awareness. Holt confirms this by stating that:

"The Christ Consciousness Grid stimulates us to evolve into conscious awareness with our open heart and with high levels of impeccability and integrity. It also helps us integrate and harmonize a true group unity as it is a unified collective consciousness. This means that we are also preparing our internal templates to integrate and harmonize all of the lifetimes we have spent within each culture on this planet, setting the stage to help us feel the oneness of all cultures simultaneously, without bias and without prejudice. And, just as we've had a lifetime or more in each culture of this planet, we have also existed on other galactic worlds and cultures. Holographically, we were born into all cultures, on all galactic worlds simultaneously. The Christ Consciousness Grid is representative of our quest to integrate and harmonize all of our terrestrial and extra-terrestrial lifetimes as a whole experience within this creation. The higher levels of life have always made their frequency available to us at all times. After all, they are us in another form. As we awaken to a higher sense of purpose and action, we naturally and eventually attune to higher grid levels until we reach the Christ Consciousness Grid and awaken the Christ Consciousness within ourselves. Life always attempts to stimulate us to achieve our highest potential and that potential is the full realization of our divinity, our divine mission and the purpose for being here at this time. Re-connecting to the Christ Consciousness Grid is the doorway that will lead us home to paradise, right here on Earth and experienced right there in the body." (Some emphasis added)

Zero Point

According to the concept of Zero Point, there is a point within the Universe where everything becomes still or at rest. It's sort of like a field of perfect balance between motion, sound, light and movement. In that space, in the "in-between," the point at which motion becomes still and sound becomes silent or darkness becomes light and hot becomes cold is the field of "Zero Point." In his book *Awakening to Zero Point: The Collective Initiation*, Gregg Braden defines Zero Point by saying it is when, "The amount of vibrational energy associated with matter, as the parameters defining that matter decline to zero." He goes on to say that to an observer, the world at Zero Point appears to be very still, while the participant experiences a quantum restructuring of the very boundaries that define the experience. He feels that at this very moment, Earth and our bodies are collectively preparing for this Zero Point experience which he refers to as "The Shift of the Ages."

Kiara Windrider author of *Doorway to Eternity: A Guide to Planetary Ascension*, describes Zero Point by saying, "It is like the odometer in your car synchronizing to 9999 before turning over to zero." It is the "in-breath" of God. It is that moment in time when everything on this planet reaches a complete state of unity where time, dimensions and reality converges and becomes one. This is what we are currently experiencing during this time of ascension. We are at the threshold where all things slowly begin to merge into one, where all dimensions simultaneously begin to resonate on the same octave. At that point, the Earth will systematically stop spinning on its axis for three days and we will lose awareness during that time. Upon resuming its rotation, the Earth will begin to turn in a different direction causing its poles to shift according to Braden. This is what is known as the "great shift." It is during this transition, while the planet is stopped that God consciousness will merge with the hearts and minds of each individual on Earth, forever infusing a "Collective Initiation." And, as the base frequency increases; Earth's magnetic field will slow down and eventually stop at 13 cycles per second which is Zero Point. Science has determined that by 2012, planet Earth will reach 13 cycles per second or Zero Point.

During this Zero Point moment of infusion, all of humanity's vibratory frequencies will increase exponentially and because all things relate to rates or vibrations, we will suddenly find ourselves being thrust into higher dimensions along with the rest of the planet. Semir Osmanagić referred to 2012 in his book *The World of the Maya* by saying; "When the 'heavens open' and cosmic energy is allowed to flow throughout our tiny Planet, we will be raised to a higher level by the vibrations."

This event only occurs within 12,960 or roughly 13,000 years according to the Earth's Equinox. As our planet crosses the Galactic Equator, the influence of the Central Sun permeates our Solar System giving all aspects of life an evolutionary increase. Throughout this transition, the shadow self or the "darker," hidden aspects of our being will become exposed, thus allowing for a full transmutation and awakening. Mankind's cellular make-up along with its genetic encoding will shift in order to sustain these new energies. Even the planet itself will recalibrate to these higher frequencies. During this precessional cycle, a unique thing happens which causes major shifts in human consciousness including shifts within the Earth. During the last 13,000 year cycle, we have been guided by the "masculine" aspect, but as we draw closer to the precession of the Equinox, we ill usher in the "feminine" energy which will guide us throughout the next cycle of 13,000 years. This transition is akin to hitting the "reset button," where all of life is offered the opportunity to heal any disharmonic wave patterns and to be brought back into a collective unity.

As spiritual beings, we too posses a Zero Point so-to-speak which is centered at the root of our being. This is the aspect of oneself that is associated with the higher dimensional physics and metaphysics of the heart. Dr. Christopher Holmes maintains that each individual is a divine emanation within the higher dimensional space of the heart. And, according to Madame Helena Blavatsky in the *Secret Doctrine*; "Material points without extension or Zero-Points are . . . the materials out of which the 'Gods' and other invisible powers clothe themselves in bodies . . . the entire Universe concentrating itself, as it were, in a single point." According to Jewish mysticism, creation emerges from a Zero Point source out of a seeming "void" which precipitates dimensions of being out of apparent non-being, everything out of nothing, '*as above, so below.*' This is what the "Tree of Life", the "Ladder of Jacob," or the "Star of David," essentially represent.

Unfortunately, for many of us, truth is stranger than fiction. But, we can always find real truth in what we consider to be science-fiction. I believe the real truth of things is shrouded in science-fiction where art is always imitating life especially in television with shows like *Stargate SG-1* or *Stargate Atlantis* that make references to Zero-Point energy in the form of Zero Point Modules or ZPMs. In fact, the Ancients attempted to extract Zero-Point energy directly from their own Universe in "Project Arcturus." Upon closer examination, we will discover how the DNA (which is the genetic programming), is set to remember the truth of who we really are. At Zero Point, a polar shift of consciousness occurs when the polarities of the energy field merges and shifts. Ancient civilizations have tried to assimilate this experience by being placed into chambers that would bring them to a place of Zero Point. This was to help mankind prepare for what the world was expected to go through sometime around "2012" according to "end time' theories and the Mayan Calendar end date of December 21, 2012.

The Photon Belt

One of the predictions surrounding the Mayan calendar is that our solar system will enter a band of light called "The Photon Belt" sometime around December of 2012. This "band of light," also referred to as a (photon ring, manasic ring, photon band or golden nebula, is what the ancients believed would send the world as we know it into an initial tumultuous situation followed by a "New Age," and a period of enlightenment. According to some New Age beliefs, Earth will pass through this belt, resulting in either Humanity's elevation to a higher plane of existence or the end of the world, or both. It is expected that once we've entered into the Photon Belt, electricity will no longer function and there will be three to five days of total darkness. This interaction might cause massive failure of electrical equipment with two to three days of total darkness or total daylight, and initiate a spiritual transition (usually referred to as "a shift in consciousness," "the shift of the ages," or just "the shift," with the time period leading up to the shift as "the quickening." This time has also been referred to as "Zero Point" by such authors as Gregg Braden and it coincides with various indigenous cultures, prophecies, the Mayan calendar, and 2012 "End time" scenarios.

For millennia, civilizations such as the Maya, the Hopi Indians, and the Dogons of Africa have predicted almost with razor like precision exactly what we were to experience in the years to come. Much of this information was provided to them by ancient visitors from distant stars and galaxies. These visitors from distant galaxies had an extreme knack for understanding the cosmos and they used the solar system to navigate their space craft. Often times, this advanced race of beings would impart knowledge of the future onto their subjects who would then record them onto tablets or commit them to memory. Many of these predictions of future calamities were recorded in scripture and other forms of sacred text. Perhaps these predictions were instigated by these advanced beings or they were simply able to know the future either through "time travel" or by reading the skies. Whatever the case, the wisdom they imparted was well documented.

The ability to know future events by reading and understanding the stars was definitely an ability possessed by ancient civilizations. The Maya whose calendar consisted of a 260-day religious calendar, twenty 30-day months with a separate 5 days at the end was one of these civilizations. Their calendars were based upon careful observation of the planets, Sun, and Moon. Mayan astronomers calculated that a year contained 365.2420 days. Scientists now know that the Mayan year was .0002 of a day too short. The Maya had an uncanny ability for determining future outcomes by discovering that time is "cyclical" rather than linear. This means we experience certain occurrences in cycles. In fact, our Universe operates on one big cycle where things happen according to a set of situations based on the cyclical nature of the solar system. This understanding is what enabled these people to know exactly when to plant crops, attack enemies, or crown new rulers among other things. To this very day, they have been able to predict when the moon will rise and set and when it will be a full moon. Scientists have known the precise moonrises and sets through-out the modern day. However, when they studied the Mayan records of when the moonrise and moonsets would occur they discovered that up to this very day, the Maya have only been .33 seconds off the actual time. One question to ask would be how could they have known this without the sophisticated telescopes and devices used by modern day astronomers? Again, they were masters at understanding the natural cycles of the planet along its predictable course.

One such prediction made by the Maya was that—"Great Birds" will come from the sky and end a great city "to the north" in 9/11/01. Of course these "Great Birds" were actually two airplanes that struck the twin towers of New York a city "to the north." The Maya have made many predictions most of which have all been accurate. But of all the predictions ever made by the Maya, the greatest one to date is by far the "end time" scenario where they postulate the world will end on or around December 21, 2012. Whether they meant a total end to all life or simply the end of time as we know it still remains to be seen.

What exactly could have given the Maya this revelation? Was it something shared with them by their visitors from the sky? Or perhaps it was simply a matter of reading the planetary cycles to determine this outcome. But why "2012" and what would happen during this time that would lead them to believe the world would actually come to an end? I'm led to believe they knew something in which we have been far too ignorant or negligent to understand. I believe that certain something could have very well been their understanding of the great 25,860 year cycle of the solar system and our entering the Photon Belt every 12,000-12,500 years. Accordingly, this Photon Belt circles the

Pleiadian system at an absolute right angle to its orbital planes. As our Sun orbits the Pleiades once every 25,860 years, it reaches the midpoint of the Photon Belt approximately every 12,500 years. It requires some 2,000 years to traverse it, meaning that after departing this realm, another 10,500 years pass before our Solar System enters it again. Oddly enough, it has now been roughly 10,000 or so years since the upheavals that brought about the total destruction of ancient Atlantis. We then have 21,860 years of darkness and 4,000 years of light (21,860 + 4,000 = 25,860) years, or one complete cycle/orbit. Coincidentally, the Photon-Belt cycle is synchronized with a number of greater cycles. For example, the 25,860 year cycle of our solar system through the galaxy, and 103,440 years marking the evolutionary peak of four cycles of 25,860 years. However, what distinguishes this particular cycle from all its previous occurrences is that it culminates, together with all the other cycles of which it is but a part—including the overall cycle of 225 million years, in one single point of convergence called the "Harmonic Convergence." It is also recognized that this point in time coincides with the Universe reaching its maximum point of expansion. Technically, the energy of the Photon Belt is etheric and spiritual in nature. It is not physical, although it does have an influence on the physical being. The 10,500 years of darkness between the 2000-year periods of light allows for spiritual evolution. Unfortunately, many of us have forgotten our divine source and purpose during these Earthly sojourns and these periods of Light serve a dual purpose. They represent a sorting-out process, gathering matured souls into the Light of the Spirit and affording the weaker, just maturing souls a stabilization period of respite and an opportunity for further spiritual growth.

Although some people speculate that we entered the sphere of influence of this Photon Belt in 1962, calculations approximate the year of the actual entry into its mainstream to be around 2011 or 2012. This correlates with the time when the Universe reaches its point of maximum expansion. Eastern belief systems speak of a contraction and expansion rhythm of the Universe as the "In-breath" and "Out-breath" of God with each breath covering a time span equal to 11,000 years. It just so happens that this time frame corresponds with the "Grand Cycles," the orbit of our Sun around the central sun Alcyone.

Knowledge of the Photon Belt was first made known in 1949 when Paul Otto Hesse made the supposition about a great "band of light" or "ring of photons" which is going to fully envelop the Earth causing a catastrophic scenario. Hesse described his beliefs about the belt and its impact in his 1949 book *Der Jüngste Tag* (English: "The Last Day"). The concept was further progressed in 1977 by Samael Aun Weor in his lecture *The Rings of Alcyone* at the Conference on Alcyone in which he cites Hesse who predicts that if the Earth enters the belt first, a "great fire in the skies, or pyrotechnic lights would occur"; but if the Sun enters first, "the radiation released would interfere with the solar rays and darkness would reign for 110 hours, after which everything would return to normal." Weor refers to the Photon Belt as "Alcyone's rings" or "the rings of Alcyone." Alcyone, Weor claims, is the principal star of the Pleiades 7-star cluster, of which our Sun, according to Weor, "is the seventh sun that circles Alcyone." Alcyone has rings made of "radiation" caused by the splitting of the electrons which releases energy by which Weor refers to as "*manasic*," a Sanskrit term for the mind that is in some way related to the "*inferior manas*" (inferior mind), or to the "*superior manas*" (superior mind) of the subtle body. Weor suggests the electrons release a type of unknown energy where he says:

> "Thereabout, in the year of 1974, three astronauts who were circling the Earth reported a type of radiation, or a type of unknown energy, unsuspected by official science. Obviously, since 1962, specifically since the 4th of February of that year, our planet Earth, and in general, the whole solar system has been on the verge of entering the terrible rings of Alcyone . . . These rings extend for some light years; they are instantly enormous. Nevertheless, at any given moment, our solar system will enter Alcyone's rings."

However, the suggestion of the Photon Belt didn't become popular in "New Age" circles until it was first published in the 1981 *Australian International UFO Flying Saucer Research Magazine* #12 in an article called *The Photon Belt Alcyone Saga* by Shirley Kemp which was later reprinted in the Nexus magazine in February 1991 as *The Photon Belt Story*. Since then, there have been countless other suggestions hinting at the possibility of a huge band of photons that could possibly affect the Earth. On May 5 and June 23, 1992 the *Phoenix Liberator* mentions the Photon Belt. The Photon Belt is also mentioned in a few *Phoenix Journal*s from the mid-1990s. On June 8, 1992, the Photon Belt appears on Usenet in the newsgroup sci. astro. In November 1992, in the channeled newsletter, *Revelations of Awareness*, the Photon Belt is mentioned in the section *The Photon Belt: "Five Days of Darkness & No Electrical Power,"* where the Phoenix Liberator claimed this event would occur on July 25, 1992. Outwardly, no known events occurred on or during that time. However, the newsletter refers to the Photon Belt in numerous issues thereafter. Ultimately, a number of predictions have been made as to the date of Earth's collision with the Photon Belt. So far, no observable effects attributable to the Photon Belt have been seen on those dates. Dates so far given have included 1992 and 1997, future dates include 2011or 2012.

In 1993, in Foster Perry's book *When Lightning Strikes a Hummingbird: The Awakening of a Healer*, Barbara Hand Clow mentions the Photon Belt numerous times in the book's foreword. In April 1994 the book, *You are Becoming a Galactic Human* by Virginia Essene and Sheldan Nidle was published which mentions the Photon Belt:

> "The Photon Belt, a huge "toroid" shaped object composed of photon light particles, was first discovered by your scientists in 1961 near the vicinity of the Pleiades by satellite instrumentation."

In January 1998, Noel Huntley, Ph.D. wrote an article called *The Photon-Belt Encounter* which describes many aspects of the encounter with the belt, which he refers to also as an "electromagnetic cloud," in great detail. Since 2000, the Photon Belt has been mentioned in other books such as, *The Pleidian Agenda* by Barbara Hand Clow. In the 2005 book *Touched by the Dragon's Breath: Conversations at Colliding Rivers* by Michael Harrington, the author mentions the Photon Belt numerous times and, in the foreword, refers to a 1987 meeting with John Redstone at "Colliding Rivers" who, the author claims, was familiar with the Photon Belt, citing it as "a spectacular band of multi-dimensional light that St. Germaine called the *Golden Nebula.*" Harrington also refers to a Native American prophecy that spoke of a dynamic wave of energy traveling through space and that when the Earth passed through this wave, great changes would occur. This "great transformation" he says, would be preceded by a "time of purification."

Given this set of circumstances, what exactly would an experience such as this mean? Well for starters, at present our planet is flying through space at an estimated 67,000 miles per hour. It is believed that upon entering the Photon Belt, we will have reached a speed of 208,000 miles per hour, or an increase of 141,000 miles per hour. This compression alone would have a tremendous affect on time and space beyond comprehension. All matter would have to undergo a tremendous transformation in order to be in harmony with the compression and accelerated speed. Every cell in our body, every molecule, every atom would be rearranged so as to (hopefully) transform our current bodies of density and morality into a vehicle of transformational light, capable of facilitating the incoming Christ consciousness. What I find to be most interesting is that our DNA would revert to a system of 12 strands and our chakras would also be rearranged and increased, going from 7 to 12. Our atoms would be increased and rearranged in order to facilitate the higher frequencies and we would no longer exist as we now do. This is something that would appear very subtly as a change in matter and a change in consciousness, where consciousness would have more effect on matter and on the material realm. As we enter the main segment of the Photon Belt, we would be raised to the fifth dimension of existence and we would become "transformed" so-to-speak. Our bodies would become etheric meaning we would no longer take on physical disease or ailments as we now do. Since our bodies would be of an etheric nature, we would vibrate at a much faster rate allowing us to take on greater capabilities such as telepathy and telekinesis. With these new forms, we would not require much sleep or food as our bodies would be pure energy. Obviously buy entering this massive source of energy we would no longer utilize archaic methods of power such as fossil fuel which destroys the planets environment. In fact the new energy would be "photon" energy based on the concept of "Anti-matter." Scientists are aware of such energy only they say it takes far too long to create this type of energy which comes from the collision of atoms. Be that as it may, one gram of anti-mater could fuel a vehicle for 100,000 thousand years and one pound could fuel the entire U.S. for three full days. With this new source of energy, inter-galactic travel would finally be made possible and traveling throughout the galaxy would become common place. Traveling to distant galaxies would be as simple as traveling across town taking minutes as opposed to light years. But by far the greatest possibility of entering into this New Age would be to finally interact with higher forms of beings and inhabitants from earlier civilizations like the Lemurians, Atlanteans and the Mayans, that now exist on higher dimensional levels. Once we enter the Photon Belt we would be in a fully realized "space age" which would allow us to reclaim our full spiritual potential. Here is a general description taken from the internet of what we could expect once we entered the Photon Belt:

➢ Enter the null zone.
➢ Alter body type of all living things.
➢ Non-operation of any electrical devices. Lights cannot be turned on. Cars will not start. When the collapse of the planet's electrical and magnetic field occurs, it will also allow all atoms on Earth to be changed. The atoms in our bodies would be modified to form new bodies—bodies that are semi-etheric—and the veil of consciousness around us would be removed. We would no longer be living in the limited 3rd dimensional reality. We would now have physical and psychic gifts that we were meant to have.
➢ Total darkness (for 2-3 days). The Sun would have disappeared from view and we would be unable to see stars in the pitch black sky. The atmosphere would become extremely compressed. This aspect is also beginning to happen now as noted by the increase in seismic activities that stretch from the 1960s to the present time. This can also be seen by the dramatic change in our planetary weather patterns.
➢ The big danger would be from nuclear materials since there is the possibility for either nuclear chain-reactions or huge and deadly radioactive explosions of fissionable materials.

Therefore, to avoid these dangers, the Galactic Federation would allow a special landing of technical ships and personnel so that these potential nuclear dangers can be alleviated.

➤ Sun cools down.
➤ Earth climate cools 'ice age type of climate.' This would occur because the Sun would undergo a change in its interdimensional polarity which would prevent the Sun's heat from reaching planet Earth's surface.

Day 3-4

➤ Atmosphere dimly lit (like dawn).
➤ Start photon effect. This photon effect is very important because it would allow us to have a new energy source. This new energy source would permit the end of our planet's fossil fuel dependency. It would also allow the capability for space travel since photon drive technology is the power system for all starships operated by the Galactic Federation.
➤ Photon energy devices would become operable.
➤ Stars would then reappear in the sky.

Day 5-6

➤ Exit the null zone; enter the main photon belt zone.
➤ Transition into a 24-hour daylight period.
➤ Every living thing is invigorated (Humans will go back to having 12 strands of DNA).
➤ Earth climate warms.
➤ Photon beam-powered ships would travel in space.
➤ Incredible psychic abilities are reclaimed (e.g. telepathy, telekinesis, etc).
➤ We would now be living with higher intelligent beings.
➤ Normally going through the photon belt would take 2000 years.
➤ However at this time our solar system would enter an interdimensional rescue bubble that would thrust it out of the Photon Belt.

➢ Our solar system would be put into a position about 3 light years from the Sirius star system (at present Sirius is approximately 8.3 light years from Earth).

➢ This would ultimately end the 24-hour daylight experience and bring the return of an approximate 12-hour daylight/12-hour nighttime schedule.

➢ We would then become fully 5th dimensional beings.

At times I wonder just how much validity there is to these types of speculations. When we take into account how the Maya were able to predict events which such accuracy, one has to wonder whether or not what they are forecasting for the year 2012 is actually true. Accordingly, this wouldn't be the first time Earth has entered the Photon Belt causing massive geological changes. With all of the "end time" speculation about Earth changes via the passing of Nibiru, Polar Shifts and the like, it's very hard not to take any of this stuff seriously.

Although the previous speculations about "end times" have not yet come to fruition, we wouldn't want to be caught unsuspecting like the boy who cried wolf. I firmly believe the world is entering a new stage of enlightenment, a "New Age" so-to-speak. Not a New World Order governed by power mongers but rather a world in which love, peace and light reign supreme. A world where polarities are balanced and we are no longer dominated by the aggressive masculine tendencies of the male ego. This new age would be much like the "Golden Age" prophesized by civilizations of old. It would be a world without false religions, wars, famine, hunger, monetary systems, caste systems, secretive governments, and militia or power mongers.

I realize that in order to arrive at such a place, the world must undergo a purging if you will of the negative or darker energies that exist as they are. This process can only come about through global changes; changes of government and regime; changes in beliefs and ways of cherishing the eternal spirit that permeates all. Mother Earth would survive as she has countless times before. This would not be the first nor would it be the last time this planet has undergone a cataclysmic cleansing of sorts. These devastational upheavals come and go according to the great cycles of the planet and the solar system. People have known about these Earth changes since time immemorial some of which took the time to document these events for future generations. We happen to be that future generation and while we can certainly be grateful to our ancestors for having provided the warnings, we can't help but to feel threatened by these coming calamities. This doesn't mean we lose faith or that we forget our eternality, it simply means that we sometimes fear what we do not know or understand. What is to come and how will we be in the coming world? These are the questions we have. An old Chinese proverb reiterates, *"We have been cursed to live in interesting times,"* and as Charles Dickens so eloquently declared:

> "It was the best of times, it was the worst of times, it was the age of wisdom, it was the age of foolishness, it was the epoch of belief, it was the epoch of incredulity, it was the season of Light, it was the season of Darkness, it was the spring of hope, it was the winter of despair, we had everything before us, we had nothing before us, we were all going direct to heaven, we were all going direct the other way—in short, the period was so far like the present period, that some of its noisiest authorities insisted on its being received, for good or for evil, in the superlative degree of comparison only."

Whether you subscribe to the notion of planet Earth approaching a huge Photon Belt or the approach of a massive sized planet causing catastrophic polar shifts or not is entirely up to you. Now is the time to evaluate these interesting times and see that they are not a curse but a blessing for everything must change and believe it or not; this is definitely change for the better.

Polar Shift

There seems to be a great deal of speculation about if and when there will be a major Polar Shift. What this means scientifically is that North, according to the geographic poles would become South and South would become North. The geographic poles of the Earth refer to the points on the surface of the planet that are intersected by the axis of rotation. In reality, the orientation of Earth's magnetic field has reversed several times, with magnetic north becoming magnetic south and vice versa—an event known as a "Geomagnetic Reversal." It is believed that "reversals" occur when the circulation of liquid nickel/iron in the Earth's outer core is disrupted and then reestablishes itself in the opposite direction. It is not known what causes these disruptions. Evidence of geomagnetic reversals can be seen at mid-ocean ridges where tectonic plates move apart and the sea bed is filled in with magma. As the magma seeps out of the mantle the magnetic particles contained within it are oriented in the direction of the magnetic field at the time the magma cools and solidifies.

In the past 15 million years, scientists found pole shifts occurred four times every 1 million years. Although this averages out to once every 250,000 years, unfortunately, switches do not occur at regular intervals. During a long period in the Cretaceous era, polarity remained constant for as long as 30 million years, though this is believed to be highly unusual. The last Polar Shift happened roughly 740,000 years ago. Some researchers think our planet is overdue for another one, but nobody knows exactly when this might occur. Much of the speculation surrounding such an event is related to the "2012" doomsday scenario. A large number of people believe there are certain markers pointing to the destruction of our existence as we know it.

Many researchers believe a Polar Shift will be brought on by "Solar Flares" where radio-activity from the Sun will cause the Earth's magnetic field to break-down. Because the Earth's magnetic field extends into space for tens of thousands of miles from the planet's poles, it not only protects the Earth from solar radiation but it also plays a fundamental role in overall climate, weather patterns, and migratory habits of animals. If the poles were to reverse *instantly,* destruction would be global, from earthquakes and volcanic eruptions to the melting of Arctic ice and vast flooding. The Earth's crust would weaken causing its plates to shift. In the book *The Orion Prophecy* by Patrick Geryl, he says that the magnetic field of the Sun undergoes a drastic change every 11,500 to 12,000 years. Once a crucial point has been reached, it reverses instantaneously. Chaotic outbursts accompany this phenomenon and an immense cloud of plasma is catapulted into space causing a shock wave of particles to reach this planet resulting in a Polar Shift. This would certainly spur on major Earth quakes, and volcanic eruptions of epic proportions.

Others feel that a Polar Shift will be caused by an even rarer event such as the passing of the planet Nibiru. Apparently, planet Nibiru which is commonly referred to as "Planet X," has a 3,600 hundred year elliptical orbit around the Sun. According to certain beliefs, this planet is on approach to re-enter the Earths orbit. Because of the size of Nibiru, its massive gravitational pull would cause the Earth to stop spinning on its axis for a brief period of time; "three days" and then resume its rotation by spinning in the opposite direction thus causing the poles to shift. In *Awakening to Zero Point: The Collective Initiation*, Gregg Braden postulates that the planet will reach a base resonance of 13 cycles per second at which time the Earth would reach what he refers to as "Zero Point," whereby a great shift would occur causing the Earth to stop rotating for three days and resume its rotation headed in the opposite direction.

In 1950 Immanuel Velikovsky postulated in his book *Worlds in Collision* that, the planet Venus emerged from Jupiter as a comet during two proposed near approaches in about 1,450 BCE. He further suggested that the direction of the Earth's rotation was changed radically, and then reverted to its original direction on the next pass. This disruption supposedly caused earthquakes, tidal waves, and the parting of the Red Sea. He went on to say that near misses by Mars between 776 and 687 BCE, also caused the Earth's axis to change back and forth by ten degrees. He supported his work with historical records but his work was harshly ridiculed by those in the scientific community.

So what exactly does all this mean? When we look back at the ancient civilizations, many of them pointed to a time where there would be an end to this world as we know it and the start of a new world or "New Age" so-to-speak. Supposedly, this has already happened four times before. The historical Mayan calendar annotates an ending of a great cycle in addition to many of the star gazers prior to them. All accounts point to some Earth shattering event that is to take place in the upcoming years. There can be found mention of this in the "Book of Revelations" as well as in predictions foretold by Nostradamus as well as the great Edgar Cayce who coined the phrase "Earth changes." In some of Cayce's predictions, he prophesied about cataclysmic events involving the whole planet. He claimed the polar axis would "shift" whereupon many areas that are now land would again become ocean floor. He also postulated that during this time, ancient Atlantis would rise from the sea. He further claimed that the California coast would slip into the sea. So what exactly will occur and how will it affect us as a whole? There seems to be a wide range of speculation and hypothesis as to what will actually happen during a Polar Shift, so let's look at what the possibilities might be and how they fit into our already existing beliefs.

One proponent of Polar Shift was Charles Hapgood. In his book *The Earth's Shifting Crust* written in 1958, Hapgood speculated that the ice mass at one or both poles over-accumulates and destabilizes the Earth's rotational balance, causing slippage of all or much of Earth's outer crust around the Earth's core, which retains its axial orientation allowing for Polar Shifts to occur. Geological evidence suggests that something like this has happened repeatedly since the formation of the planet; the magnetic poles seem to have shifted at least 171 known times. According to research performed by Hapgood, these shifts happen over a 5,000 year period with about 20,000 to 30,000 years of no movement at all. Based on his theory, the spinning Earth core maintains its usual momentum and the magnetic poles remain in place, but there appears to be a Polar Shift because the crust has slid over the magnetic poles. Supposedly, this theory has never been disproven. However in a later book titled *The Path of the Pole*, Hapgood retracted his statement by claiming that the weight of the polar ice would be insufficient to bring about a Polar Shift. Hapgood maintained that the forces that caused the shifts in the crust must be located below the surface. Although he was unable to fully explain exactly how this could occur.

According to Patrick Geryl, sudden reversals and Polar Shifts are natural to the Earth. These shifts happen with "clock-like" regularity and are based on the harmonic cycle of the magnetic fields of the Sun. Geryl asserts that Polar Shifts are determined based on the sunspot cycle theory or the magnetic field theory, which the Maya and the Old Egyptians were privy to. He says that thousands of years ago our ancestors knew that when the magnetic field tilts, a worldwide destruction was subject to occur. His description is as follows:

> "A solid central core rotates in the center of the Earth. It is surrounded by a liquid iron-like layer, on top of which the Earth's crust is continuously drifting. This whole structure therefore appears to be a huge rotating dynamo. In addition, the liquid layer rotates in the electrostatic field of the Sun, recharging itself. However, this is not at all efficient: more electrical potential is lost than regained. Just like a battery that is almost empty, it is difficult to recharge and it becomes exhausted more easily and quickly. This is the situation with the "battery" of the magnetic field of the Earth. For this reason one sees the force of the magnetic field diminishing, almost 60% over the last two thousand years. At this rate there will not be much left within a couple of decades. And then one can expect a reversal of the poles. But nobody knows in what way this will actually happen, nor what the consequences will be, in contrast to the Maya and the Old Egyptians who knew the terrible consequences only too well."

Geryl states there are mathematical certainties that correlate with periodical Polar Shifts. Based on his findings, the mathematical matrix ends on the day of the next polar reversal and just like one would count down the launching of a rocket, the ancients were able to count down to the end of times. To the Maya, the last day on the calendar is when the magnetic north of the Earth will suddenly become south. This marked not only the end of their civilization, but also the whole civilized world.

We know that the Earth is essentially a huge magnet with the opposite poles being North and South. At any given time, this electric field can be short-circuited by an immense burst of energy coming from the Sun. This would be the cause of a catastrophic Polar Shift where the magnetic North Pole changes places with the magnetic South Pole. This is supported in the book *Earth under Fire* where astronomer Paul La Violette writes:

"Field flips have been accomplished experimentally, by shooting large quantities of loaded particles on a strong bipolar magnet. These particles are then caught in the magnetic fields and cause a "ring-stream" in them. At a certain moment this stream speeds up to such an extent that the field of the magnet reverses completely."

In a similar setting, the field of the Earth can also reverse. Geryl adds that not only will the poles shift, but the Earth will actually begin to rotate in the opposite direction. This supports Braden's theory as well. He says this will occur when the "ring current" pushes the inner core of the Earth in the opposite direction similar to that of an electric motor. Once this occurs he says:

"All securities we presently have at hand, like—amongst others—food, transport, and medicines, will have disappeared in one big blow, dissolved into nothingness. As will our complete civilization. It cannot be more horrifying than this; worse than the worst nightmare. More destructive than a nuclear war in which the entire global arsenal of nuclear weapons has been deployed in one blow."

According to ancient beliefs, the planet always experiences a shift as it enters into a new age. This happens roughly every 26,000 years or so according to Mayan calculations. This is known as the "Precession of the Equinox." Drunvalo Melchizedek asserts that the shift that we are beginning to experience is the adjustment from "masculine" energy to "feminine" energy. For the last 13,000 years, our planet has been governed and led by an outwardly aggressive masculine energy which has catered more or less to the condition that we now find ourselves in. Based on the attributes of masculine energy, we have existed under the regime of a more outgoing, assertive and aggressive nature but as we begin to usher in the female aspect, we will be governed by a more intuitive and inward type of guidance. This is not to say that our world leaders will all be female per se; but rather the energy in which we live by will be of a more intuitive feminine nature. The aspects of male and female energy have very little to do with gender and everything to do with the

Universal balancing of forces. This is considered by many conscious minded people to be a time when the planet and its inhabitants will undergo a positive physical and spiritual transformation heralding the beginning of a new Golden Age. The "New Age" or "Higher Consciousness" movement describes this time as an awakening of the collective and planetary, consciousness. In his book *Something In This Book Is True*, Bob Frissell says that by 2012, our whole planetary octave is going to shift up. He says that we will all have to go through what he calls the "great, great void" into the next octave and we can only go through as Spirit in complete oneness to God and all life.

It's no mystery that we are living on a ticking time-bomb waiting to go off. This may or may not be brought on by the polar ice masses or perhaps a passing comet, asteroid or even planet Nibiru. Needless to say, all the critical elements are all in place. Coincidentally, many of the scientific predictions of a Polar Shift in *Earth Changes* are eerily similar to the predictions of Edgar Casey, Nostradamus, Michael Scallion, and ancient Hopi and Mayan prophecy. All of which is expected to bring an "end time" of chaos and destruction, prior to the widespread enlightenment anticipated by the "New Age" movement. Is this simply conjecture, or is it the place where physics and metaphysics actually agree? It's safe to say that we can ill afford to ignore these "coincidences." The question to ask ourselves is: Are we prepared both physically and spiritually to accept a catastrophic Polar Shift?

Resonance and Vibration

Our Universe is a system of vibration. This world of vibrations is the world of resonance. There are countless waves and octaves of sound and light constantly occurring all around us at any given moment. This oscillation or "harmonic" motion has a tremendous affect on every form throughout the galaxy. Vibration, frequencies, rates and tones cater to our very existence in the form of light, heat, sound and all forms of matter. Everything gives off a vibration.

Even the smallest of matter has a pulse. Everything wields a certain electromagnetic attraction toward each other, and generally speaking, the less the attraction between molecules, the greater their motion relative to one another. This, in turn, helps define the object in relation to its particular phase of matter. The basic building blocks of the Universe seem to be either waves or vibrating strings, and most of the things they make up move in bigger waves and vibrations.

Resonance takes place at a level invisible to the human eye. This is so because the particles in which matter consists are nothing more than vibrating "strings" on the smallest scale and molecules or balls of energy graduating to a larger scale and finally physical matter in the form of what appears to be solid objects to include the human body. Basically, when molecules are moving at high speeds, with very little attraction for one another, gases are formed. Although with liquids, the rate of motion is moderate which determines the loose molecular structure. On the other hand, in a solid, there is little relative motion, and therefore molecules put forth massive attractive forces. Consequently, the molecules that make up a solid tend to vibrate in place. Though we seldom witness it directly, our entire Universe is in a constant state of motion, and where solid objects are concerned, this motion is manifested as vibration.

Technically speaking, whenever the vibrations produced by one object come into alignment with that of another, this is called "resonance" which is a very powerful analogy for understanding how various types of energies and spaces operate. So, resonance is simply a matter of one object or force getting in tune with another object. This is akin to the concept of a tuning fork. Whenever you strike a musical note let's say on a stringed instrument, other stringed instruments in the immediate surroundings begin to vibrate or resonate along with the pitch. It sets the "tone" so-to-speak. The same holds true for all forms of vibration. If you were to hum a perfect E, then you can actually see the string on a guitar start to vibrate at the same frequency. This is because it is resonating with your voice.

Resonance helps to explain all manner of familiar events, from the feedback produced by an electric guitar to the cooking of food in a microwave oven. Gregg Braden describes in his book *Awakening to Zero Point* how when two electronic modules are placed near one another, with one vibrating quicker than the second, something interesting begins to happen where the module of lower frequency will have the tendency to match that of the higher pitch through resonance or entrainment. This also holds true with the human energy system.

Another form of resonance is when you hear the sound of the ocean in a seashell when it's placed up to your ear. The human ear can hear sound produced up to 36,000 wavelengths per second, anything beyond this becomes inaudible. But just because you can't hear sound, doesn't mean it doesn't exist. There are always sound waves with a range of frequencies beyond what the human ear is capable of discerning. These inaudible sound waves fill the seashell causing it to vibrate and since the seashell has a set of natural frequencies, a resonant situation is created. The result is the sound of the ocean coming from the vibration within the seashell. In fact, the sound is loud enough to hear. So the next time you hear the sound of the ocean in a seashell, remember that all you're hearing is the amplification of one of the many background frequencies in the room resonating within the shell.

The dictionary defines resonance in terms of physics as: *"The increase in amplitude of oscillation of an electric or mechanical system exposed to a periodic force whose frequency is equal or very close to the natural frequency of the system."* In essence we are nothing more than electromagnetic beings oscillating between constant frequencies of higher and lower pitches and vibrations. Be that as it may, the living Earth is also vibrating at a particular rate and as it denizens, we too are affected by any oscillations or instabilities in its frequencies. This is known as "homeostasis." Braden attests to this where he says:

> "The net result of this increase is that each cell of our bodies seeks to match the rhythmic 'heartbeat,' or reference frequency, to that of the Earth. Moving into the resonant pattern of a higher tone, each life form, including human, is attempting to map out a new rhythm, or 'signature' frequency."

What's important to know about the concept of resonance is that whenever an object is vibrating at the same natural frequency of a second object, it forces that second object into vibrational motion. Applying this science to the electromagnetic field in which we all exist will help us better understand how individuals can be affected by the vibrations coming from others through "inductance." This principle explains why we can sometimes feel as if our energy is very low or that we're depressed whenever we come in contact with certain people that are resonating on a much different frequency than the one we're accustomed to. Certain people have the ability to drain us of our vital energies simply because they may be functioning more towards a negative polarity while we're trying to maintain a vibration that is consistent with higher frequencies and beliefs. As they begin to draw upon our energy, our vitality becomes lowered causing a shift in our moods, attitudes and overall outlook towards life.

Terrence McKenna writes in his book *True Hallucinations*, that resonance is a mysterious phenomenon in which a vibrating string seems magically to invoke a similar vibration in another string or object that is physically unconnected. It suggests itself as a model for the mysterious property that related one time to another even though they may be separated by days, years, or even millennia. He became convinced that there is a wave, or a system of resonance, that conditions events on all levels. This wave is fractal and self-referential, much like many of the most interesting new curves and objects being described at the frontiers of research mathematics. This "time-wave" is expressed throughout the Universe on a number of discrete levels. It causes atoms to be atoms, cells to be cells, minds to be minds, and stars to be stars. What he suggests is a new metaphysics, a metaphysics with mathematical rigor; something that is not simply a new religious conviction. Rather this insight takes the form of a formal proposition.

Everything resonates, the question is, what are we resonating or sending out as our vibration. We each have the ability to attract into our being anything we desire through the practice of sending out powerful vibrations with our thoughts, words and deeds. Consequently, whenever we find ourselves in the presence of someone that is not in alignment with that in which we believe, our efforts can become thwarted as long as we allow ourselves to be subjected to their contrary ideas. If the wave and the oscillation have different frequencies, then sooner or later they will drift out of phase and the motion of one will work against that of the other. The wave will actually reduce the energy of the other through destructive interference. Conversely, a vibration matching the resonant frequency of the first wave will cause larger and larger vibrations. This occurs as an enhanced coupling between quantum states with the same energy. One analogy would be if you were to drop a pebble into a lake, it would cause a ripple or a wave to travel across the lake. By simultaneously dropping another pebble into the lake, you create another wave sending out ripples to meet with those of the previous pebble. If the waves are in sync, then they will combine energies causing greater momentum as a unified force. By the same token, if the waves are not in alignment, then the force generated by each wave will ultimately cancel the other out. The key is to always stay conscious of the energy around you especially the energy coming from the people you most frequently associate with. My good friend always says "If you hang around 9 broke people, you'll be number 10." The same holds true for all forms of association. If you hang around 9 negative people, you'll end up being number 10 and so on. Positive people resonate comfortably around other like-minded people. In fact, they typically gravitate towards one another. And like the pebbles in the lake, their combined energies become much stronger as they unify. Subsequently, negativity breeds more negativity. German philosopher Arthur Schopenhaur speaks to this by saying:

> "People of similar nature, on the other hand, immediately come to feel a kind of general agreement; and if they are cast very much in the same mold, complete harmony or even unison will flow from their intercourse . . . This explains two circumstances. First of all, it shows why it is that common, ordinary people are so sociable and find good company wherever they go. It is just the contrary with those who are not of the common run; and the less they are so, the more unsociable they become; so that if, in their isolation, they chance to come across someone in whose nature they can

find even a single sympathetic chord, be it never so minute, they show extraordinary pleasure in his society. For one man can be to another only so much as the other is to him. Great minds are like eagles, and build their nest in some lofty solitude."

This is in no way placing judgment on anyone's actions but rather it helps to draw a comparison between two "like" and "opposite" frequencies creating resonance and vibration. For we know that no one is truly all "negative" or all "positive" as people tend to fluctuate between frequency patterns based on their awareness.

Be that as it may, there are certain independent studies that show the Earth's fundamental vibration has gradually been accelerating. Historically, planet Earth's frequency has been stabilized somewhere around 8 Hz. or cycles per second. The amount of time it takes to complete one cycle is called a period, and the number of cycles in one second is the frequency of the oscillation. Frequency is measured in Hertz (Hz.) named after the German physicist Heinrich Rudolf Hertz. Throughout history, 8 cycles has become the Universal constant. Based on the principle of Fibonacci sequence where you advance to the next number in a series by adding the last two integers such as 1+1=2+1=3+2=5+3=8+5=13 and so on, Braden feels that the Earth's target frequency will be 13 cycles per second with this becoming our new "base resonant frequency." Accordingly, this is the frequency that may trigger resonance with the new grid heralding the close of the present cycle of evolution and the beginning of the "New Age."

In summary; *"The only thing that matters about the whole fucking Universe is the frequency, the resonance—down at the atomic level holding our flesh together. Science has found the frequency of the atom's vibration, everything is a constant vibration."*—DJ Spooky

Schumann Resonance

In the previous chapter on resonance I mentioned Schumann's Resonance (SR) so I want to take this time to thoroughly explain what this is exactly. Our planetary electromagnetic resonance is named after physicist Winfried Otto Schumann who predicted it mathematically in 1952. What he was able to determine was that resonances occur because the space between the surface of the Earth and the conductive ionosphere acts as a closed waveguide. He postulated that the limited dimensions of the Earth caused a sort of waveguide to act as a resonant cavity for electromagnetic waves in the Extremely Low Frequency (ELF) band. Schumann discovered that this cavity is naturally excited by electric currents in lightning. This may sound extremely technical but what I'm trying to point out here is that the planet has a "tone" or a frequency much like a heart beat. Just as a tuning fork has natural frequencies for sound, Earth has natural frequencies or Schumann Resonances for electromagnetic radiation. Depending on how you look at it we either developed into this electromagnetic environment or Divine Intelligence created us to live in sync with it. One thing is for certain and that is; we are all enclosed by this natural frequency pulsation. As such, Earth is a living being with vibrations that coincide with that of the entire electromagnetic spectrum of all living things on the planet.

All biological processes are a function of electromagnetic field interactions. Any perturbation or fluctuations in the global resonance will have a direct affect on all living beings since our individual vibrations are governed by it. These fields serve as the relationship between our world of form and all patterns of information. It is the bridge between resonances and brain frequencies which exist in our human DNA blueprint that evolved within the Earth's environment. Understanding this will allow us to gauge exactly what appears to be happening at this time in our ascension. As we begin to see how resonance and vibration determine the state or condition of a thing, we will begin to embrace what a higher frequency actually means.

In *Zero Point*, Braden delineates how the different frequencies are associated with the different states of consciousness. He calls them "frequencies of awareness." If we look at the human brain, we know that there are four different states of awareness each having a signature frequency range. In the "Delta" state which is a deep relaxed state, the brain waves range between .5-4 Hz. In the "Theta" state we become a little more aware but yet we're still in a relaxed state with our brain waves ranging between 4-8 Hz. From this point, we reach a more awakened "Alpha" state with our brain waves ranging between 8-12 Hz. And finally, once we reach "Beta" consciousness, we are in a fully awakened state of awareness with our brain waves ranging between 12-25 Hz. Having gone from a base planetary frequency of 7.8 Hz to what is now somewhere around 11 Hz, according to Braden, we are collectively moving toward the vibration of 13 Hz where all life upon Earth is just beginning to wake up. The Hindus refer to this time as *"Turiya"* which is the fourth or wakeful state. To give you a better understanding of how certain waves affect our state of awareness, here is an overview of the various waves of resonance and how they pertain to our overall state of consciousness as described by (Miller and Miller):

Gamma waves (25-60 Hz) appear to relate to simultaneous processing of information from different brain areas, e.g., involving memory, learning abilities, integrated thoughts or information-rich task processing. Gamma rhythms modulate perception and consciousness, which disappear with anesthesia. Synchronous activity at about 40 Hz appears involved in binding sensory inputs into the single, unitary objects we perceive.

Beta waves (12-25 Hz) dominate our normal waking state of consciousness when attention is directed towards cognitive tasks and the outside world. Beta is a "fast" activity, present when we are alert or even anxious, or when engaged in problem solving, judgment, decision making, information processing, mental activity and focus. Nobel Prize winner Sir Francis Crick and other scientists believe the 40 Hz beta frequency may be key to the act of cognition.

Alpha waves (8-12 Hz) are present during dreaming and light meditation when the eyes are closed. As more and more neurons are recruited to this frequency, alpha waves cycle globally across the whole cortex. This induces deep relaxation, but not quite meditation. In alpha, we begin to access the wealth of creativity that lies just below our conscious awareness. It is the gateway, the entry point that leads into deeper states of consciousness. Alpha waves aid overall mental coordination, calmness, alertness, inner awareness, mind/body integration and learning. Alpha is also the home of the window frequency known as the Schumann Resonance [SR], which propagates with little attenuation around the planet. When we intentionally generate alpha waves and go into resonance with that Earth frequency, we naturally feel better, refreshed, in tune, in sync. It is, in fact, environ-mental synchronization.

Theta waves (4-8 Hz) occur most often in sleep but are also dominant in the deepest states of meditation (body asleep/mind awake) and thought (gateway to learning, memory). In theta, our senses are withdrawn from the external world and focused on the mindscape—internally originating signals. Theta waves are associated with mystery, an elusive and extraordinary realm we can explore. It is that twilight state which we normally only experience fleetingly as we rise from the depths of delta upon waking or drifting off to sleep. In theta, we are in a waking dream; vivid imagery flashes before the mind's eye and we are receptive to information beyond our normal conscious awareness. Theta meditation increases creativity, enhances learning, reduces stress and awakens intuition and other extrasensory perception skills.

Delta waves (.5-4 Hz) are the slowest but highest in amplitude. They are generated in deepest meditation and dreamless sleep. Delta waves confer a suspension of external existence and provide the most profound feelings of peace. In addition, certain frequencies within the Delta range trigger the release of a growth hormone which is beneficial for healing and regeneration. This is why sleep, deep restorative sleep, is so essential to the healing process.

The existence of Schumann's Resonance is an established scientific fact but many people are unaware of the importance of this frequency and it's ramifications on human life. It's not merely an occurrence caused by lightning in the atmosphere, but a very important electromagnetic wave acting as the background frequency that influences the brain. A physician named Ankermueller was able to make the connection between the Schumann Resonance and the alpha rhythm of brainwaves. Shortly after that, Dr. Herbert König demonstrated a correlation between Schumann Resonance and brain rhythms. In 1979, he compared human EEG recordings with natural electromagnetic fields of the environment and found that the main frequency produced by Schumann oscillations is very close to the frequency of alpha rhythms. Upon further investigation, he eventually arrived at a frequency of exactly 7.83 Hz, which is even more interesting because this is the frequency that applies to all mammals. Based upon this information there have been many other studies relating to the Earth's magnetic field and the implications it has on the human brain. One such study involved ancient Chinese teachings which state that we actually need two environmental signals which is the "Yang" or masculine signal from above and the "Yin" or feminine signal from below. That of the stronger signal correlates to the Schumann Resonance surrounding our planet. Based on this theory, in order for us to achieve optimal health, both of these signals must be in balance. In his book *Informative Medicine*, Dr. Ludwig writes that research carried out at the University of Dusseldorf showed that the one sided use of Schumann "Yang" wave simulation without the geomagnetic "Yin" signal caused serious health problems. On the other hand, the absence of Schumann waves creates a similar situation. This was confirmed by a study conducted on students who volunteered to live in underground bunkers totally screened off from the magnetic fields whereby their "circadian rhythms" or the rhythms associated with daily cycles deviated causing them to suffer emotional distress and migraine headaches. Upon being re-exposed to Schumann's Resonance of 7.8 Hz, their health was able to stabilize itself.

So to reiterate, the significance of Schumann's Resonance and how knowing where we are presently, can help us understand the influence of an increasing frequency. I want to recapitulate some of the points made with regards to "Zero Point." Essentially, time will appear to speed up causing a 24 hour day to feel much shorter. This is because Schumann's Resonance (SR) has been 7.8 cycles for thousands of years, but since 1980 it has been rising to where it is presently at 12 cycles or "quickened time." Once it reaches 13 cycles, or "Zero Point" according to Braden it will stop. This occurrence has been predicted by ancient cultures for thousands of years. There have been many shifts including the one that always occurs every 13,000 years at each half of the 26,000 year, "Procession of the Equinox." This will result in a shift of the magnetic poles which will probably happen within the next few years or so according to ancient predictions. Some believe that after Zero Point, the Sun will rise in the west and set in the east. Evidence of this can be found in the annals of ancient history. Once the planet reaches 13 cycles, it will undergo an ascension that will probably introduce us to the 4th dimension. This could be either a curse or a blessing because on the 4th dimension everything we think or desire will instantly manifest. This includes love as well as fear so our intentions will be of the utmost importance. Subsequently, as a result of this approaching shift, our physical bodies are changing. Our DNA is being reprogrammed to 12 strands and a new light body is being created as discussed in previous chapters. This allows for much greater insight and intuition. Some say that by the year 2012, we will have entered the 5th Dimension after the shift to the 4th Dimension at Zero Point. This is not to incite fear but to better prepare ourselves for the changes that will usher in the new age of light. Physicists Richard Allen Miller suggests:

> "We are extremely complex electrodynamic beings that are sensitive to natural and artificial electromagnetic fields. Schumann Resonance frequencies coincide with our human brain waves and this affects over-all brain-wave generation which regulates equilibrium and balance. This accounts for the strong correlation between human behavioral disturbance and geomagnetic field instability or isolation from Schumann's Resonance. As human beings, we have extraordinary potentials we have hardly begun to study, much less understand. Creative gifts, intuitions and talents that are unpredictable or emergent may become stabilized in generations to come. Hopefully, we can learn to understand both our emergence from an essentially electromagnetic environment and facilitate our potential for healing, growth and non-local communication."

Chapter Three

Higher Truth

Higher Truth

"Know the truth and the truth will make you mad."
—*Julian Huxley*

Truth is a funny thing; just when you think you have it all figured out, another form of what you thought was the "ultimate truth" slowly begins to emerge. I've come to understand how truth is transcendental in that it constantly expresses higher and higher versions of itself to the ardent seeker. As I become more willing to accept the truth regardless of how unorthodox it may appear, I begin to breach certain boundaries of understanding and what I once believed to be a finite understanding suddenly becomes infinite. The deeper I dig, the more I realize there is no end to understanding. Truth evolves according to ones awareness. Although I know truth is constant meaning it can never be changed, what *I* know to be true is constantly expanding into greater and greater knowledge. Therefore, nothing is truth until *I* realize it.

At times, I think I have a pretty firm grasp on a particular subject and then suddenly without warning what I know turns out to be just the tip of the Iceberg because lurking beneath the surface is a mass of substance and foundation just waiting to be discovered. 90% of all truth is below the surface. Much of what we know is very shallow and convoluted due to misinterpretation, religion, enculturation, the media, and societal influences. In fact, much of what we presently know about religion has long since been lost in translation. If we truly want to know the truth then we will seek it beyond the confines of conventional thought. Everything we think we know about life and the beliefs we hold will suddenly become questionable. Trust me; what we know about the truth is definitely subject to revision. Today, we can hold a certain belief based upon where we are in our process of discovery and for whatever reason although that belief doesn't necessarily change altogether, it does have a funny way of evolving into a more complex understanding as we continue to seek. In our digging, we will find there really is no bottom. How could there be? To hit bottom is to say we can reach a point where there is nothing more to learn. In that instant, we stop growing. Once we decide there is nothing more to learn, our minds become closed to an infinite realm of wisdom and knowledge eager to be discovered. The insatiable desire to know more can never be quenched for there is no amount of knowing that could ever satisfy a seekers thirst.

Truth is encoded in our genetic make-up. It is a part of us. That thing that happens to us whenever we hear something that resonates in our being is truth. That feeling we get when someone is trying to convince us of something we know to be false, is truth. Whenever we feel as if we are betraying our very nature simply by accepting a doctrine or a belief incredulously, that's truth resisting deceit. Imagine this; our whole entire being is founded on truth and truth alone. It's woven into the fabric of our chemistry. Within each cell of our illustrious body temple is the truth of the entire Universe hidden away waiting for our beck and call. We are sacred because we *are* the truth. We hold within our possession the keys to all mysteries, the answers to every question we could ever possibly have about life, the Universe and all consciousness. We are created in the image and likeness of all there is.

Seek truth, and with all your seeking, get understanding. As we begin to ask of our divine selves to know more about this reality and all that it holds, truth will make itself privy to us. New teachers will emerge in our field of awareness and certain books will suddenly become available to us. Classes and workshops will be presented to help us discover the truth we seek. A whole new vista of beliefs and understandings will miraculously become a part of our awareness. Thus we will never be the same. There is a higher truth than the one we now hold. Not a better truth but rather a higher form of what we already know to be true. Our direction is upward bound to a higher, loftier existence. In reality what we are seeking is merely a higher version of ourselves. This truer more pristine aspect of *Self* can only be discovered by letting go of the dogma and worn-out thought patterns of generation upon generation of false teachings. There is nothing to know outside of ourselves. We're harboring all the answers deep inside our being. We hold within our fundamental nature, the answer to any question we could ever possibly have. We are an algorithm, a mathematical phenomenon clothed in flesh. This higher truth we seek is ourselves. There are many things about

Higher Truths that we have been completely unaware of. So, in this chapter I will attempt to address some of the more esoteric subjects such as; *Avatars, The Inner Guru, Sanat Kumara, Shamballa, The Great Brotherhood of Light, The Ascended Masters, The Hathors, Maitreya, Jesus Christ?, The Merovingian Agenda, The Illuminati, The Global Elite and A New World Order.*

Avatar

Imagine this . . . we are eternal. We have existed in pure form as an aspect of the great whole. We are pure love, light and energy resting in the bosom of the One and suddenly, we're inspired to individuate into physical form. And so, we decide to orchestrate our coming forth. So we wait. We have an idea in our conscious mind of what type of experiences we would like to have. We're fully aware of the multitude of choices and so we ponder what it is we would like to understand better by manifesting into a human form. We decide that we would like to have this experience as a male and alternate our gender with each incarnation thereafter. We pick a channel in which to come forth based upon the vibrational frequency of our parents and the genes they will provide us with. We know all the various nuances of our experience but not the experience itself. We know that choosing an earthly experience will involve stepping down our vibration to that of the environment. Our earthly bodies will be heavy and dense causing us to feel encumbered and trapped without the ability to be inter-galactic. We will take on an emotional body that will be uncomfortable at times and we will be subjected to the human condition. Our ability to create will be hindered by the slowing down of our vibration and everything will be on a delayed response. Our three dimensional awareness will lack all the nuances of a fully twelve dimensional consciousness and at times it will feel as if we are disconnected from our source. We fully understand these forfeitures and yet we decide to manifest into human form so that we may have an earthly experience. And so, in spite of giving up what we know for what we don't, we incarnate into human forms donning our life suites as *Avatars.*

In Hinduism, the word *"Avatar"* literally means, the deliberate "descent" of a deity primarily from Heaven to Earth. The Sanskrit noun *"avatāra"* is derived from the verbal root तृ "to cross over," combined with the prefix *"ava"* "off, away, down." In the Bhagavata Gita it reads; *"Whenever righteousness wanes and unrighteousness increases, I send myself forth, in order to protect the good and punish the wicked. In order to make a firm foundation for righteousness, I come into being age after age."* (4. 7-8)

The concept of Avatar within Hinduism is most often associated with Vishnu, the preserver or sustainer aspect of God within the Hindu Trinity or Trimurti. Although in reality we are all deities living in human form for the purpose of our evolution into greater aspects of ourselves. For clarification, I want you to understand what is being suggested here. We are created in the image and likeness of the Divine. We are an aspect of it. The only difference is one of degree so the part can not be different from the whole. This means we are divinity but we have chosen to forget this very important aspect of ourselves by becoming human. Deities are depicted in a variety of forms, but are frequently expressed as having human form. While some faiths and traditions consider it blasphemous to imagine or depict a deity as having any concrete form, we are each divine in our own rite. Deities are usually considered to be immortal. As pure energy in human forms, our essence can never die. Deities are commonly assumed to have personalities and to possess consciousness, intellect, desires, and emotions—doesn't this sound like you?

Deities, incarnations, and manifestations, it's all the same. We have deliberately manifested into human form for the sole purpose of evolving into higher forms of ourselves. Earth is just one of the many places where life can be experienced. There is a vast array of worlds and realities that exist beyond the limited confines of earthly thinking and understanding. We limit ourselves when we only subscribe to the possibilities of what is known. The Universe is a myriad system of planets, inhabitants, existences and realities that we have hitherto not even begun to understand. It seems too farcical to imagine having come from divinity and to be here living as a deity in human form. But it's true; we are part and parcel to God which makes us gods in heritage. *"Know ye not that ye are gods."* We possess all the attributes of divinity but we are limited in our abilities because of the laws of this planet and the Universe. This does not mean we lack the quintessential make-up of divinity. It merely means that while we are here, in this form, we must abide by the laws governing this realm of existence. This is what makes living in human form as spiritual beings so difficult to embrace because we come from a place where any and everything is possible. Having accepted this earthly assignment, we've forfeited those limitless possibilities to a certain degree. Many of us can actually sense the loss and our physical bodies feel inhibited. The Earth plane begins to weigh on us and we long for the time when we were in our rightful essence. Be that as it may, we are still divinity incarnated in human form for the purpose of evolution. We have donned our life suits and are here experiencing life as humans. Deep in the recesses of our cosmic memory, we feel the truth of these words as something begins to surface in our consciousness reminding us of the truth that we are all *Avatars*.

Inner Guru

"O myself, you are an embodiment of God's Light; know your true origin"

—*(Guru Granth Sahib 441)*

The truth is not out there somewhere, it's inside us. We spend our entire lives seeking wisdom, seeking answers, constantly striving outward to find something that can only be obtained by going within. We seek counselors, teachers, rabbis, Imams, pastors, scholars, and wise ones in order to help us understand something that can only come from within. It's not our fault; we were conditioned to behave in this manner since the very beginning. Here today, I want to introduce you to a truth that may have eluded you for your entire life. That truth is that everything we've been seeking is already inside us. There's is nothing outside the knowledge of our higher selves. That is, all the answers for our evolution and to all of our life's situations are nestled in our heart's wisdom. The only requirement to accessing this wisdom is a sincere childlike desire to know the truth. And; *"unless we become like a little child, we shall not enter into the kingdom of heaven."* This means everything we thought we knew about the truth becomes subject to revision. It means that all of our degrees and accolades thus far have only served our intellect and not our hearts. The real truth that we seek can only be found in the pureness of our hearts through the higher self.

Within the recesses of our hearts lies an ancient wisdom just waiting for us to turn our gaze inward. It's very liberating once we come into the understanding that we all have this higher aspect within us. Each and every one of us is a *"Guru"* unto himself and whether we realize it or not, we are all hardwired to receive higher communication from our inner selves moment by moment. As the inner guru, we already know everything that has ever been known. We also know everything that is yet to be learned because to the guru within, everything is happening simultaneously so there is no past or future only the present. As we begin to embrace this knowledge, we will come to understand that nothing is outside of our being, everything is within us. When this knowing takes place, the truth of who we really are will begin to unfold. We will begin to experience strange and miraculous things. Life will become the most loving teacher we could ever imagine. The outside world will begin to communicate in various ways because the inner world is alive and directly connected to the outer world. The two will be in constant communication on our behalf. The world will suddenly expand and open up to us in ways that we never dreamt possible. Music will speak to us directly, bill boards will be strategically positioned along our paths, animals will speak to us in the silence and all manner of life will suddenly start collaborating for our evolvement.

When we call upon the inner guru and start trusting its guidance, the very Universe itself will begin to conspire on our behalf. We will notice a sense of calm come over us and we will finally see that anything that could ever happen in life is whole, perfect and complete and everything is unfolding exactly as it should. I've experienced many things in my life that I felt were horrible experiences until I was able to reflect back on what I've learned as a result of having the experience. One of the worst experiences I've ever had in life was becoming addicted to drugs. Although this experience has now turned out to be one of the greatest lessons I could ever have. I never knew that having that experience would serve to be my greatest form of learning thus far. Without that experience, I know for certain I wouldn't have chosen the path of a Life Coach and Spiritual Counselor. Often times what we see as a calamity in our lives later turns out to be our greatest period of growth. But it's hard to see this while we're immersed in the lesson. The inner guru knows the wisdom behind everything we could ever possibly experience. In fact, many of the situations we find ourselves in are actually orchestrated by the inner guru. You see, we receive certain promptings to do certain things without understanding the how or the why and yet by trusting this inspiration, we find that it was really the inner guru guiding us in a way that we could not fully understand at the time.

When we look at some of the meanings associated with the word "*guru*," we can see how we are all gurus within ourselves. In Sanskrit, a guru is regarded as "having great knowledge or wisdom in a certain area." This knowledge or wisdom is usually used to guide others as a teacher. However, a guru is somewhat different from a teacher or a preacher. He or She serves as a beacon of spiritual light in the world and teaches us, the universal spiritual principles that underlie all religions and cultures. But upon deeper examination, we find that the word "*guru*," has a more cryptic meaning where "*gu*," actually means darkness while "*ru*," means light. The two serve as a principle for the development of consciousness where it leads the creation from unreality to reality, from the darkness of ignorance to the light of knowledge. This connotation is used primarily in the Hindu belief but it is also accepted in Sikhism, Buddhism and certain other religious movements. Guru Nanak, founder of the Sikh religion said: "*Even if a thousand suns and moons rose, they would be unable to remove the darkness of ignorance within the heart. This can only be removed through the grace of the Guru.*" While many people believe that finding a true guru is considered to be a prerequisite for attaining self-realization, they fail to understanding that self-realization is when we discover that "we" are the inner guru. To further illustrate this point many traditions claim "*Guru, God and Self*" (Self meaning soul, not personality) are one and the same. According to Sikh belief there is no difference in spirit between such a guru and God:

> "The guru is God and God is the Guru; there is no distinction between the two" says Guru Ram Das (GG, 442). "God hath placed Himself within the guru, which He explicitly explaineth" (GG, 466). "Acknowledge the Transcendent God and the guru as one." (GG, 864). "The real personality of a human being is the atman, the physical body is only a temporary dwelling place for the atman which is eternal and is a spark from the Eternal Flame, the Supreme Atman or God." (GG, 441).

As such; the atman of the guru remains ever in tune with the supreme light from which it has sparked off. It is thus believed that God is accepted as residing within man. God is the source of all light or consciousness. God kindles that light, in the chosen human body. It is in this sense that there is no distinction seen between ourselves and the guru.

Spiritually, a guru is one characterized as someone who dispels spiritual ignorance or darkness, with spiritual illumination or light. This knowing can only come from within as no one can truly have the answers for another person's growth while on this spiritual journey. Some may provide instructions on how to obtain this knowledge but no one can truly guide another person in self-realization for it defeats the very nature of it being realized by the "*Self*." A real guru will instruct a person to seek within for the answers understanding that it is a pre-existing knowingness that did not require asking for an answer in the first place. The wise ones who have realized this truth will impart the knowledge to you. A guru is a teacher who shows the way but he or she is not an intercessor, but an exemplar and a guide. They indicate the path to liberation and they are capable of leading the believers to the highest state of spiritual enlightenment. Any so called guru who requires someone to remain under their tutelage is not fully serving the student but rather keeping them in a state of servitude which causes the teacher to feel superior and haughty.

Throughout history, many of the purported gurus discovered their higher selves through introspection and by seeking the answers to their own dilemmas. Never did they seek outside guidance for they knew and understood that the same universal intelligence is available to us all. All anyone has to do is to trust their inner knowingness.

When the word "*guru*," is used as a noun, it means the imparter of knowledge. When used as an adjective, it means "heavy," or "weighty," as in "heavy with knowledge." The concept of the "*guru*" can be traced as far back as the early Upanishads or Hindu teachings where the idea of the divine teacher on Earth first manifested from its early Brahmin associations. But the real unseen guru encompasses the entire Universe and is with us at all times during life and even after we transcend this life. It is actually our higher selves and it guides and supports us throughout our lives. At some point, upon coming into a greater awareness, it slowly lifts us from our worldly life into a spiritual way of life and it guides and prompts us according to our spiritual level. If we are proactively seeking spiritual growth, our inner guru will be more active by guiding us according to what our needs are. A recent study indicated:

> "Out of the entire population of the world, few take up spiritual practice that is universal and beyond the confines of formal, organised religion. Among these, very few people through their spiritual practice (regardless of their religion of birth) attain a spiritual level of over 70%. The unmanifest guru then works completely through some of these evolved individuals who are then known as the manifest guru or the guru in human form. In other words, a person has to be at least of the 70% spiritual level, to qualify as a spiritual guide or a guru."

Thus as we become more reliant on the inner guru, we become teachers and beacons of spiritual knowledge for all of humanity as we slowly move into total alignment with the Universal Mind and the intellect of God.

Sanat Kumara

Speaking of Gurus, Sanat Kumara is regarded as the "*Maha-Guru,*" or the greatest guru or head and savior of all evolution in this fourth globe of the Earth Scheme. In Sanskrit *Sanat* means "eternal" *Kumara* means "youth" this would make *Sanat Kumara* the "eternal youth." He is described as "the greatest of all the Avatars, or Coming Ones." Sanat Kumara serves as the prototype for all world saviors to include the Buddha, Maitreya and the Christ. Sadly, his role as a savior is not known by most of humanity and only the more highly evolved beings are able to glimpse the real source of his light and the existence of those through whom it is focused.

Roughly eighteen and half million years ago in the middle of the Lemurian epoch; our planet was in such despair and darkness that practically all of humanity was caught up in a low state of existence. We were literally living as cavemen even though we were highly advanced spiritual beings that chose Earth as our playground of growth and expansion. Something very drastic was needed in order to reestablish the God centered connection that we once knew. It was at that time that a great being of light volunteered to serve as the conduit to help bring our planet back to a place of consciousness and enable us to continue upward on our spiritual journey. As legend has it, Sanat Kumara came as an Avatar, from the Venus chain, when our planetary scheme reached its lowest point of physical manifestation. Purportedly, the beings living on the etheric plane of Venus are hundreds of millions of years ahead of us in their spiritual evolution and according to Theosophy; Venus is the most spiritually advanced planet of our solar system. Sanat Kumara being one of the "Seven Holy Kumaras," agreed to assist by holding the Earth within his own light and blanket of wisdom. He therefore took physical incarnation and came down to this dense physical planet and has remained with us ever since. The Tibetan writings tell us that he is; "The divine prisoner of this planet, held here until the last weary pilgrim has found his way home." In other writings it says that he will stay ". . . *as long as may be needed.*" Although Sanat Kumara incarnated in form, he is pure in nature. Therefore, he could not descend to this dense physical level but took an etheric body instead. He along with six other Kumaras are said to reside at *Shamballa* on the etheric plane above the Gobi Desert or the "Center where the Will of God is known." It is here that they form part of a large-scale, coordinated effort to nurture spiritual evolution on this planet. Supposedly, Shamballa can be visited by anyone who is skilled in white magic that can transport their etheric body through a technique of etheric projection.

The Planetary Council of Light also known as the "Seven Holy Kumaras" agreed that it would be this compassionate being along with several others that would later serve as the saviors of this world. And so, Sanat Kumara along with 144,000 others traveled from the etheric plane of Venus on a mission to help save humanity. In Theosophy, the beings that helped Sanat Kumara organize the expedition from Venus are called the "Lords of the Flame." These highly evolved beings are known throughout the world as great spiritual leaders such as; Gautama Buddha, Maitreya, Mithra, Krishna and the supposed Christ which have been incarnating again and again to bring forth the highest truths and help mankind out of their darkness. This could very well be the reason why many of these figures share the exact same birthdates; some of the same attributes and in many cases are considered to be the same personification over and over again. Sanat Kumara himself is seen in all the major religions, as "*Skanda/Kartikkeya*" in Hinduism, "*Brahma-Sanam Kumara*" in Buddhism, "*Ancient of Days*" in Judeo-Christianity and "*Ahura Mazda*" in Zoroastrianism. It is also considered that Sanat Kumara is "*Al Khdir*" by Sufi Muslims according to Dakshinamurti.

Upon Sanat Kumara's arrival on Earth, humans had been reduced to barbaric cavemen where we had lost touch with the frequencies of our soul and we were locked into fear and survival. Through the Holy Kumara's help under the guidance of Sanat, we were gradually reconnected with our souls. Soon after, more and more people began to reconnect thus creating a consciousness field that gradually made it easier for others to follow. Eventually, the spiritual density slowly began to lift.

So, who exactly were these beings of extreme light and compassion that were willing to take on such an enormous task and how did they get here? Well, they are considered to be an etheric race of beings that traveled here from the planet Venus. They favored Norwegians and Scandinavians having very pale white skin and deep blue eyes so they were often referred to as the Nordic Aliens. Theosophist Benjamin Creme favors the idea that these Venusians pilot flying saucers from their civilization and are capable of stepping down their vibrational level to the 3rd density of the physical plane. Thus, adherents of Creme's ideas postulate that Sanat Kumara and these "*Lords of the Flame,*" came from Venus in some type of space craft.

Another description of Sanat Kumara is given by Jelaila Starr who describes him in her book, *The Mission Remembered: Book Two* as being ". . . the son of a priestess/healer from the house of Ananda and a slave to a high ranking Melchizedek." She asserts that Sanat Kumara started a new bloodline of the house of Ananda with the purest of the Draconian lines which represented the purest lines of both Reptilian and Humans. She believes that his purpose was to integrate the two. This integration would provide a blueprint or template so-to-speak that would help incorporate both the light and the dark aspects of ones being as portrayed through the Reptilians and the Humans. Upon completion, Earth humans would be able to experience peace and joy on a much more profound level. In addition, we would have the power to change creation itself and to mold reality in any form that we chose. This was primarily the purpose of Sanat Kumara's intervention, to serve as a reminder of our connection to source for all people on the Earth plane.

Sanat Kumara is linked with the star system Sirius which is the heart center of the Cosmic Logos. Starr believes that he came to Earth through the Orion black league by way of the etheric Sirians of Sirius B. Robert Temple author of, *The Sirius Mystery*, states; "There is definitely a relationship of very ancient date between our Lord of the World, Sanat Kumara, and the Lord of Sirius, and this exists in spite of the fact that our planet is not a sacred planet." It is further believed that Sanat Kumara is the custodian of the will of the "Great Brotherhood of Light" on Sirius. This council is composed of Ascended Masters and volunteers from other worlds who have joined together to advance spiritual evolution on Earth. Supposedly, this group of highly advanced Masters is working for the Spiritual Hierarchy of our planet, under the direct leadership of Sanat Kumara.

Theosophists believe these Masters are able to serve this purpose by utilizing the cosmic power of the "Seven Rays." Accordingly, Sanat Kumara harnesses the mystical power of the "Seven Rays" from the Solar Logos and distributes it to the Ascended Masters who then guide the spiritual evolution of humanity by focusing this power to those of us that are receptive to it. Another supporter of Theosophy A.E. Powell believes that Sanat Kumara is in constant telepathic communication with the "Spirit of the Earth" the goddess known as *"Gaia."* However, C.W. Leadbeater and Alice A. Bailey who are also Theosophists believe that Sanat Kumara maintains telepathic rapport with the Solar Logos which is the consciousness of the Sun itself. Whatever the case may be, Sanat Kumara under whatever name you choose, has provided the opportunity of greater acceleration in acquiring light, wisdom and greater consciousness. He, along with all the Ascended Masters invites us to merge into the "I AM," consciousness where we can experience the joy and splendor spoken of through the integration of both light and dark. We have nothing to lose and everything to gain. We stand to achieve tremendous growth and acceleration on our path of enlightenment while releasing the karmic pain and struggles of previous lifetimes. In addition, we stand to serve the Earth as a beacon of light by helping to raise the consciousness of individuals that are unaware of this great opportunity.

This is an unprecedented time and Sanat Kumara, by any name, is calling upon us, his most beloved supporters, to remember his ideal as our great teacher and friend. He, along with his cohorts, eagerly stands by ready to assist by helping us bring greater light to our planet. We are tremendous beings of light event if we haven't awakened to this idea. If you are reading these words, chances are, you are among the 144,000 that have willingly gotten caught up in the lower vibrations of this planet while seeking to uplift it. We are *"Lords of the flame,"* but we must ignite our passion once again if we are to fulfill our divine purpose. I ask that you search yourself for the recognition of who you really are. Re-"cognize" this knowledge through your own personal experiences and they will attest to your greatness. We will all come to find that just below the surface of our physical selves is an Avatar suffering from millions of years of amnesia. But something is stirring. Something is moving within our celestial framework that is allowing us to awaken to this truth. We must remove all doubt and silence any fears if we are to remember the mission we so willingly accepted. By *"re-member,"* I mean that we actually realize that we are *"members"* of the body of God and we become reunited with it in consciousness. And whether or not Sanat Kumara is an actual being or merely a moniker to help jolt our memories into this realization; now is the time for us to awaken to our true nature and resume our mission as light bearers. We are here to hold the planet in our consciousness; but how can we do that if we ourselves are unconscious?

Shamballa

In February of 1972, The Staple Singers released a song that went: *"I know a place, y'all ain't nobody crying, ain't nobody worried ain't no smiling faces lying to the races. If you're ready now, I'll take you there . . . What good times, happy times . . . I'll take you there. Just take my hand and come on . . . I'll take you there. Can you see it? Wipe the tears from your eyes . . . I'll take you there . . ."*

In practically every religion there is talk of a very special city where only the pure at heart can reside. A place of extreme beauty where the streets are paved with gold and everyone is happy. In her book, *Shamballa: The Spiritual Axis of The World,* Victoria LePage provides some very heartfelt commentary on this subject. She writes; "Nearly all races have enshrined in their folklore a sacred paradisiacal place, hidden and incorruptible, closely corresponding to Shamballa—a gateway to a higher world that only those gifted with mystical vision can fully enter." Some call it "Utopia" while others refer to it as *"Shangri-La,"* but for the purpose of this writing, I shall refer to it simply as *Shamballa.* In any case, my goal here is to present all sides so that we may consciously draw our own conclusions. So, *"If you're ready now . . . I'll take you there."*

This description of Shamballa was found in Wikipedia:

"The people who live in all these countless cities and counties have great wealth, happiness, and no sickness. The crops of good and everyone passes with Dharma. As all the kings are religious ones, there is not even a sign of non-virtue or evil in these lands. Even the words 'war' and 'enmity' are unknown. The happiness and joy can compete with that of the gods . . . In addition; all the new products for daily *samsaric* use which have been manufactured spontaneously without any effort are to be found. The villages of Shamballa are made up mostly of two story houses of the kind found in India. Men wear white or red cotton robes; woman white or blue dresses decorated with pleats and various designs. All the people of Shamballa lead wholesome lives, and there is no crime, famine, or disease. These satraps all teach the Kalachakra to their subjects. Most residents of Shamballa achieve Buddhahood in their own lives by means of various tantric teachings, including the Kalachakra."

There are many different beliefs and ideas surrounding this mystical city. For centuries, people have sought to discover the fabled paradisiacal city of Shamballa the purported home to the "Lord of Planet Earth" Sanat Kumara. During the end of the Middle Ages, the Roman Catholics would send missionaries to convert the Tibetans and the Chinese to Christianity. Each time, the missionaries brought back reports of a wondrous place somewhere in Middle Asia. They described it as a natural paradise in which all the inhabitants were full of wisdom, where justice reigned and suffering and old age were unknown. However, getting to the mystical land of Shamballa was very difficult and dangerous and only the pure were granted admission. Many *lamas* and teachers claimed to have visited this sacred land in dreams and visions, and some even on foot. Although many Theosophists postulate that Shamballa only exists on the etheric plane which represents the fourth or higher sub-plane of the physical realm while others believe it exist in the inner level of the Earth.

In Tibetan Buddhist tradition, Shamballa is a mythical kingdom hidden somewhere in Inner Asia or the Himalayas. They speak of it in some of their ancient text such as the "*Kalachakra Tantra*" and the ancient texts of the "*Zhang Zhung*" culture. In the Bön scriptures they speak of a closely related city called Olmolungring. In any event, Shamballa eventually became an extraordinary kingdom whose reality is visionary or spiritual just as much as physical or geographic. However, many believe Shamballa is not a physical place that one can actually find. Nevertheless, we know it to be a pure land within the human realm but unless one is of pure spirit, he cannot actually arrive there.

Shamballa actually has several different meanings to include "outer" and "inner" as well as "alternative" meanings. According to the "outer" meaning, Shamballa actually exist on the physical plane, but it is believed that only people with the appropriate *karma* can reach it and experience it as such. Having said that, it's safe to say that the "inner" and "alternative" meanings refer to more subtle understandings of what Shamballa represents in terms of one's own body and mind that being the "inner," and the meditation practice representing the "alternative."

Noted Theosophists Helena P. Blavatsky also believes Shamballa is a physical location on Earth, albeit one which can only be penetrated by a worthy aspirant. Alice A. Bailey who is also a Theosophist, believes Shamballa is an extra-dimensional or spiritual reality on the etheric plane. She believes it to be a spiritual center where the governing deity of Earth Sanat Kumara resides as the highest avatar of the Planetary Logos. This Planetary Logos is said to be an expression of the will of God. As such, there is a council of spiritual beings that receive spiritual energies through the lens of the Solar Logos which in turn reflects that purpose to our Planetary Logos, who then implement it as God's perpetual will on our planet. These highly evolved beings are 6th degree *Arhats* or spiritual practitioners who have realized *nirvana* through the culmination of the spiritual life. These evolved beings receive directives from Sanat Kumara, where they lower the frequency and make it available to the 5th degree masters who then relay it to other members of the Spiritual Hierarchy. This energy then gets distributed directly to humanity on our planet at certain designated times. Accordingly, this is a brief outline of what they consider to be the higher will for this planet:

> To establish, through goodwill, right human relations on the Earth, and with all kingdoms of nature.
> To share and circulate the resources of the Earth so that each incarnated soul has enough to live in joy and dignity.
> To help every soul understand the purpose of life as the evolution of consciousness.
> To help each soul transform their *karma*, evolve their consciousness, and realize their potential as fully as possible in service to all life.

Unfortunately though, as this energy gets distributed to humanity, it is often corrupted based on the choices of humanity rather than its higher use. This higher wisdom is being misappropriated by the powers that be and self seeking governmental agencies that are utilizing this energy to implement a plan for world domination as opposed to synthesis.

In Sanskrit, Shamballa is a term comprising *swayam + bhala* meaning "self benefited" or *swayam + bala* meaning "self powered" but it is most commonly considered to be a place of peace, tranquility and utter happiness. And in fact, all the inhabitants of Shamballa are considered to be extremely enlightened beings. According to legend, Shamballa is ruled over by a line of Kings of Shamballa known as *"Kulika"* or *"Kalki King"* which is a monarch who upholds the integrity of the *Kalachakra* tantra. This being is believed to be none other than Sanat Kumara himself. In the esoteric tradition, Shamballa is known to change its location from time to time according to changes in landmass and geological conditions, but presently its communities are said to lie in the highlands of Asia in a network of *ashrams*, training centers and monasteries often hundreds of miles apart and closed off to the outside world. In fact spiritual adepts have gathered there for thousands of years without exposure. In truth, Shamballa serves as the focal center of the greatest mysteries, philosophies and the most advanced scientific knowledge known to man. There is believed to be a vast network of caverns and tunnels that exist under the mountains where subterranean caverns have sheltered secret schools of magic from the earliest times. British Esotericists J.G. Bennett called Shamballa "The Hidden Directorate," because he believed it was responsible for secretly starting new truths and establishing new energies in society, thus directing the course of history from behind the scenes.

In his book *Blue Blood, True Blood: Conflict and Creation*, Stewart A. Swerdlow gives an entirely different account of Shamballa. According to his understanding, due to an upheaval that occurred between the Reptilians and the Atlanteans, the Reptilians migrated to the Earth's interior where they created an underground civilization. He believes this is where the legend of Hell and demons living under the Earth was formulated. Accordingly, these cities are constructed along the interior wall of the Earth's crust. What caught my attention was what he says next. Swerdlow postulates that there are primary entry points at the North and South Poles which can actually be seen from outer space. This, he believes, is the reason why commercial aircraft are not allowed to fly over these areas as opposed to the alleged reason of magnetic disturbances. Within the center of the Earth is a residual energy that serves as an inner Sun. This globe of energy is what causes the *aurora borealis* more commonly referred to as the "Northern Lights." According to Swerdlow, there are countless cave entrances to this inner city through the Rocky Mountains and the Sierra Mountains in western United States as well as other openings in the Ozarks and Appalachian Mountains. Other entries include the Alps, Himalayas, Andes and the Caribbean. He believes there to also be numerous sub-oceanic entry points in the Pacific Ocean, the Caribbean Sea and the Atlantic submarine mountain ranges. This could very well be the reason why there have been so many accounts of Unidentified Submerged Objects (USOs) emerging from and entering the Ocean. Subsequently, many of the locations referred to by Swerdlow are heavily guarded by the secret government. In Swerdlow's account, there are also entrances under the Denver Airport, the Giza Plateau in Egypt, major Air Force complexes around the world and many of the Temples in India and China. And while the intentions of the Reptilians mentioned by Swerdlow are somewhat different than those of the *Kumaras*, his account is eerily similar to all accounts of a city existing beneath the surface where a race of highly evolved beings resides.

So there you have it, Shamballa revealed. In this view, it serves as the guardian of our planetary evolution where divine beings channel the energies of the planet and direct humanity towards ever renewed opportunities for self-development. Whether or not you find any truth in these accounts is entirely up to you. Truth can always be judged based upon how it feels within ones self. I can't say whether or not either of these explanations is based on truth are fallacy. I can only say that I wouldn't put anything past the government as they have been known to cover up such things. In terms of whether or not there is an actual race of beings existing within the etheric planes of the Earth, I can only speculate. Needless to say, I myself have not been counted among the ones privileged enough to experience this reality. Nevertheless, I remain forever hopeful that someday I shall be counted among the esteemed witnesses of this illustrious dwelling place. Until then, I trust that there *is* such a place where . . . *"ain't nobody crying, ain't nobody worried and ain't no smiling faces . . . lying to the races."*

The Great Brotherhood of Light

Whether you believe it or not, there are actually higher spiritual beings that exist on different dimensions that directly affect the third-dimensional Earth plane. These beings serve as the conduit from which higher vibrational information can be transmitted to individuals that are receptive to higher guidance and wisdom. This group of illuminated individuals possesses an extreme telepathic ability which enables them to be sensitive to mind currents and to register the thoughts of those who personify the Universal Mind. They have the ability to function on thought frequencies beyond our planetary body. Their goal is to uphold and execute the ideas of Divine Mind. Therefore, they are in constant telepathic rapport with the Solar and Planetary logos as well as immediate telepathic rapport with each other. As the spiritual executives of the Supreme plan, they constantly oversee human and planetary affairs. This council is known by many names but here I will simply refer to them as "The Great Brotherhood of Light."

This Brotherhood does not solely consist of male energy but rather it is derived from many different adepts to include both feminine and masculine beings. In fact, there is a group of Ascended Masters made up of all feminine energy called the "Ladies of Shamballa." Be that as it may, they have been assisting humankind here on Earth for millions of years. Members of this spiritual body are believed to be individuals who have actually lived in physical bodies who have gained the wisdom and mastery in order to become immortal and free of the cycles of incarnation and karma. They have since "ascended" into becoming the complete and permanent union of the physical self with the "I AM" presence which is the ultimate goal for all incarnated souls.

The Great Brotherhood of Light possesses a supernatural power which enables them to spread light and wisdom throughout humanity. Their sole purpose is to help beings of lower densities of light evolve into greater expressions of their God-Self. Subsequently, they have been assisting this planet long prior to it ever coming into the third dimension. And since the Universe is constantly expanding and evolving into more and more diversity, this Brotherhood of Light also provides its assistance to thousands of other forms of existence throughout the cosmic Diaspora.

The Great Brotherhood of Light is an enlightened community of adepts that can reside here on Earth or on the Etheric Plane. But more importantly, they are benevolent beings whose primary concern is the spiritual development of our species as a whole. As spiritual adepts and ascended masters, many of the members of The Great Brotherhood of Light have gained higher levels of understanding and experience by having evolved from the physical world. Therefore, their wisdom comes from countless experiences of being human. Before deciding to move on to higher dimensions, they elect to assist those of us still evolving. While some actually do go on to higher levels of evolution on other spheres of existence, those that choose to remain become teaching masters. Unfortunately, very few of these masters are known to us because they travel through light. They are of a much higher dimensional vibration and since the human eye can only see certain vibrations, they remain invisible to the naked eye. At present, this Brotherhood is considered to be the highest and purest form of intelligence that is aiding Divine Mind in all realms of existence. Some of these souls have willingly returned to physical form to open the world to enlightenment, wisdom and knowledge. These enlightened beings are bringing forth truth, light and higher forms of wisdom to the world.

In 1954, Geraldine Innocente founder of The Bridge to Freedom Church and purported messenger of The Great Brotherhood of Light channeled this message from Sanat Kumara:

> "Thus we took our abode upon the sweet Earth. Through the same power of centripetal and centrifugal force of which I spoke (cohesion and expansion of the magnetic power of Divine Love), We then began to magnetize the Flame in the hearts of some of the Guardian Spirits who were not sleeping so soundly and who were not too enthusiastically engaged in using primal life for the satisfaction of the personal self. In this way, the Great Brotherhood of Light began. The Three-fold Flame within the heart of Shamballa, within the Hearts of the Kumaras and Myself, formed the magnetic Heart of the Great Brotherhood by whom you have all been blessed and of which Brotherhood you all aspire to become conscious members."

The Great Brotherhood of Light consists of members of the "Heavenly Host" which is the Spiritual Hierarchy directly concerned with the growth and development of our species. This Spiritual Hierarchy consists of several types of beings that have contributed to our genetic make-up through our DNA. Therefore, they have a vested interest in our progress for we are their progeny. As such; they have assumed responsibility for the cosmic destiny of the human race, both individually and collectively. This is the reason why whenever we are in need of some type of assistance, the Brotherhood provides the necessary teachings and spiritual help. It's no mystery that whenever we extend our reach towards Divinity, it always draws nearer to us. Throughout history and our quest for light and wisdom, the Spiritual Hierarchy has always provided the necessary guidance and incentive towards fuller spiritual living. The Brotherhood's intention is to help us open our own personal "channel" so that we may come in contact with our true God source energy. This will enable us to be "dependent" on nothing outside of ourselves and each person will be empowered in their own life as a result of their individual connection to truth.

I shall close with these words from the website Jeddahmali. com:

> "We have come to a time in humanity's journey when the gap between Heaven and Earth is closing. Truth has been available to all throughout the ages but only understood by a few. Our purpose, in this communication, is to remind mankind of the key principles that govern your whole experience here on Earth. Life is not currently viewed in its true light; there is so much more going on than many are aware of. In the next few years, there is an unprecedented opportunity for the people of Earth to move out of struggle and into freedom, which is the birthright of Man. The time has come for mankind to wake up from a long sleep and see the whole truth; to shift the entire paradigm of human consciousness from limitation to freedom. There are many who have come to assist you in this, a whole host of advanced spiritual beings who are offering their encouragement, support and inspiration. We wish to share with you the many wonders of your existence and to give you our heartfelt reassurance that all is well. It is a very exciting time in the evolution of the Earth. Mankind is becoming Godkind."

And, I might add; it is through the assistance of The Great Brotherhood of Light that this realization is finally becoming known.

The Ascended Masters

One cannot speak of The Great Brother/Sisterhood of Light without mentioning the Ascended Masters. In fact, the two are synonymous. Both of these facets are associated with the Spiritual Hierarchy in different aspects. While the Spiritual Hierarchy is comprised of all Council members, there are different degrees of carrying out the Universal plan. Information trickles down from the top just as in any organizational structure. This is not to say there is a rank-and-file but rather there are highly evolved beings that are designated to help implement learning on a higher level as well as information dissemination. When it comes to executing the wishes of the Council, the Ascended Masters have elected to be the vehicles for these teachings where they function from a higher plane of existence in order to assist humans in their gradual movement toward enlightenment. These beings are not confined to time and space. They have incarnated just as you and I have by way of the birth canal and they live among us fulfilling the inner calling of their God presence throughout each embodiment. As true masters, they have conquered all the lesser things of this world by incorporating the lessons of life, balancing karma, fulfilling their Dharma and becoming God incarnate. They stand by ready to support us in accomplishing this same goal and they will forever continue to extend their compassion until we have achieved individual and planetary ascension.

Throughout our existence here on this planet, there have been countless masters that have volunteered to provide mankind with higher wisdom. These Ascended Masters have been compared to angelic beings in Christian folklore where they act as a source of revelation and authority. They are often viewed as respected teachers of spiritual wisdom and they are highly revered for their level of understanding. The Ascended Masters are extremely compassionate and solely dedicated to uplifting humanity. Some of the more familiar masters include such figures as; Thoth, Maitreya, Buddha, Sananda, Krishna and Jesus. Many people believe that each of these masters is the embodiment of the same being but we'll leave that for another discussion. Be that as it may, the Ascended Masters serve as teachers of wisdom to those that are receptive to their instruction.

In the glossary of *Doorway to Eternity: A Guide to Planetary Ascension* by Kiara Windrider, he defines an Ascended Master as a person who has succeeded in unifying the physical body with the light body. This pretty much describes the process of "ascension" hence the term "Ascended Master." Windrider's description of ascension is the process of raising the frequencies of the physical body so as to merge with its higher dimensional counterpart, the light body thus allowing for it to transcend the ordinary limitations of the physical body. This is the process that each Ascended Master has undergone in order to have the epithet of Ascended Master bestowed upon them. As such, they are believed to be spiritually enlightened beings that once inhabited human bodies but have undergone a process of spiritual transformation as in the case of Thoth, Maitreya, Buddha, Jesus and many others. That being the case, they know passion and they feel just like we do. They are real, visible, glorious, tangible beings of extreme light. They are living and caring beings that have such love, compassion, wisdom and power that the human mind could never comprehend. They function throughout the Universe with complete freedom and infinite power.

These adepts once lived upon the Earth just as you and I now are but they were able to transcend the lessons of life during their physical embodiments. They have since "Ascended" into a level of expression higher than that of the common human. They have essentially become pure, eternal, all-powerful, divine and perfect beings. This has allowed them to gain mastery over the physical plane by being able to balance at least 51% of negative karma thus fulfilling their Dharma or divine purpose. This process has enabled them to become "God-like" by becoming unified with his or her own "God Self," or the "I AM" presence. Once they are freed of negative karma, they can then choose how and where in the Universe they would like to serve. Many of these evolved masters have elected to continue developing with the souls on Earth in order to guide them on the path of soul development and self-transcendence. As such; they are the true teachers of mankind, directing the spiritual evolution of all those who desire to reunite with divine consciousness. Two proponents of these teachings, Alice Bailey and Benjamin Creme assert that there are sixty such beings that they refer to as the "Masters of the Ancient Wisdom," who have reached the fifth level of initiation or above. Helena P. Blavatsky, founder and Secretary of the Theosophical Society referred to them as the "*Mahatmas*" or "Masters," that were physical beings living in the Himalayas. She says of them:

> "... They are living men, born as we are born, and doomed to
> die like every mortal. We call them "Masters" because they

are our teachers; and because from them we have derived all
the Theosophical truths . . . They are men of great learning,
whom we call Initiates, and still greater holiness of life."

Although Blavatsky refers to these adepts as being men, this is
not to imply in any way that there are no female masters.

Ascended Masters can belong to particular orders some of
which include the Melchizedeks and the Elohim. The Melchizedeks
purpose is to bring higher wisdom to humankind by influencing
the arts, sciences, education and technology. They represent the
"Triune" consciousness of wisdom which makes up the fundamental
human life force. The Elohim are considered to be the most
powerful aspects of the consciousness of God and they include the
"Elementals" which are the Sylphs that control the air, the "Gnomes"
that control the Earth, the "Undines" that control the water, and the
"Salamanders" that control the fire element. These four aspects are
said to govern our four lower bodies. Also under the Elohim are the
"Beings of Nature"—the Four Beings of the Elements, who are the
"Twin Flames" who have dominion over all of the evolutions of
the Gnomes, Salamanders, Sylphs, and Undines. The Elohim carry
the greatest concentration, the highest vibration of light that we can
comprehend in our state of evolution. There is also the Karmic Board
or "The Lords of Karma" who metes out justice, mercy and judgment
on behalf of every incarnation. It is believed that all life streams
pass before this board before each incarnation on Earth to receive
their assignment and karmic allotment for that lifetime. Each soul
then passes before the Karmic Board again at the conclusion of each
lifetime to review their performance. According to ascendedmaster.
com, these are the purported members of the Karmic Board:

> Goddess of Liberty
> Ascended Lady Master Nada
> Cyclopea, Elohim of the Fifth Ray
> Pallas Athena, the Goddess of Truth
> Portia, the Goddess of Justice
> Kuan Yin, the Goddess of Mercy

The same source delineates the Spiritual Hierarchy below by describing each facet and what its functions are. It begins by describing this planetary spiritual hierarchy as a governmental structure with far more complexities. Here is a detailed breakdown from this website:

The Council of Nine: A tribunal of teachers governing our immediate super-galactic and galactic region, subject to change in evolving "new programs" of the Father's Kingdom.

The Council of Twelve: Sons of Heaven working to supervise the creation and regeneration of the lower worlds. It is this complete Council of Twelve, embodying the Twelve Rays, which enables this creation, this one Cosmic Day, to exist.

The Council of Twenty-Four: A council governing spiritual civilization in the Sun Universe and is not to be confused with the 24 Elders.

The Council of One Hundred and Forty-Four Thousand: A tribunal of Ascended Masters administering the program of the "Ancient of Days;" The infinite mind working through the Creator God; The hierarchy of the "Higher Heavens" that governs the hierarchies of the mid-heavens and the lower-heavens, assessing the final "soul programs" of man and master alike.

The Council of Light: The collective name for the above councils which govern this galaxy and other regions of distant Universes. These are not solar or planetary councils.

The Order/Brotherhood of Enoch: Initiates the faithful into new worlds of consciousness by creating the spiritual-scientific scrolls of knowledge. The brotherhood builds the pyramid grids on the planets necessary to evolve the biomes of intelligence.

The Order/Brotherhood of Melchizedek: Is in charge of the consciousness reprogramming that is necessary to link physical creation with the externalization of the divine hierarchy

The Order of Michael/Brotherhood of Michael: Guards the galaxies from biological/spiritual interference from the lesser forces of light except where necessary to test/train for soul advancement. (I can neither deny nor confirm the validity of these statements. My goal here is simply to present you with my findings. However, it is up to you to discern within your own knowing whether or not you choose to accept this as truth).

The concept of Ascended Masters has long since been a mystery for us. For many years we haven't been able to figure this group out. Fortunately today, through the process of channeling we have been able to learn a considerable amount about them. Over the last several hundred years or so, these masters have been supporting our spiritual evolution by spreading light and wisdom through their initiates. They have earned the right to be the representatives of our spiritual hierarchy and it is through them that we are able to gain a better understanding about the evolution of the planet as well as ourselves. As we learn more about the Ascended Masters, we will begin to see just how much of an integral part they have played in bringing the planet and all of us to our present state of awareness. Once we begin to accept them, we will come to understand just how crucial they have been in the role of spiritual intermediary.

We are all capable of ascension through the assistance of these Ascended Masters who speak and channel inspiration to us usually in the dreaming or meditative state. Typically this is accomplished through the creative mind which is the intuitive side of the brain known as the right hemisphere or feminine side. Simply put, ascension means a return to the higher frequencies which is essentially a return to the feminine aspects of our souls. Connecting with an Ascended Master is a process of tapping into these higher forms of knowledge that are intrinsically ours. The Ascended Masters are the source we tap into when we want to trigger that higher knowledge within ourselves. People all over the world today are looking for a deeper and more meaningful way of connecting with spirit and it is the masters desire to present us with a path of initiation that will help us raise our awareness by accelerating and reuniting us with our Higher Selves. But, we must to be willing to do the necessary work. And then, when the student is truly ready to learn, the Master will appear.

The Hathors

Another group that is assisting this planet in its ascension is a highly evolved race of beings from Venus known as the Hathors. While there is some affiliation with the goddess Hathor, they are not to be confused with her. This group is a 3rd dimensional race of beings from another Universe that came in through the Sirius portal and then went to Venus. This was revealed in the book, *Channeled Messages* by Tom Kenyon and Virginia Essene where they channel this message from the Hathors:

> "We are the Hathors. We come in love and with the sounding of a new dream reality for your Earth. If you are ready to build the new world, we invite you to join us on a journey of the mind and heart. We are your elder brothers and sisters. We have been with you for a very long period of your evolution on this planet. We were with you in eons past—even in the forgotten days before any trace of us is known in your present written history. Our own nature is energetic and interdimensional. We originally came from another Universe by way of Sirius which is a portal to your Universe, and from Sirius we eventually proceeded to your solar system and the etheric realms of Venus. We are what you might term an 'ascended civilization' a group of beings existing at a specific vibratory field, even as you have an energy signature. It is simply that we vibrate at a faster rate than you. Nonetheless, we are all part of the mystery, part of the love that holds and binds the entire Universe together. We have grown as you have grown, ascending to the One Source of all that is. We have grown in joy and through sorrow, as have you. We are, in terms of the vastness, a little higher on the spiral of awareness and consciousness than you are; therefore, we can offer you what we have learned as friends, mentors and fellow travelers on the path that leads back to remembrance of All That Is."

Venus is a highly evolved 5th dimensional planet that inhabits some of the most enlightened beings in the Universe. It is considered to be the focal point for all life in our solar system. In terms of advancement, the Hathors are several million years further along in their development. They exist in both the physical form and non-physical form on the etheric level where thought is the primary cause of creation. They are beings of tremendous love and they hold the highest vision for humanity. Drunvalo Melchizedek describes the Hathors as being the primary mentors within the Left Eye of Horus Mystery School that have assisted us in the unfolding of our consciousness. He says they are on the level of "Christ Consciousness" and they only use vocal sounds as their way of communicating and carrying out feats within their environment. Unfortunately, as we became more physical in nature, we somehow lost the ability to see them which makes it difficult to respond to their teachings. But, as we begin to raise our consciousness, we are slowly beginning to reestablish contact with this race of cosmic teachers.

Hathors are interdimensional beings that are assisting Earth's ascension through extreme love and compassion. One of their primary methods for assisting us is through the use of sound and breathing. Much like the Dolphins, Hathors use sonar to accomplish everything. Through their incredible understanding of sound and breath, they are able to create a continuous sound without stopping for up to an hour. They understand that sound is the primordial basis of all creation, for it was the sound *"Om"* that created all of nature and therefore, it is sound that will restore it. The sound made by this method creates a tone that not only heals the body but also restores the balance of nature. This is also a balancing of masculine and feminine energies which when brought into balance within the human body are actually balancing the (electric) male principle and the (magnetic) female principle which is our overall electromagnetic make-up. The Hathors are able to help balance the male and female aspect by holding a consistent harmonic. And since they are androgynous beings, they have successfully undergone this process themselves by balancing both aspects of their divine selves.

The Hathors are intergalactic beings that have been here on this planet for many thousands of years under the direction of Sanat

Kumara. While Egypt was being formulated, the Hathors were very instrumental in helping to develop its civilization. But this was long prior to the inception of the Pharaohs. During that time there were only two primary gods which were Horus and Hathor. Horus was the sky god while Hathor was the sky goddess but as politics became more prevalent, Hathor was later reduced to the station of fertility goddess. In fact, the female goddess in general was relegated to the Earth. Initially, the gods and the goddesses from heaven were both considered "equals" until eventually the male principle was associated with a higher loftier station in the heavens thus rendering him more important, while the female goddess was reduced to a lower station here on Earth.

The Hathors have since mastered the art of sound and love by working directly with the feeling nature of the Universe and they are presently assisting everyone seeking higher consciousness, to do the same. They have come in our time of ascension and personal transformation in order to assist us in understanding who we are, and why we are here. These great beings of love and light have been with us, serving from the elevated planes of consciousness for eons. The Buddhists call this; "The Pure Realms of Light and Sound." Today, they are rekindling their relationship with us, as we become more willing to seek greater independence within our own spiritual nature. Obviously, dealing with a transition of this magnitude involves raising our vibratory field. But, how exactly does one accomplish this? One message suggests; "The simple act of appreciation for what is in our lives will shift our vibratory field faster and more effectively than any sacred geometry . . . the cultivation of appreciation for the smallest things in our lives will give us the greatest results." Ultimately the Hathors message is simple and that is that we are not to be overly concerned or worried. Despite how badly things may appear or how serious our situation has become. We are all eternal beings and we will go on indefinitely. There is no judgment or eternal damnation awaiting us, only an opportunity to return once again in order to do a better job of it in the next incarnation.

Maitreya

According to Buddhist philosophy, it is prophesized that a figure is to appear here on Earth, achieve total and complete enlightenment and stay on to teach the basic principles of cosmic and individual existence as Divine Law. This stream of consciousness is the express reality of none other than the Master Maitreya who was among the first of humanity to actually take initiation, way back in early Atlantean times and has been at the forefront of humanity ever since. He is known as a *"Bodhisattva"* which is one who has already reached a very advanced state of grace or enlightenment but holds back from entering nirvana so that he may help others. This is an extreme act of love. In fact; the title Maitreya literally means "Loving One," derived from the Sanskrit, *"maitri,"* meaning radiant kindness and love. While western tradition is unfamiliar with such teachings, mention of Maitreya is found in the canonical literature of all Buddhist sects.

There's a long held belief which says that many of the great ascended masters we know as Krishna, Confucius, Zoroaster, the Buddha, Mohammed and even that of Jesus the Christ was essentially one-in-the same personification through a process known as "Overshadowing." In order to understand this, I need to explain that Jesus of Nazareth and the Christ was essentially not the same person. I'm aware that many Christians may find it hard to accept this fact but the title "Christ" does not refer to an individual at all but rather the name of a function in the Spiritual Hierarchy or group of advanced beings who guide and orchestrate the evolution of humanity from behind the scenes. Whichever being is seated at the head of this Hierarchy automatically becomes the "World Teacher" during the term of office. It is believed that Maitreya, who embodies the Christ Consciousness, has held this office for over two million years. It is further believed that he manifested himself as Jesus the Christ as a means to usher in the "Piscean Age" through the process of "Spiritual Overshadowing," where it was actually *his* consciousness that informed and guided the actions and teachings of Jesus. It was, therefore, the consciousness of the Christ, Maitreya, which was seen and experienced by those around Jesus. Jesus and Maitreya the Christ were (and are) one in the sense that they, each on his own level, work together in perfect concord to further the divine Plan. Many of the events from Jesus' life and his words have been greatly misinterpreted because of this unknown connection to Maitreya the Christ. This is why people question whether Jesus was God or man, or perhaps both together. Some even question whether Jesus ever existed at all. Whatever the case, If he did in fact exist, Jesus was simply a man just like you and I who, as a result of the process of spiritual evolution, became enlightened as everyone eventually does.

Many others have also chosen the path of enlightenment. One such figure is Sai Baba, a guru in south India. Sai Baba and Maitreya both embody the Christ principle, the energy of Love with Sai Baba being at the cosmic level, and Maitreya being at the planetary level. Sai Baba embodies the energy of Love at a cosmic level and Maitreya embodies this energy at the planetary level. His duty is to prepare all of mankind for the work of the Christ. By awakening the principle of Love in humanity, Sai Baba will prepare people for the initial work of Maitreya. As the Initiator, at the first two planetary initiations, Maitreya will lead humanity gradually out of the human kingdom into the Hierarchy, the Kingdom of Souls, or the Kingdom of God. That is his major work in the coming Age of Aquarius. These two Great Ones work together in daily contact, complete harmony and shared purpose in the evolution of mankind.

The appearance of Maitreya has been expected for generations by all of the major religions. Christians speak of this event as the "Second Coming" or the return of the Christ, and presume his return to be imminent. The Jews await him as the "Messiah" while the Hindus look for the coming of "Krishna." Buddhists expect him as Maitreya Buddha; and Muslims anticipate the Imam "Mahdi" or Messiah. While there are many different interpretations in terms of the actual name of the one to return, the fact remains that all beliefs point to a figure that is to return for the sake of mankind during a time when humanity will have reached its lowest point and the arrival of some type of Savior or Messiah is widely accepted. So, even though the names may be different, it is a common fact that they all refer to the same individual: The World Teacher, or in this case, Maitreya.

Maitreya's coming is characterized by a number of physical events. The oceans are predicted to decrease in size, allowing for him to traverse them freely. This event is to allow the unveiling of the true *"dharma"* to the people which in turn will permit the construction of a new world. His coming is to represent the end of the middle time in which we currently reside. Many religious traditions claim that Maitreya is already present in the world, but is waiting to make an open declaration of his presence in the near future. They believe he is here to inspire mankind to create a "New Age" based on sharing and justice. Through channeled communications, Maitreya himself has said that he is a teacher from the world beyond ours. He has been known in many cultures as *"Lord Maitreya"* but he doesn't declare himself as a Lord, just an ascended energy, who has come to the Earth plane to teach. He prefers only to be known as the "Teacher" but not as a religious leader, or to found a new religion, but as a teacher and guide for people of every religion and even those of no religion. As an ascended master, Maitreya has risen to a high station in the Spiritual Hierarchy, which qualifies him to speak on a higher plane of consciousness. He has said that, *"It does not matter who I am, what matters is the message, it is not about personalities, but the message."*

Since 1974, British artist Benjamin Crème has been writing about Maitreya helping to make people more aware of his existence. Crème says Maitreya descended in July 1977 from his ancient retreat in the Himalayas and took up residence in London where he has been living and working as an ordinary man. Of course very few people are actually aware of his true status. Crème believes Maitreya has been gradually emerging into full public view without infringing on humanity's free will. Perhaps it has been the energy of this extraordinary being that has been the stimulus for some of the dramatic changes throughout the world over the years. Crème feels Maitreya will make his true identity known to the world on the "Day of Declaration" where everyone will know him for who he truly is. Crème says on the Day of Declaration, Maitreya will finally present his credentials to all of humanity and "every eye shall see him." Accordingly, everyone will simultaneously hear his voice inwardly—telepathically in their own language and we will all feel his omnipotent love whereupon hundreds of thousands of spontaneous healings will systematically take place throughout the world.

Upon declaring his identity to the entire world, Maitreya will then begin serving humanity openly rather than from behind the scenes as he now does. Gautama Buddha is quoted as saying:

> "Now in those days, brethren, there shall arise in the world an exalted one by name Maitreya (the kindly one) an Arhat, a fully enlightened one, endowed with wisdom and righteousness, a happy one, a world-knower, the peerless charioteer of men to be tamed, a teacher of the devas (angels) and mankind, an exalted one, a Buddha like myself. He of his own abnormal powers shall realize and make known the world, and the worlds of the devas, with their Maras, their Brahmas, the host of recluses and Brahmins, of devas and mankind alike, even as I do now. He shall proclaim the norm, lovely in its beginning, lovely in its middle, and lovely in the end thereof. He shall make known the wholly perfect life of righteousness in all its purity, both in the spirit and in the letter of it, even as I do now. He shall lead an Order of Brethren numbering many thousands, even as I do now lead an order of Brethren numbering many hundreds."

What then are we to think . . . ? Is the world truly in need of a savior to make itself known in order for humanity to find an equilibrium? It's no mystery that practically all world religions speak of the return of some form of savior that will one day rid the world of all its woes thus bringing about a "Heaven-on-Earth" scenario. But is this really necessary? Is it not true that we must each seek to work out our own salvation and that no one can ever help us to reach self-realization? I'm of the opinion that while there is in fact some form of spiritual hierarchy that oversees planetary evolution; each individual soul has the responsibility of working out its own salvation, that being his or her evolutionary plan. Nothing outside of ourselves can save us from ourselves. I do however, subscribe to the idea of ascended masters otherwise I wouldn't be expounding on it here in this book. Only my interpretation is somewhat different in that these "masters" are no different than you or I and they have each manifested here in order to reach the level of awareness that they have achieved through self-realization. This is something that all of us are capable of through practice and mastery. Granted this may take several life-times, it is the purpose of our being, our sole/ soul reason for existing. We are all masters in our own right seeking to ascend to higher levels of consciousness through the examples we know as the Christ, Buddha, Krishna, Muhammad, and countless others. They were no different than we are today and we will all reach the same level of awareness whenever we decide to live and dwell as the masters we truly are.

Jesus Christ?

"It has served us well, this myth of Christ."

—*Pope Leo X*

What if the figure we know as Jesus never even existed? What would this revelation do to our faith and our way of believing? While this question may seem unrealistic to some, the reality is, recently I had to ask myself this very question. Fortunately for me the answer didn't come in that instant but it came slowly over a period of time in a gradual gentle sort of way. Had it come to me in an instant, it probably would have been too devastating for me to handle considering my entire belief system was based on the teachings of "Christianity" which are founded on the life and teachings of Jesus the Christ. What had to happen for me was that I first needed to break free of the stranglehold Christianity had over me. This came in the form of Islam. And although I went from one form of belief system to another, this adjustment allowed me to first accept Jesus as merely a prophet as opposed to him being the actual "Son of God," and the Savior to the world. With this change in my belief, I was one step closer to freedom. After several years, my seeking led me to realize that even Islam was not the only proponent of truth and there was an even greater aspect of my being that was still seeking to find truth in whatever form it might present itself. At that point, I started to open up to the possibility of simply being the spiritual entity that I am without the labels or the dogmas and the systematic ways of thinking. It was in making that adjustment that I became able to handle the truth of what I otherwise wouldn't have been able to handle. That truth being that the figure I was raised to believe in, cherish and worship as the "Son of God," was nothing more than a mythological plagiarism from Egyptian paganism which was based upon the Sun.

But let's say for the sake of argument that you are not ready to accept this ideology as I have, I mean after all, it is a huge and bitter pill to swallow. But what would it take to convince you that this is in fact true? Sadly enough, there is probably nothing that can be said that would thoroughly convince anyone of this truth outside of the Roman Church actually admitting it themselves and of course we know this will never happen. But why is that? Well, there are a number of reasons, one of which is to keep us from ever discovering who we truly are as spiritual beings. This discovery alone would wrench the power from those that have worked so diligently to keep us weak and powerless. Secondly, if the billions of Christians were ever to find out that everything they've believed in for the past 2000 plus years has all been a sham, there would be sheer and utter pandemonium. Therefore, this secret has to remain a top priority in order to maintain the control they've wielded over us for all these years. And so, the greatest lie ever perpetrated against Man goes unknown and even if we were to discover this grave injustice, we still couldn't bring ourselves to accept it. Sadly enough, there are billions of people, much like myself, who've accepted the story of Jesus seemingly without question.

There was a time in our history when the very mention of there *not* being a Jesus would have been cause enough to commit murder. Once the Christians gained absolute political power in the fourth century under Emperor Constantine, anyone opposing these newly established Christian doctrines was forced into believing by removal, imprisonment or threat of death. Fortunately though, through the works of people like Acharya S. and her book the "*The Christ Conspiracy: The Greatest Story Ever Sold*," and films like

Zeitgeist by Peter Joseph and countless others that are now coming to the forefront to expose this lie for what it truly is, we are finally able to break free from this delusional tyranny of falsehood in the form of not only Christianity, but all manner of organized religions. *"If a single person suffers from delusions, we call that insanity but when an entire people suffer from delusions, we call that religion."* If you ever want to enslave a people, give them a religion and build a foundation based upon fear and you will never again have to worry about exercising overt control. For they will indoctrinate themselves into this belief without question, passing it on from one generation to the next causing it to further ensnare all those that would come into that way of thinking.

I once read of a lady who was preparing a ham for dinner and before putting the ham into the pot, she cut off all four edges. Not really understanding why she went through this ritual each time she prepared a ham, she called her mother of whom she got the practice from. *"Mom . . ."* she said: *"As a child, I can remember watching you cut the edges off the ham. What was the purpose of that?"* *"Come to think of it,* says her mom, *I'm not sure why I started cutting off the edges."* *"You'll have to ask your grandmother, I got it from her,"* she says. So, that's exactly what she does. She calls her grandmother and says, *"Grandmother, I've been cutting the edges off the ham whenever I prepare it and mom says she got it from you, what was the purpose of cutting off the edges?"* Of which her grandmother replies, *"Because my pot wasn't big enough."* This is the exact same mentality we have with all of our beliefs. We inherit them from our parents who in turn inherited them from their parents without fully understanding what they were doing or why.

Practically all my life, I believed in the figure known as "Jesus Christ." Although my perception of Jesus had changed quite a bit over the years, I never thought I would arrive at the conclusion of Jesus being a myth altogether. In fact, my intentions in writing this book was to discuss Jesus as one of the ascended masters, but as I began to research this figure, with each book I read, and every link I visited, I came to discover an entirely different truth. More and more scholars, historians and writers were providing historical information claiming how Jesus is nothing more than an amalgamation of previous Sun deities. This aroused my curiosity, so I began to look in a different direction and I was truly amazed at what I discovered. One thing I learned was that the question of whether or not Jesus actually existed would never be confronted or tolerated by the religious believer. Christian fundamentalists would argue tooth and nail against such an idea without ever having done the research necessary to determine if in fact there is any validity to this claim. Sadly, their faith has blinded them to the point where they are unwilling to listen to reason and so the question of reliable evidence gets obscured by tradition, religious subterfuge, and outrageous claims.

So, what led me to believe that Jesus never existed, well for starters there is absolutely no physical evidence to support whether or not Jesus actually existed; no artifacts, no written work from Jesus himself or even from anyone during the time of his purported existence. Not one single historian, philosopher, scribe or follower who lived before or during the alleged time of Jesus ever mentions him. In his book *The Christ: A Critical Review and Analysis of the Evidence of His Existence*, John E. Remsburg compiled a list of forty-two writers who lived and wrote during the time or within a century after the time of Jesus and not one of them ever mentioned him. All the claims supporting the existence of Jesus were written long *after* his death by other people, some of which were written hundreds of years posthumously. Speaking of which; there is no actual court record that shows Pontius Pilate ever executing a man named Jesus. To this very day, there is not a single contemporary writing that mentions Jesus. Historians find it hard to believe that a figure of such importance would not be written about by anyone during that time and the writings that did come about well after his death were from unknown authors, people who had never met an earthly Jesus, or from fraudulent, mythical or allegorical writings. All of these accountings were derived from hearsay which is information derived from other people rather than on a witness' own knowledge.

The most convincing accounts of a historical Jesus come from Mathew, Mark, Luke and John the four canonical gospels of the bible all of which were not in their original form but were strongly influenced by the early Church fathers. In fact, the Encyclopedia Biblica declares that ". . . *the order of events in the life of Jesus according to the evangelists is contradictory and undependable and the chronological structure of the Gospels is worthless.*" The facts show unerringly that Matthew, Mark, Luke and John did not write what they knew but what they heard and imagined. There were several other gospels that existed during that time but for whatever reason, only these four gospels became Church cannon for the orthodox faith while most of the others were burned, destroyed, or lost. Elaine Pagels, Professor of Religion at Princeton University writes: "Although the gospels of the New Testament like those discovered at Nag Hammadi are attributed to Jesus' followers, no one knows who actually wrote any of them." Not only do we not know who wrote them, but none of the unknown writers ever claims to have actually met Jesus. Not to mention, none of these were the actual manuscripts but rather duplicates of the originals after they had been severely modified. Based upon the findings of biblical historians, there were no actual writings mentioning Jesus until a hundred and possibly even two hundred years after his alleged crucifixion. Again Pagels writes that "The first Christian gospel was probably written during the last year of the war, or the year it ended. Where it was written and by whom we do not know; the work is anonymous, although tradition attributes it to Mark . . ." It was the Church that first began to portray the authors as the apostles Mark, Luke, Matthew, & John, but scholars know from critical textural research that there is no factual evidence that the gospel authors could have ever served as the apostles described in the gospel stories. How can gospels which were not written until a hundred to two hundred years after Jesus is supposed to have died, have the slightest value as evidence that he really lived. So I'm led to believe that the gospels are nothing more than made up hearsay based on fictional, mythological, and falsified stories rendering them historically worthless. They are fraught with contradictions which are entirely unreasonable and there is nothing in them that can be considered true while there is much in them that can certainly be considered false.

What actually made it into the bible was determined by the priests who were often members of secret orders. So, it was the fathers of the Church that determined what would appear in the bible which provided the opportunity and motive for them to change, alter, and fabricate passages that would help strengthen the position of the

Church or the members of the Church themselves. This allowed the Church to have power over the masses and no one would ever question the Church because in most cases this would be seen as "heresy" which was punishable by death. Regardless of what the Church claimed, most people simply believed what their priests told them without question. Ignatius Loyola of the 16th century wrote in his Spiritual Exercises: "To be right in everything, we ought always to hold that the white which I see, is black, if the Hierarchical Church so decides it." Martin Luther said: "What harm would it do, if a man told a good strong lie for the sake of the good and for the Christian Church . . . a lie out of necessity, a useful lie, a helpful lie, such lies would not be against God, he would accept them." But deception is still deception by any other name.

Another interesting fact to note is that the bible does not provide a description of the human shape of Jesus. One would think that if people actually witnessed this figure perhaps there would be some mention of his physical attributes to include his stature, his eyes, or even his hair color. But there are none made. I find it a bit odd that none of the purported disciples mention what Jesus looked like and yet they are credited for knowing exactly what he said. This only serves to confirm the fact that they never actually saw him and there were no eyewitness accounts during the time of Jesus' theoretical existence. It wasn't until centuries later that pictures began to emerge depicting what Jesus looked like and these images came from cult Christians with a wide range of variations. Nevertheless their images of this "so called" figure did nothing more than mimic the pattern of other Greek mythological figures according to their own cultural image. One such figure was that of Hercules who could very well be the prototype for Jesus. Many of the myths about Hercules strongly resemble Jesus in many areas. Hercules' mother was a pure woman who had a union with Zeus/God giving birth to him much like Jesus and Mary. Hercules was sought after by "Hera" similar to that of Jesus and "Herod." Hercules traveled the Earth as a mortal helping mankind and performing miracles as did Jesus. In Greek Mythology, Hercules supposedly died, rose to Mt. Olympus and became a god, which happens to be very similar to Jesus who died and rose to heaven and is now worshipped as God. Hercules was perhaps the most popular hero in Ancient Greece and Rome and yet we know he never truly existed. This is also the case of the mythical Jesus where Church historian Johann Lorenz Mosheim writes, "The Christ of early Christianity was not a human being, but an 'appearance,' an illusion, a character in miracle, not in reality but a myth."

Many people believe that an actual Jesus lived but this is not the historical Jesus we're speaking of here but rather a character based on earlier mythologies of the Middle East and Egypt during the first century and before. Many of these stories appear similar to the Jesus savior story. Much of this was already discussed in previous chapters where I discuss how early Christians lived within pagan communities and how Jewish scriptural beliefs coupled with the pagan myths of the Egyptians gave rise to Christianity. Whether one is aware of it or not, there were countless savior stories being promulgated long before the alleged life of Jesus none of which were originated by Christians. For example, the religion of Zoroaster, founded circa 628-551 B.C.E. in ancient Persia, instituted the belief in a devil, the belief of a paradise, last judgment and resurrection of the dead. Even Mithraism, which is an offshoot of Zoroastrianism, had a tremendous influence on early Christianity. Pagan Mithraism had a deity of light and truth which was the son of the Most High who fought against evil and presented the idea of the Logos. It also had the burial in a rock tomb, resurrection, sacrament of bread & water (Eucharist), the marking on the forehead with a mystic mark, the symbol of the Rock, the Seven Spirits and seven stars, all before the advent of Christianity. All of the gods of antiquity to include; Osiris, Hercules, Mithra, Hermes, Prometheus, Perseus and others compare greatly with the mythical Jesus figure. According to Patrick Campbell in, *The Mythical Jesus*, all these figures served as pre-Christian sun gods, yet all allegedly had gods for fathers, virgins for mothers; had their births announced by stars; got born on the solstice around December 25th; had tyrants who tried to kill them in their infancy; met violent deaths; rose from the dead; and nearly all got worshiped by "wise men" and had allegedly fasted for forty days. When early Christian apologist Justin Martyr recognized the similarities between Christianity and Paganism he wrote to the pagans:

"When we say that the Word, who is first born of God, was produced without sexual union, and that he, Jesus Christ, our teacher, was crucified and died, and rose again, and ascended into heaven; we propound nothing different from what you believe regarding those whom you esteem sons of Jupiter (Zeus)."

Practically all reports of Jesus have their parallels with past pagan mythologies which have existed long prior to Christianity. Another well known biblical scholar Earl Doherty reveals in his book, *The Jesus Puzzle*: *Did Christianity Begin With A Mythical Christ*, that early pre-Gospel Christian documents prove that the concept of Jesus sprang from non-historical spiritual beliefs of a Christ derived from Jewish scripture and Hellenized myths of savior gods. He writes, "Christian documents outside the gospels, even at the end of the first century and beyond, show no evidence that any tradition about an earthly life and ministry of Jesus were in circulation." He goes on to say that none of the New Testament writers ever describes a human Jesus. None of the writers ever mentions a Jesus from Nazareth, an earthly teacher, or as a human miracle worker and nowhere do we find these writers ever quoting Jesus. Not one of them ever describes any details of Jesus' life on Earth or his followers. In fact, none of them even used the word "disciple" only the term "apostle" which simply means messenger. In the letter to the Hebrews 8:4 we find there was certainly some doubt of the existence of Jesus by saying, "*If Jesus had been on earth, He would not be a priest.*" There's clearly some doubt as to the validity of Jesus' existence and many simply accept this traditional way of thinking and believing without question while Bible scholar Robert J. Miller says that "What one believes and what one can demonstrate historically are usually two different things." So as we continue to seek the answer to such hard questions, we come to find that countless scholars have begun to take a more honest approach in looking at the evidence or the lack there of.

There's no question in my mind that when the Church was originally established, the early Church fathers collected all the writings they could find and managed them as they pleased. We know for certain that these manuscripts were added to, altered, abridged and adorned with other writings. "Some scholars say so many revisions occurred in the 100 years following Jesus' death that no one can be absolutely sure of the accuracy or authenticity of the Gospels, especially of the words the authors attributed to Jesus himself," writes Jeffery L. Sheler of the *Catholic Papers*. American abolitionist Moncure D. Conway writes:

> "The library of such books has grown since then. But when we come to examine them, one startling fact confronts us: all of these books relate to a personage concerning whom there does not exist a single scrap of contemporary information—not one! By accepted tradition he was born in the reign of Augustus, the great literary age of the nation of which he was a subject. In the Augustan age historians flourished; poets, orators, critics and travelers abounded. Yet not one mentions the name of Jesus, much less any incident in his life."

I find it very interesting that no one took the time to write about such a prominent figure during a time when poets and writers flourished. So the fact remains, there is no documented evidence to support the claim of an historical Jesus outside of the tainted and fabricated Christian bible. Therefore it was not Jesus that produced the Church but rather the Church that produced the story of Jesus. According to Tim C. Leedom author of, *The Book Your Church Doesn't Want You To Read*, ". . . we can recreate dimensions of the world in which he lived, but outside of the Christian scriptures, we cannot locate him historically within that world." Therefore, I'm led to believe that Jesus was nothing more than a fictitious character in the tradition of pagan mythology and almost nothing in all of ancient literature would lead one to believe otherwise. Subsequently, ". . . anyone wanting to believe Jesus lived and walked as a real live human being must do so despite the evidence, not because of it," says Bible critic C. Dennis McKinsey in The Encyclopedia of Biblical Errancy. But unfortunately, belief and faith replace common knowledge in many people's minds and there is absolutely nothing that could ever change their way of thinking.

Finally, I share in this statement made by an unknown writer on the subject of Christianity where he says:

> "The Christian religion has been and is a mighty fact in the world. For good or for ill, it has absorbed for many centuries the best energies of mankind. It has stayed the march of civilization, and made martyrs of some of the noblest men and women of the race: and it is today the greatest enemy of knowledge, of freedom, of social and industrial improvement, and of the genuine brotherhood of mankind. The progressive forces of the world are at war with this superstition, and this war will continue until the triumph of truth and freedom is complete. The question, of did Jesus Christ really live, goes to the very root of the conflict between reason and faith; and upon its determination depends, to some degree, the decision as to whether religion or humanity shall rule the world."

The Merovingian Agenda

So who exactly are the orchestrators behind this great deception and what is their aim? Upon learning about the Jesus myth and how religion itself was instituted as a means to keep people docile and under control, I wanted to research this "unseen hand" even further in order to better understand the body in which it is attached. I wanted to understand their position and their ultimate goal. As I began to probe into this elaborate web of deception and subterfuge, I became angered by the fact that there are those among us that would seek to manipulate and cajole an entire planet of people into believing in a fairy tale for the sole purpose of power. Speaking from a purely spiritual standpoint, this would indicate that the very people responsible for all the deception and subterfuge that are seeking to gain power are functioning from a place of fear and panic. In order to seek power, one would first have to feel as if they were lacking in power. This mentality would call for a greater exertion of power to help compensate for the lack thereof. This, I believe is the reason for all the clandestine activity being carried out by these secret societies.

It's no mystery that secret societies exist. Although many of us have never really taken the time to actually understand what their purpose is, the fact remains that people meet in secret to discuss hidden, surreptitious agendas in which they plan to have carried out. These clandestine organizations are a religion in and of themselves where they practice certain rituals and faithfully cater to the beliefs of their group. They are sworn to secrecy and they take oaths vowing never to expose their hidden agendas. These sects have existed since the beginning of the modern world and they have continued to guide and direct the situations of the world from behind the scenes. Their unseen hand controls everything from religion to economics and all things in between to include the media, all forms of government and even the very books we read. There is no place on the planet where their reach is not felt. They help build nations only to be in a position to dictate how that nation is to be run. They establish governments with many of their members as the so-called elected officials. They control the legislature which allows them to create laws that only serve to further their causes. They control the airwaves so they can monitor every bit of information that is being disseminated to the general public. Our very lives are controlled and governed by a sadistic group of power hoarders seeking to rule the entire world.

In order to better understand how this system of control first began, it's necessary that we go back to when the first ruling families came into power. My purpose here is to show you how far reaching this system actually is and to help uncover some of the originating factions. You will discover that many of the high ranking government officials belong to this elite society. In fact 33 of the 44 presidents here in the United States alone were and still are connected to this sinister group through blood ties. Recent studies have discovered blood ties linking 44th President Barack Hussein Obama to the Bush family as well as countless other ties connecting many of the United States presidents. This means that in spite of the many billions of people that have existed on the planet and the vast genetic pool in which to draw from, an overwhelming seventy five percent of the nation's presidents have all been related through the same bloodline. But which bloodline am I referring to, the royal bloodline of the Merovingian family of course. Unfortunately, this is not a new practice, in fact, if you look at the origin of the word "kingship," you will find that it is derived from the ancient Sumerian culture wherein "kingship" was identical with "kinship" and *"kin"* means blood relative. Talk about keeping it in the family.

According to tradition, it was Merovech who founded the Salian Frankish Merovingian dynasty which are thought to be descendants of reptilian extraterrestrials. His son Childeric I brought the house to prominence by defeating the Visigoths, Saxons and Alemanni thus becoming known as the "famed fighter." This vitally important battle would ultimately determine the religious and political future of Europe, the U.S. and the entire world. Since that time, Nicean Christianity has remained the indisputable religious, social and legal authority in Western society. Later, the Merovingian house would become known as the principal seat of global Luciferian power and it is believed that Lucifer carries out his accusations against humanity through this vehicle. Be that as it may, there are 13 ruling families that serve as the royal lineage of most European royal families and many of America's political and financial movers and shakers support the overall plans of this established global elite group. These families are listed here according Stuart Swerdlow's *"Blue Blood, True Blood: Conflict and Creation.* They are; Rothschild, Bruce, Cavendish, De Medici, Hanover, Hapsburg, Krupp, Plantagenet, Rockefeller, Romanov, Sinclair, Warburg and Windsor. The mandates of this hierarchy are carried out by "The Committee of 300" which employs the use of many other factions to include The Illuminati, The Bilderberg Group (BG), The Council on Foreign Relations (CFR), The Royal Institute of International Affairs (RIIA), The Federal Reserve, The IRS, The CIA, The Freemasons, and The Trilateral Commission (TC), all of which serves the pleasure of the Merovingians who believe in . . . *"a theocracy wherein nations would be no more than provinces, their leaders but proconsuls in the service of a world occult government consisting of an elite."* The entire world serves their goals without even knowing while they desperately pursue world domination in the form of their *"Novus Ordo Seclorum"* or "New World Order."

The primary vehicle for carrying out the mandates of the Merovingian agenda is The Illuminati who according to Lyssa

Royal and Keith Priest in *The Prism of Lyra* are a group of extraterrestrials that believe they have territorial rights over planet Earth. Interestingly enough, Webster's dictionary defines this group as *"persons possessing or alleging to possess, superior enlightenment."* Accordingly, the foundation of The Illuminati was established during a period when various extraterrestrial groups were primarily fighting for control of the Earth. And as such, these ET's overall purpose has been to deter Earth humans from their natural evolutionary processes.

Today, the Illuminati have become the target of many conspiracies but people are too conditioned or too stupid not to take this information seriously. This mentality has allowed the Illuminati to "hide in plain sight" without reprisal or fear of detection. Many signs of this group are very visible to the adept person who knows what to look for such as dragons, owls, eagles, snakes, bees, the Eye of Ra, checkered floors, the numbers 7, 13, 33, octagons, pyramids, obelisks and domes all of which many of our governmental and religious structures are patterned after. The pyramid structure is in fact identical to the systems that exist in the Reptilian Draconian Empire. This very symbol with the "All-Seeing," reptilian eye is even located on the back of the American one-dollar bill.

Many of the countries today were artificially created in order to further the goals of the Merovingians. Among these are; the United States, Switzerland, Israel, Italy, The United Kingdom, Africa, Central and South America and all of the Arab countries just to name a few. These countries were established solely for the purpose of generating wealth for the ruling families. One of their primary wealth building schemes is to manufacture wars in which they themselves fund through their central banking system. In many cases, they have been known to finance both factions in a war which was instigated by them from the start.

The original 13 colonies of the United States were actually established for these 13 ruling families. As a matter of fact, the original American flag actually had 13 stars and 13 stripes and we can see from the American dollar bill that the eagle is holding 13 arrows with 13 stars, 13 stripes, 13 leaves on the olive branch, with 13 steps of the pyramid leading up to illumination, with 13 letters in the two great mottos; *"annuit coeptis,"* and *"E pluribus unum."* But why so much emphasis on the number 13 and why is this number so significant in these secret orders? Well, the York Rite of Freemasonry has 13 degrees and the Bavarian Order of the Illuminati also has 13 degrees. The way they understand it, the number 6 represents man. The number 7 represents divine perfection or God. Thus it can be seen that the number 13 is a combination of man and divine perfection (6 + 7 = 13) which is exactly what "Illuminism" actually is, man becoming as the gods.

Upon further investigation, it can be found that the United States is actually a corporate asset of the Virginia Company which was established in 1604 in England by the Rothchilds. Today the assets of the Virginia Company are owned by the Holy Roman Empire through the Vatican. America like many other wealth building countries is nothing more than a pawn in the global scheme of the Merovingian agenda.

Earlier I mentioned how this bloodline is extraterrestrial in nature meaning it is not of this planet. In some of Zecharia Sitchin's work, he talks about a group of extraterrestrials called the *Nefilim* who apparently came to planet Earth in order to mine for gold. Talk of these extraterrestrials can be gleaned all throughout the Old Testament by Noah, Moses, Abraham, Isaiah, Ezekiel, and Daniel just to name a few. While they were here, they created a hybrid human by grafting their genes onto the already existing primates. This genetic enhancement jump started the evolutionary process by millions of years providing for an advanced human breed called "*homo sapiens*," and it was from this cross-breeding that the Nefilim came into power where they were worshipped as gods in Sumer, Ancient Egypt and continuing to the Phoenicians, the Babylonians, Troy, Greece, The Roman Empire and the British Empire. David Icke has done extensive research on this bloodline in his book *The Biggest Secret*, where he shows how this bloodline continues from the Nefilim down to Philip of Macedonia and his son Alexander the Great, to Cleopatra, Julius Caesar, Mark Antony, Herod the King of the Jesus myth and the Piso family who allegedly had a hand in writing the gospel stories. Coincidentally, Constantine the Great was also a part of this bloodline which would account for why in 325 CE he held what is called the Nicean council where these false gospels were formed into what is being practiced today as Christianity. Eventually, this bloodline would continue to include The Merovingians of France who have claimed royalty as direct descendants of Jesus but in reality this bloodline is of the reptilian race from the Draco constellation. This bloodline has been traced down from Charlemagne (Charles the Great) with 33 of the United States presidents ranging from George Washington to Barack Obama having the same blood ties. Not to mention all of these presidents have been members of the Masonic order. This just goes to confirm what I've known all along which is that presidents are not selected by ballot but rather "chosen" by blood. This type of clandestine activity has continued to infiltrate countries, governments and presidencies for thousands of years and they have managed to do so primarily through the well connected and resourceful members of the infamous Illuminati.

Illuminati

The Illuminati is a group of individuals considering themselves to be the "Enlightened" ones although they once called themselves *"Perfectibilists."* They were established in 1776 by Jesuit, Adam Weishaupt who patterned the group after the Freemasons where much of their membership was drawn from. Some argue that Weishaupt didn't devise the Illuminati, but only revived it; which is in fact true because the Illuminati can be traced back to the Knights Templar, to the Greek and Gnostic initiatory cults, to Egypt and even Atlantis.

Today membership in secret societies is well into the thousands but many of these members are not privy to the actual dealings of the organization. There is believed to be two orders, the ones that "know" and the ones that "think they know" because they have secret grades and levels of initiation. As such, their symbol is the pyramid structure where people on one level of the pyramid do not know what the people on the level above them know. For them, the Pyramid symbolizes illumination with the majority of initiates at the bottom with the road to illumination becoming narrower and narrower the higher up you go until you pass through the illumination of the Sun to ultimate illumination on the other side. One important distinction must be made here and that is; while anyone can join a secret society, no one can actually join the Illuminati. You are born into it based upon your bloodline. Accordingly, some of its members include such notables as Winston Churchill, the Bush family, Barack Obama, the Rothschild family and David Rockefeller just to name a few.

The Illuminati have been written about and discussed more prevalently in recent times and you can find information about them just about anywhere you look, although this wasn't always the case. Since their inception, they have become the political movers and shakers cleverly carrying out the mandates of the thirteen wealthiest families in an effort to bring about their long awaited "New World Order." They are the ones that rule the world from behind the scenes and they are the real decision makers. They establish the rules for presidents and governments to follow while they cleverly avoid public scrutiny. Many of them are related by bloodlines going back thousands and thousands of years and they are very careful at keeping those bloodlines as pure as possible from generation to generation. Therefore, the continuing "Generative" process is represented by the letter "G" in the Masonic symbol. The involvement in this clandestine organization is so far reaching that many people cannot bring themselves to accept just how powerful they really are. The very mention of this group causes people to immediately shut down from fear and skepticism. Many people cannot bring themselves to accept the fact that practically all world affairs are orchestrated by a select few and more importantly that this elite group of individuals does not have the well being of the people in mind. They're very heinous in that they created the different religions and sects and cults so we would be too busy worshipping false gods rather than being concerned about their dealings. They established the churches and put themselves in charge in order to entrap people and to spread conflicts between different belief systems. It's no mystery that practically all the wars throughout history have been steeped in religion.

Over the years, the Illuminati have managed to amass huge fortunes through their Central Banking Institutions. Today they own all the International banks, the oil-businesses, the most powerful businesses of industry and trade, they infiltrate politics and education and they own most governments in one way or another. They even own and control all of the major media outlets to include Hollywood and the music Industry. In politics they sway presidential elections by providing sponsorship and media coverage to whichever candidate they would like to put into office. Much of this sponsorship comes directly from drug monies since they control that industry as well. They will stop at nothing even if they have to steal the election like they did in Florida when President George W. Bush won over Al Gore. The leading candidates for Presidency are carefully selected by their blood ties to the thirteen Illuminati families. Recent studies show that almost all the Presidents of the United States from the beginning and up to present time are of the same royal bloodline, and they are all related through ancestry and family trees. Therefore, elections are a sham just to give the appearance of having a say in who becomes the next president. It's all a game pretending to follow the Constitution through the illusion of democracy.

The main objective of the Illuminati is a "one world government" where they can serve as the rulers and everyone else is considered to be nothing more than a slave for labor. When their off-planet ancestors first colonized the Earth some 300,000 years ago in Mesopotamia, they set out to create an inferior race in which to do their labor. They called this hybrid reptilian mammalian a *"Lulu,"* which was merely meant to be a beast of burden and their mentality has remained this way ever since. In terms of who this race of beings actually is, the bible describes them as the "fallen angels" that interbred with the daughters of men here on Earth to create the *"Nefilim"* who were the giants that walked the Earth. (Genesis 6:4) They were also referred to as the "Watchers." Thus, they were the result of hybridization between reptilians and humans. They are, according to the Bible, believed to be the ascendants of extraterrestrial rulers, leaders and warriors who lived here before the great flood. Interestingly enough their progeny are still here to this very day seeking to control the Earth.

Ultimately, the Illuminati would like to eliminate any type of caste system where people are able to achieve a certain level of existence thereby creating one ruling class with everyone else as the lower class. This way, they can control economies, major industries, the media, religions and all other aspects of human existence. It is even believed by some that they are seeking to reduce the world's population to roughly 500 million people through pestilence, and disease which is not too far fetched although this would greatly contradict their plan to make the entire population working class slaves. Nevertheless, world domination has been their aim for thousands of years and it was never meant to be accomplished in a single generation but rather it was to be the culmination of years of control and manipulation that was to be reached over several generations. They have hidden behind the scenes of history for a very long time beginning with the "Brotherhood of the Snake," a secret society dating back to ancient Sumer. According to Icke, this group is controlled by the reptilians and is the core center of today's global secret society network. It was from this original Brotherhood that Freemasonry, the Rosicrucian's, The Knights Templar, Ordo Templi Orientis, Knights of Malta, Skull & Bones and many more orders were established. One of their primary goals is to keep spiritual knowledge away from the masses because to them, it is to be shared only by a select few. This esoteric and powerful information is only exchanged among the initiated. This is to ensure that the selected few (which is almost always the ruling families), can reach the goals they decide for themselves and for others. This select few has since become the power elite and has ruled over mankind unsuspectingly for thousands of years.

Due to industrialization and modern technology, the Illuminati have been able to make long strides in the last decade. But, in order to completely pull off their plan they must first lower the standard of living in developed countries, like the United States and Europe which would give them a more authoritative position allowing them to control us more easily. Once this happens, the living standards of the third world countries will be raised to the same standard as the developed countries creating one standard of living world-wide. This is necessary because in order to create a one world government, the living standard must be similar all over the world thus allowing them to have a uniform world in which to rule.

Their first attempt at a one world government was in 1920 with the "League of Nations" (which was the precursor to the United Nations), but they were unsuccessful. But they didn't stop there. Over the years, they have continued to pursue a one world government and they have recently moved into place by establishing the "United Nations" (UN), which is nothing more than a front organization for the Illuminati to unite the countries of the world into one government. If you recall, both World War I and II were both attempts to establish a world government. After World War II, people were at their wits end so they welcomed the United Nations when it was founded. The official policy of the UN was to safeguard the peace, so as not to create another world war. But what we find here is a typical example of how the Illuminati work. They use a tactic that David Icke calls "problem-reaction-solution," where first they create the "problem" by starting a war which in turn brings about a certain "reaction" from the population, who is now in need of a "solution." So they create a solution to the problem they themselves created by founding the United Nations (UN) bringing us one step closer to their agenda and a One World Government. According to sociologist Hadley Cantril in his 1967 book *The Human Dimension—Experiences in Policy Research*; government Psycho-political operations are propaganda campaigns designed to create perpetual tension and to manipulate different groups of people to accept the particular climate of opinion that these secret groups are seeking to achieve in the first place. Canadian writer Ken Adachi (1929-1989) said, "What most Americans believe to be 'Public Opinion' is in reality carefully crafted and scripted propaganda designed to elicit a desired behavioral response from the public." This is the same exact method they used to implement the Patriot Act in 2001 which removed many of our civil liberties by manufacturing the 911 incident which has now been exposed for being an "inside job" by the American government under the Bush administration. Illuminati member Henry Kissinger once stated at a Bilderberg Group meeting in 1992 that:

> "Today, Americans would be outraged if UN troops entered Los Angeles to restore order; tomorrow, they will be grateful. This is especially true if they were told there was an outside threat from beyond, whether real or promulgated, that threatened our very existence. It is then that all people of the world will plead with world leaders to deliver them from

this evil . . . . individual rights will be willingly relinquished for the guarantee of their well-being granted to them by their world government."

They will stop at nothing and they have no problem letting the people know that this is their aim. People like George Bush Sr. and a few other major players like Mikhail Gorbachev and Gordon Brown have openly called for a New World Order, which is referring to this One World Government. In a speech given by George H.W. Bush Sr. on September 11, 1990 he says:

> "Until now, the world we've known has been a world divided—a world of barbed wire and concrete block, conflict and cold war. Now, we can see a new world coming into view. A world in which there is the very real prospect of a new world order. In the words of Winston Churchill, a 'world order' in which 'the principles of justice and fair play . . . protect the weak against the strong . . .' a world where the United Nations, freed from cold war stalemate, is poised to fulfill the historic vision of its founders. A world in which freedom and respect for human rights find a home among all nations."

This is not a new development and they have diligently pursued their agenda for hundreds if not thousands of years as depicted by the phrase *"Novus Ordo Seclorum,"* which means *"New Order of the Ages,"* or loosely translated to mean *"New (Secular) or Worldly Order,"* on the Great Seal of The United States back in 1782.

Since the very beginning of all civilizations, there has always been a ruling class that has sought to have dominion over the masses. They feel it is their birthright to rule and lord over the people. The Illuminati believe we are sheep in need of a Shepherd. This mindset has caused them to treat the masses like nothing more than gullible and ignorant "Sheeple" that will never wake up and realize that we've been duped into believing in false propaganda and outlandish lies. Now is the time for all of us to understand once and for all who is behind this intricate plan of deception and world domination. I often asked myself; is it really my responsibility to bring such things to bare? Or, is it spiritual to be discussing such things? I for one know the feeling I get when I discover how sinister their plot is. So I just want to inform you that yes, my writing about such things is in fact spiritual because knowledge is power. Not just the knowledge of secret societies and clandestine organizations but the knowledge of who these individuals are and what their primary agenda consist of. Because in knowing the truth about the *why*, we can then begin to understand *what* is necessary in order to bring about a greater awareness for unity and higher consciousness. We must come to realize that it is through a lowered state of awareness that they are able to continue operating and once we awaken to their existence and then their agenda, we can collectively work to expose them for who they truly are. Unfortunately, many of us would much rather be entertained than to be educated which is exactly where they want us to be. This way, they can continue to pull the wool over our eyes without fear of reprisal.

In his book *Blue Blood, True Blood: Conflict and Creation*, Stewart Swerdlow raises a very interesting analogy when he says that everyone and everything is a reflection of our own mind-pattern. In other words, whatever we see being manifested in the outer-world of reality is essentially a manifestation of our global consciousness. This would mean that most of what happens in our world such as the famines, wars, strife, and control seeking, is merely just a culmination of our global consciousness being reflected back to us through world events. Based on this correlation, we are the ones responsible for everything that happens in the world to include the hidden agendas and the clandestine activities that are being carried out all over the world. Since we are all connected, the external world is an exact replica of the internal situation of all mankind. It is nothing more than a reflection of our own fears, hidden agendas and pursuit of power collectively being played out the world over.

Be that as it may; one thing is for certain and that is, there is definitely a conspiracy against mankind that has been culminating since ancient times and the Shadow Government and the power elite are real and they are controlling the world from behind the scenes. There is definitely something fishy going on within our government and governments abroad. Something reeks of a stench that is real and pungent to the nostrils of conscious minded people who are fed up with the antics of their politics or as a friend of mine says, "*poly-trics*." This chapter is my attempt at exposing this intricate web of deceivers and manipulators for who they truly are. I firmly believe that once we become aware, the battle is half won. But, it is our responsibility to either heed this warning or simply go on living in a falsified stupor of fairytale and fiction with the wool snuggly pulled over our eyes. You decide.

The Global Elite

"A nation can survive its fools, and even the ambitious. But it cannot survive treason from within. An enemy at the gates is less formidable, for he is known and he carries his banners openly. But the traitor moves among those within the gate freely, his sly whispers rustling through all the alleys, heard in the very halls of government itself. For the traitor appears not traitor, he speaks in the accents familiar to his victims, and he wears their face and their garments, and he appeals to the baseness that lies deep in the hearts of all men. He rots the soul of a nation, he works secretly and unknown in the night to undermine the pillars of a city, he infects the body politic so that it can no longer resist. A murderer is less to be feared."

—Cicero, 42 B.C.

Over 200 hundred years ago, William Pitt once said; "Unlimited power is apt to corrupt the minds of those who possess it." This was a truism of Lord Acton's statement which implied that "power tends to corrupt and absolute power corrupts absolutely." Many people find it hard to believe that there is a very small group of people who secretly run the world with all-powerful and unrestrained dictatorial powers. They dispute the extent of this operation believing it to be too "fantastic" or too "enormous" to be real. They still choose to believe that our government and its coterie of chosen politicians carry out the democratic process in favor of the people. But, you will find that the Global Elite is diametrically opposed to our interests as they are motivated by nothing more than greed and the lust for power and control. This is why they have worked in the shadows acting as the planners and instigators behind the monetary system, wars, globalization, industrialization, and the entire economy for hundreds if not thousands of years. They seek to usurp control of the planet through the avenues of major corporations, faulty politics and academics. They own big business to include such names as; Coca Cola, Ford Motor, Deere & Co., Hewlett-Packard, Cargill, Chase Manhattan Bank, Cummins Engine, Texas Instruments, Honeywell, Bechtel Corporation, Weyerhaeuser, General Motors, Boeing, and many others. They control governments and they educate the general public in the way they would have us think through avenues of the media which includes; The New York Times, Time-Warner, Chicago Sun-Times, Los Angeles Times, Foreign Policy Magazine, Comcast, CBS, Atlantic Media, The Rand Corporation, Washington Post, Dow Jones & Company, U.S. News and World Report just to name a few.

In order to carry out their plans and schemes, the Global Elite devises organizations and societies which assist them in fulfilling their common interests. These include such groups as the Bilderberg Group (BG), the Trilateral Commission (TC), the Council on Foreign Relations (CFR), and The Royal Institute of International Affairs (RIIA). These groups have become self-perpetuating from generation to generation with many of its members having been groomed from birth or hand selected for their overall loyalty to the world agenda.

In recent years, the pinnacle of the Global Elite has been the Trilateral Commission (TC). This organization was founded in 1973 by David Rockefeller and Zbigniew Brzezinski and it consists of approximately 300 members from North America, Europe and Japan. They were established primarily to help stimulate the dialogue between Western Europe, Japan and the United States. It is this very group that helped found the New International Economic Order that has given rise to globalization today.

Prior to the formation of the Trilateral Commission (TC), there was the Council on Foreign Relations (CFR), which was the most significant body of the Global Elite in the United States. Since its inception back in 1959, the (CFR) has been very clear about a need for world government. This is indicated here in a quote made by one of their members, "The U.S. must strive to build a new international order . . . including states labeling themselves as 'socialist' . . . to maintain and gradually increase the authority of the United Nations." Coincidentally, the United Nations (UN) headquarters in New York was originally donated by the Rockefeller family which happens to be the prime instigators for global control. Don't you find it a little strange that an organization which was established to help promote world peace and government is being funded by the Rockefeller family which happens to be one of the major families responsible for seeking a One-World government?

To give you a better indication of how they've managed to usurp our government, did you know that back in 1976, out of the 54 original U.S. members of the Trilateral Commission (TC), member Jimmy Carter was chosen to win the presidential election. And then, after he was put into office, he brought 18 fellow members of the Commission into top-level cabinet and government agencies. Then in 1988 George H.W. Bush Sr. was elected to the presidency which further strengthened their influence in the U.S. Then again in 1992, (TC) member William Jefferson Clinton became president further contributing to the causes of the Commission. In 2000, George W. Bush Jr. assumed the presidency and although he is not a "known" member of the Trilateral Commission (TC), Vice President Dick Cheney is. Finally, in 2008, President Barack Hussein Obama who happens to be a "known" member of the Trilateral Commission (TC), the (CFR), as well as the Bilderberg Group (BG), was voted into office. Sadly enough I happen to like President Obama as an individual, although I cannot in good conscious support him knowing that he is helping carry out the wishes of the Global Elite. In truth, I believe President Obama is nothing more than a diversion to help pacify and distract the American people while the powers that be continue their pursuit of globalization.

To further add insult to injury, you should know that (TC) members are "not" elected nor representative of the general population of the U.S., in fact there is no enrollment or application process to belong to the Trilateral Commission (TC) one is merely chosen or invited to join. However, the selection process is highly discrete and all candidates are thoroughly screened before invitation is delivered. This way, they can ensure that anyone who is or who has ever been a member of the Commission is in the core of the Global Elite. Today, the Commission effectively dominates the Executive Branch of the U.S. government and the Federal Reserve System, and they are closely aligned with the Bank for International Settlements, which controls the world's currencies and money supply. This is exactly where they set out to be when they first formulated these secret organizations and the Council on Foreign Relations (CFR) has remained steadfast in creating a one-world government based solely on a centralized global financing system. Amschel Rothschild once said: "Give me control of a nation's money and I care not who makes its laws." He knew that once you have successfully indebted a nation, they will always be at your mercy. This is done through the constant lending of currency with exorbitant interest rates. Ultimately, the nation becomes weakened by its inability to pay its debts thereby surrendering control to the banks which are owned by the Global Elite. This is being done on a global scale with nations being indebted to international banking institutions that are owned and run by members of the global hierarchy. In this way the banking cartel are able to usurp governments when they default on their debt in which case they eventually take over control and rewrite policies to suit their needs and further their causes.

According to recent commentary, these are the overall objectives of the Global Elite:

> ➤ One international identity (observing) one set of universal values.
> ➤ Centralized control of world populations through (mind control) in other words, controlling world public opinion.
> ➤ A New World Order with no middle class, only (rulers and servants) and no democracy.
> ➤ A zero-growth society without prosperity or progress, only greater wealth and power for the rulers.
> ➤ Manufactured crises and perpetual wars.
> ➤ Absolute control of education to program the public mind and train those chosen for various roles.

➢ Centralized control of all foreign and domestic policies.
➢ Use the United Nations (UN) as a *"de facto"* world government imposing a (UN) tax on world citizens.
➢ Expand NAFTA and WTO globally.
➢ Make NATO a world military.
➢ Impose a universal legal system.
➢ A global welfare state where obedient slaves will be rewarded and non-conformists targeted for extermination.

This comes as no surprise. When you weigh it all out, you have to admit that the people of the world are up against a pretty formidable foe. Just take into consideration how the Global Elite have consisted of practically every presidential candidate on both sides, senators, congressmen, top officials of the FBI, CIA, NSA and other leading government agencies, including state, commerce and the judicial as well as the treasury systems. How can anyone stand against such an all encompassing machine? James Warburg, son of (CFR) founder Paul Warburg once told the Senate Foreign Relations Committee: "We shall have world government whether or not we like it by conquest or consent." In his Memoirs, David Rockefeller wrote:

"Some even believe we are part of a secret cabal working against the best interests of the United States characterizing my family and me as 'internationalists' and conspiring with others around the world to build a more integrated global political and economic structure—one world, if you will. If that's the charge, I stand guilty, and I am proud of it."

Trilateral Commission (TC) co-founder Zbigniew Brzezinski wrote in his book *Between Two Ages—America's Role in the Technotronic Era*:

"People, governments and economies of all nations must serve the needs of multinational banks and corporations. The Constitution is inadequate . . . . the old framework of international politics, with their sphere of influence . . . . the fiction of sovereignty . . . . is clearly no longer compatible with reality . . . ."

Bear in mind if the Global Elite are able to effectively establish a "One World Government," the Constitution would become null and void as it could no longer stand under this type of tyranny. All of our rights as citizens would be completely wiped out totally eliminating our personal and civil liberties. There would be a drastic change for citizens of the United States unlike anything we've ever witnessed before. This country would become a totalitarian state resulting in the removal of all civil liberties. All rights, all policies and all decisions would be governed by the Global Elite Network, and no one would be allowed to escape those policies. This is the objective of the Global Elite and they will stop at nothing to help bring this idea into fruition. It doesn't matter to them that we're aware of their plot to take over the world. In fact, because of our recent awareness of their existence, they've now begun to pursue their agenda more feverishly than ever before.

Whenever I talk about the Illuminati, the Global Elite and the Shadow governments, I'm always left with the same feeling which is one of powerlessness and inertia. I look up into what used to be "clear blue" skies but are now polluted with chemical trails and I'm reminded of the deeds of a heinous group of individuals being carried out through chemical extermination. I read about it with every turn of the page and click of the mouse until I became infuriated at the impudence of these select few. On the one hand I'm conflicted because I'm of the opinion that whatever I focus on expands. As such, I could be giving this situation far too much power. However, on the other hand, I cannot sit idly by just allowing this to take place without shedding light on it. I cannot turn a blind-eye on what I believe to be a plot to enslave the human race. I believe that my contribution to the solution is to provide as much exposure as I can through the vehicle of my books and by speaking about this reality each opportunity I get. This I believe, will help raise public awareness making it that much more difficult for the plot to be carried out. David Icke illustrates this concept in his book *The Biggest Secret*, by saying:

> "Overt control . . . always has a finite life, because in the
> end there will be a challenge and rebellion against it. Covert

control . . . can go on forever because you don't rebel against something you don't know exists. A person who thinks he is free will not complain that he is not."

In the long run we will find that as the global mind begins to shift more towards a vibration of harmony and peace as opposed to fear and dissention, that much sooner will we be able to eradicate the very mindset that seeks to dominate the world and its inhabitants. Ultimately, you will find like I did that throughout the course of history to include un-documented history, history of the cosmos and all of antiquity, there has always been strife in one form or another. There has always been a select few that feels superior and wants to impose their will upon the supposed lowly. But if the people are fortunate, they soon overtake that regime. However, if they are not fortunate in their uprising, history has shown time-and-time again how the strong have enslaved the weak and how certain groups of people somehow end up being relegated to a low position in the hierarchy of existence. That group of people in this case is the entire human race.

A New World Order

"We will have a world government whether we like it or not. The only question is whether that government will be achieved by conquest or consent."

—*Paul Warburg*

The phrase *"Novus Ordo Seclorum"* is Latin for "New Order of the Ages." It was first selected as a motto in 1782 by a committee consisting of such members as Benjamin Franklin, Thomas Jefferson and John Adams among many others all of which were noted freemasons. This phrase also appears on the reverse side of the Great Seal of the United States as well as the back of the American dollar bill. *"Novus Ordo Seclorum"* can also be loosely translated to mean *"New Secular Order,"* or *"New World Order."* In the preceding chapters we discussed the theory of who is behind this "New World" agenda and how it will affect not only American citizens but all citizens of the world. In this chapter I would like to take a closer look at some of methods that are being instituted in order to carry out this plot. I will address the primary organizations that have been cleverly manipulated into position for the sole purpose of implementing this new sovereignty. Whenever I mention the idea of a New World Order, many people immediately think "conspiracy." They believe this idea to be something fabricated by paranoid people seeking some type of attention. However, this New World Order is not just a conspiracy, but a real world reality. It is not some "theory" as the powers that be would have us believe. In fact, it's not a conspiracy at all rather it's an agenda, and anybody willing enough to unplug from the delusional "matrix" can see the evidence all around them. Sadly enough, very few people are able to think for themselves nowadays, and fewer are willing to confirm the validity of this information with their own research. What is more, most people are afraid to even accept this as truth because they would prefer *not* to know. As such, people don't want to discover anything that may infringe upon their delusional comfort zones. They feel that if they're not aware of it, then it doesn't exist for them. This is equivalent to a frightened child putting his head under the cover in order to make his fears go away. Not to mention people don't like to admit to themselves that they have been deceived. Many of us like to deny any unpleasant reality which is why people prefer fantasy and what feels good instead of the truth. Therefore, the greatest weapon the Illuminati possesses in their pursuit for a one world government is people's disbelief in their existence. "How fortunate for governments that the people they administer don't think."—Adolf Hitler

In reality, the word "conspiracy" actually means: the act of conspiring together: an agreement among conspirators, or: a group of conspirators. So in order to distinguish whether or not there is a real threat being perpetrated against humanity, we would first have to see who these conspirators are and how they intend to carry out their plans. For many people, this plot is so heinous, they can't seem to bring themselves to believe it even exists. They can't quite understand how a select few can possibly wield such power over the vast majority. The truth is, they can and they do because we are so busy living our precious oblivious little lives with our heads in the clouds not really realizing that the very freedoms we love and cherish are being corrupted from the inside out. With every cleverly planned act of terrorism or threat to our freedom by a supposed outside force, they move that much closer to the total eradication of all civil liberties. They have incited wars, financial break-downs, acts of terror and mass murder upon innocent people in the pursuit of a one world government and they will stop at nothing until their new regime is firmly in place.

In 1992, Dr John Coleman published *Conspirator's Hierarchy: The Story of the Committee of 300* where he describes the New World Order as being:

> "A One World Government with one-unit monetary system, under permanent non-elected hereditary oligarchists who self-select from among their numbers in the form of a feudal system as it was in the Middle Ages. In this One World entity, population will be limited by restrictions on the number of children per family, diseases, wars, famines, until 1 billion people who are useful to the ruling class, in areas which will be strictly and clearly defined, remain as the total world population.

> There will be no middle class, only rulers and the servants. All laws will be uniform under a legal system of world courts practicing the same unified code of laws, backed up by a One World Government police force and a One World unified military to enforce laws in all former countries where no national boundaries shall exist. The system will be on the basis of a welfare state; those who are obedient and subservient to the One World Government will be rewarded with the means to live; those who are rebellious will simply be starved to death or be declared outlaws, and thus a target for anyone who wishes to kill them. Privately owned firearms or weapons of any kind will be prohibited."

Often times, people think a plan of this magnitude cannot possibly be happening. Their initial response is usually; *"how can they do that,*" or "*why doesn't someone stop them?*" The reality is, they can do it because (a); no one believes in or is even aware of their plan with the exception of a few people who have been reasonable enough to understand what is happening, and (b); who is there to stop them when they control all forms of government including the presidency, military, judicial, banking, media, drugs, the FBI, CIA, NSA, DEA and any other form of privatized government. Naïve people often say to themselves that such a plan could never be carried out but they fail to remember what happened to the Jews during WWII where over six million people were killed during a program of systematic state-sponsored extermination under the guise of "ethnic cleansing" by Nazi Germany. The genocide of these six million people was a massive killing of two-thirds of the population of nine million Jews who resided in Europe long before the Holocaust. They were subsequently led to concentration camps and their eventual slaughter by Adolph Hitler who was a known member of the order which was funded by Prescott Sheldon Bush the father of George H.W. Bush Sr. If you think that's an atrocity, today the Global Biodiversity Assessment calls for human population to be reduced from 5.6 billion to 1 to 2 billion within the next decade so they plan to exterminate 90% of the worlds population through vaccines, disease, chemical warfare, starvation and execution. When the time comes for them to openly declare their dominion, anyone protesting or resisting enslavement will be terminated without question.

Recently, the NWO has been implementing ways in which to monitor and control the entire population. They would like to render us passive, docile and unable to think for ourselves which makes it easier for them to maintain control. Our society has become a real live Orwellian "1984" scenario only far worse. Big Brother is actually listening and watching. We now have cameras everywhere we look surveying our every move, computer chips in everything for the purpose of tracking our whereabouts and behaviors, digital phones, televisions, computers and radios for two-way communication and ease of monitoring and they are moving ever so close to micro-chipping human beings with the Radio-Frequency Identification (RFID) chip in order to control all aspects of movement and monetary access. Not to mention the magnetic strip on every form of I.D. including credit cards, driver's licenses, rewards cards and ATM and Debit cards. Our whole entire world is being governed and monitored by the very people we entrust with our freedoms. Our privacy is being violated at every turn and we don't even realize it. We're so caught up in thinking everything is so "hunky-dory" when in reality we are in a race against time. Although, at the rate we're going, it won't be long before we are totally enslaved and we won't even realize when or how it happened. It was Goethe who said: "None are more hopelessly enslaved than those who falsely believe they are free." On the other hand, "A nation of well-informed men, who have been taught to know and prize the rights that God has given them, cannot be enslaved. It is in the region of ignorance that tyranny begins."—Benjamin Franklin It's time for us to pull our heads out of the sand before it's too late and finally realize the plot that is being carried out right before our very eyes. In his farewell address to the nation on January 17, 1961, President Dwight D. Eisenhower informed us by saying:

> "Throughout America's adventure in free government, our basic purposes have been to keep the peace, to foster progress in human achievement, and to enhance liberty, dignity and integrity among peoples and among nations. To strive for less would be unworthy of a free and religious people. Any failure traceable to arrogance or our lack of comprehension or readiness to sacrifice would inflict upon us grievous hurt, both at home and abroad.

> Progress toward these noble goals is persistently threatened by the conflict now engulfing the world. It commands our whole attention, absorbs our very beings. We face a hostile ideology global in scope, atheistic in character, ruthless in purpose, and insidious in method. Unhappily, the danger it poses promises to be of indefinite duration. To meet it successfully, there is called for, not so much the emotional and transitory sacrifices of crisis, but rather those which enable us to carry forward steadily, surely, and without complaint the burdens of a prolonged and complex struggle with liberty the stake. Only thus shall we remain, despite

every provocation, on our charted course toward permanent peace and human betterment.

In the councils of government, we must guard against the acquisition of unwarranted influence, whether sought or unsought, by the military-industrial complex. The potential for the disastrous rise of misplaced power exists and will persist. We must never let the weight of this combination endanger our liberties or democratic processes. We should take nothing for granted. Only an alert and knowledgeable citizenry can compel the proper meshing of the huge industrial and military machinery of defense with our peaceful methods and goals, so that security and liberty may prosper together.

You and I, my fellow citizens, need to be strong in our faith that all nations, under God, will reach the goal of peace with justice. May we be ever unswerving in devotion to principle, confident but humble with power, diligent in pursuit of the Nation's great goals."

What is to follow is a breakdown of the greatest plot to ever be carried out against mankind; a plot so shocking and enormous in its scope that it's literally mind boggling to the average unsuspecting person. This plot is so intricate in detail that it involves every aspect of our lives from; the military, government, the media, our health, food and water supplies, economics, agriculture, civil liberties, commonwealth, providence, and the violation of our individual privacies which are being threatened daily by the monitoring devices throughout our societies which include; illegal wire tapping by the CIA in conjunction with the NSA and AT&T, censoring our email communications, the two-way monitoring devices such as our televisions and the computers we each have in our homes, bar codes and magnetic tracking devices in our purses, our wallets, our vehicles (GPS) and eventually our bodies (RFID). Our very lives are being cleverly and systematically controlled by a group of individuals whose only aim is to acquire wealth and total world domination. Like it or not, this is real, and whether we chose to accept the reality of it is entirely up to us. So again; *"We face a hostile ideology global in scope, atheistic in character, ruthless in purpose, and insidious in method, which now commands our whole attention, and absorbs our very beings."*

❖ *Fluoridated Water*: I'd like to start by looking at some of the ways the NWO plan to carry out their method of "dumbing down" the people and their global approach to "population reduction." One of the ways they have been able to do this is by adding Fluoride to our water supplies and telling us that it helps strengthen our teeth and prevent tooth decay. However, the largest survey ever conducted in the US (over 39,000 children from 84 communities) by the National Institute of Dental Research showed little difference in tooth decay among children in fluoridated and non-fluoridated communities. And, despite being prescribed by doctors for over 50 years, the U.S. Food and Drug Administration (FDA) have never approved any fluoride product designed for ingestion as safe or effective. As a matter of fact, The US Public Health Service first endorsed fluoridation in 1950, before one single trial had been completed. According to *The Fluoride Deception* by Christopher Bryson:

"As part of its atomic bomb research, the Atomic Energy Commission (AEC) sponsored experiments to test the health effects of putting fluoride in drinking water. Fluoride, which was a common byproduct of atomic bomb manufacture and of chemical manufacture in general, and was widely used as a rat poison, had numerous known adverse health effects at the time. The AEC was worried about lawsuits filed by workers at their bomb manufacturing facilities, and residents who lived nearby, who were being exposed to large amounts of fluoride and were experiencing severe health problems, and in some cases dying, as a result of exposure. Initial water fluoridation tests were performed on the citizens of Newburgh, New York and took place from 1944 to 1956 as part of a classified operation known as *"Program F."* With the assistance of New York Department of Health personnel, they then gathered blood and tissue samples from the citizens of Newburgh to test the effects. According to a 1948 issue

of the *Journal of the American Dental Association*, mention
of the adverse health effects of fluoride was censored by the
AEC as a threat to national security."

What they fail to tell us is that Fluoride is a cumulative poison
where 50% of the fluoride we ingest each day is excreted through
the kidneys. The remainder accumulates in our bones, pineal gland,
and other tissues. If the kidney is damaged, fluoride accumulation
will increase, and with it, the likelihood of harm. In addition to this,
Fluoride has been shown to be mutagenic or a physical or chemical
agent that changes the genetic material which causes chromosome
damage and interferes with the enzymes involved with DNA repair
in a variety of cell and tissue studies. Furthermore, the mutagens
cause mutations and mutations cause cancer. Therefore, mutagens
are typically carcinogens. In a study done on animals, experiments
showed that fluoride accumulates in the brain and exposure alters
mental behavior in a manner consistent with neurotoxic agents. Five
studies from China show a lowering of IQ in children associated
with fluoride exposure.

Fluoride actually serves as a form of population control because
studies showed that when Fluoride was administered to animals
at high doses, it wreaks havoc on the male reproductive system
and it damages sperm and increases the rate of infertility. One
epidemiological study (which is the study of patterns of health and
illness) from the U.S. found increased rates of infertility among
couples living in areas with 3 or more ppm fluoride in the water.
Two other studies found a reduced level of circulating testosterone
in males living in high fluoride areas. One of the major problems
with fluoridation is once fluoride is put in the water it is impossible
to control the dose each individual receives. This is because some
people (e.g. manual laborers, athletes, diabetics, and people with
kidney disease) drink more water than others, and secondly, we
receive fluoride from sources other than the water supply. Other
sources of fluoride include food and beverages processed with
fluoridated water, pesticide residues on food and fluoridated dental
products.

How can they do this without knowing how it will affect certain
individuals? Fluoride is in fact a drug so how can they administer

drugs without being able to regulate the amount a person takes. No doctor should ever prescribe a drug without first asking a person what other drugs they are taking to ensure that ingesting fluoride will not lead to more severe medical issue. This is standard medical procedure for the prescribing of all medication, and this is the very reason why most of western Europe has ruled against fluoridation and as one doctor aptly stated, "No physician in his right senses would prescribe for a person he has never met, whose medical history he does not know, a substance which is intended to create bodily change, with the advice: 'Take as much as you like, but you will take it for the rest of your life because some children suffer from tooth decay.' It is a preposterous notion." In 1978, Dr. Arvid Carlsson one of the leading opponents of fluoridation in Sweden, and part of the panel that recommended that the Swedish government reject the practice said;

> "I am quite convinced that water fluoridation, in a not-too-distant future, will be consigned to medical history . . . Water fluoridation goes against leading principles of pharmacotherapy, which is progressing from a stereotyped medication—of the type 1 tablet 3 times a day—to a much more individualized therapy as regards both dosage and selection of drugs. The addition of drugs to the drinking water means exactly the opposite of an individualized therapy."

While many people are aware of the harmful affects of fluoride, they are fearful of speaking out for fear of being targeted by the global authorities who control the World Health Organization (WHO), the Food and Drug Administration (FDA), as well as the Center for Disease Control (CDC). Many scientists, doctors and dentists who have spoken out publicly on this issue have been subjected to censorship and intimidation. Most recently, Dr. Phyllis Mullenix was fired from her position as Chair of Toxicology at Forsythe Dental Center for publishing her findings on fluoride and the brain. And, Dr. William Marcus was fired from the EPA for questioning the government's handling of the National Toxicology Program's fluoride-cancer study. Tactics like this would not be necessary if those promoting fluoridation were on secure scientific ground. We should understand that the NWO supersedes the Food and Drug Administration and the World Heath Organization, therefore there is no other authority which can intervene or suggest otherwise. The actions of the world's leaders fringes upon carelessness and ruthless tactics that are downright illegal and according to the Union's Senior Vice President, Dr. William Hirzy; ". . . we hold that fluoridation is an unreasonable risk. That is, the toxicity of fluoride is so great and the purported benefits associated with it are so small—if there are any at all—that requiring every man, woman and child in America to ingest it borders on criminal behavior on the part of governments." (Information provided by Paul Connett, PhD Professor of Chemistry St. Lawrence University).

❖ *Poisonous Sweeteners*: Another way in which the global elite plan to carry out their scheme is by adding certain chemicals to our foods that result in cancer and poor health. One of which is the sweetener Aspartame and its dangers have been a well guarded corporate secret since the 1980s. The research and history of aspartame dangers is conclusive as a cause of illness and toxic reactions in the human body. Aspartame poisoning results in aspartame fibromyalgia, aspartame restless leg syndrome, aspartame and migraines, aspartame and vaginal irritation, aspartame and tumors, aspartame allergy, aspartame multiple sclerosis, bladder cancer aspartame, aspartame and central nervous system, aspartame & infertility, aspartame and weight control, aspartame and weight gain, and aspartame Parkinson's Disease. The chemical structure of aspartame causes the body to mimic these disease symptoms, but the bottom line is its aspartame disease. Aspartame is by far one of the most dangerous substances ever foisted onto an unsuspecting public. In 1974 after several animal studies which clearly identified the dangerous effects of this substance (with side effects including: brain tumors, gran mal seizures, and even death due to cardiac arrest from an over stimulated nervous system), the FDA knowingly approved it for public consumption.

❖ *Biological Warfare*: If they can't kill us with the food, pharmaceutical drugs, pesticides or water supply, then they'll kill us from above by blanketing major cities with toxic chemicals. On any given day, the blue skies are being congested by the intentional spraying of chemical substances. Even as I sit to write these words it's barely 7:15 a.m. but still I can see just outside my window where they've already streaked the beautiful blue skies of Southern California with this toxic substance. These are commonly referred to as "chemtrails" and they are not to be confused with condensation trails or "contrails" for short. Condensation trails are artificial clouds that are the visible trails of condensed water vapor made by the exhaust of aircraft engines. As the hot exhaust gases cool in the surrounding air they may precipitate a cloud of microscopic water droplets to form smoke-like trails. These contrails usually evaporate within a matter of seconds and sometimes minutes depending on atmospheric conditions. Chemtrails however, do not evaporate and linger for hours after being dispersed. Eventually, they spread out forming a cloud-like mist which blankets the skies and eventually becomes interspersed in the air we breathe and ultimately falls to the ground becoming saturated into the food and water supplies. Chemtrails can easily be distinguished from contrails because they persist several hours and sometimes half a day forming cirrus-like clouds. In addition, chemtrails are usually sprayed in a criss-cross pattern to form a layer as the trails are dispersed.

As early as the 1940s, the US government has been experimenting with biochemical warfare by spraying hazardous chemicals on its unsuspecting citizens. According to Alexander Cockburn in *Germ War: The US Record*, from 1942 to 1944, the U.S. Chemical Warfare Service conducted experiments which exposed thousands of U.S. military personnel to mustard gas, in order to test the effectiveness of gas masks and protective clothing and they refused to pay disability benefits to the victims of the experiments. This was also done in an experiment called "Operation Dew," where they were attempting to study the behavior of aerosol-released biological agents.

According to commentary posted on the internet, there are two types of spraying: high altitude spraying, meaning 20,000 feet and above and low altitude spraying each with seemingly different purposes. Low level spraying contains molds and fungi and produces varying symptoms including: headaches worse than migraines, heartburn, heart conditions, heart arrest, flu-like symptoms, extreme fatigue, diarrhea, pain and swelling of muscles and joints, dizziness, nausea, stiff neck, nagging sore throat, general malaise symptoms last up to three months and beyond, not typical of flu. Exposure to this type of spraying can also include: respiratory tract problems, severe infections to the throat and sinuses, swelling of the lymph glands, coughing fits, shortness of breath, sinus headaches, general respiratory failure and damage to the heart and liver. These symptoms are not readily treatable by known antibiotics. More importantly, exposure to Ethylene Dibromide (EDB) which is one of the key components of chemtrails makes people more susceptible to other biological agents due to severe lung irritation. It's a systematic break-down of the immune system that renders us unable to fight off disease where we ultimately become more prone to other chemical agents. Countries reporting spraying include Australia, Canada, England, France, Germany, Holland, Ireland, Italy, Mexico, New Zealand, Scotland, Spain and the United States. The US has reported spraying in virtually every state and virtually every major US city including surrounding suburbs. These are just a few of the dastardly plots being used for the purpose of population reduction in line with a New World Order.

While very few people can deny the fact that we're being sprayed, the reasoning often varies. Some of the reasons put forth are so ludicrous, even a child can see through them. They range from protecting the planet from the harmful effects of the Sun by dispersing a mist consisting of a mirror like substance to help deflect the Sun's UV rays thus slowing down the effects of Global warming. But since Global warming is also a cock-and-bull story manufactured and spearheaded by Al Gore to bilk citizens out of millions of dollars for clean energy related carbon tax and components, we know this scenario is far from the truth. Others actually believe the government is surreptitiously vaccinating billions of people against some impending biological threat in the future but because of the huge liability which could result in a multitude of lawsuits, they have chosen not to inform us. I highly disagree with the notion of the NWO who has very little concern for anything, being so worried about its serfdom that it would risk the possibility of a massive lawsuit just to inoculate us. This is highly improbable. In terms of the population reduction theory of which I tend to favor, some people argue against this scenario stating that the very chemicals being used against us could also harm those responsible including their families. They question the logic of knowingly subjecting themselves to such toxic exposure. My response is, there are two possible solutions; one would be to simply inoculate themselves as well as their families from the harmful effects, much like taking a flu shot, and secondly, if the genetic composition of these people is of a different molecular structure catering to David Icke's theory of them having reptilian blood-lines, then they probably have some type of immunity in their systems and they wouldn't be affected in the same ways that you or I would anyway. Both scenarios seem plausible.

❖   *The Alphabet Regime*: Some of the power structures that have been created to help institute this global take-over include such names as the Central Intelligence Agency (CIA), Federal Bureau of Investigations (FBI), Drug Enforcement Agency (DEA), National Security Agency (NSA), Homeland Security (HS), United Nations (UN), Federal Emergency Management Agency (FEMA), North American Free Trade Agreement (NAFTA), North Atlantic Treaty Organization (NATO), European Union (EU), Council on Foreign Relations (CFR), Bilderberg Group (BG), Trilateral Commission (TC), Columbia Broadcasting System (CBS), American Broadcasting Company (ABC), National Broadcasting Company (NBC), Cable News Network (CNN), World Trade Organization (WTO), World Health Organization (WHO), International Monetary Fund (IMF), Bank of International Settlements (BIS), Internal Revenue Service (IRS), Center For Disease Control and Prevention (CDC), Food and Drug Administration (FDA), Environmental Protection Agency (EPA), Federal Trade Commission (FTC), Information Awareness Office (IAO), High Frequency Active Auroral Research Program (HAARP), National Aeronautics and Space Administration (NASA) and the Transportation Security Administration (TSA), just to name a few. And while all of these agencies play a very intricate part in the global puzzle for world domination, I will only take the time to elaborate on some of its key components.

❖ *Federal Reserve System*: The Federal Reserve Act was enacted on December 23, 1913 and is the Act of Congress that created the Federal Reserve System, the central banking system of the United States of America, which granted it the legal authority to issue "legal tender." It was signed into law by President Woodrow Wilson who later went on record as saying:

> "I am a most unhappy man. I have unwittingly ruined my country. A great industrial nation is now controlled by its system of credit. We are no longer a government by free opinion, no longer a government by conviction and the vote of the majority, but a government by the opinion and duress of a small group of dominant men."

The first thing we should know about the Federal Reserve System, is that it is not a part of government but rather it is a "private" institution consisting of a banking cabal that was merely granted authority to issue legal tender and control of the nations monetary system. But, according to Abraham Lincoln; "Any government should create, issue and circulate all the currency. Creating and issuing money is the supreme prerogative of government and its greatest creative opportunity. Adopting these principles will save the taxpayers immense sums of interest and money will cease to be the master and become the servant of humanity." Subsequently, he was shot and killed by an orchestrated assassination as was President John F. Kennedy for the very same reason by the same invisible power associated with the central banking cartel. However, once the central bank was able to gain control of issuing the money, from time-to-time they would methodically affect economies by increasing or decreasing interest rates. This would halt the rate of circulation of all currency by reducing spending thus catering to recessions and depressions such as the one we're now experiencing in addition to several previous recessions not to mention the great depression of 1929.

Currently, the Federal Reserve System has printed and produced far more currency than we have gold to support. Initially, money was printed based on the gold standard which is a monetary system in which the standard economic unit of account is a fixed weight of gold. This served as collateral for the amount of printed money in circulation. We couldn't carry gold around, so they started issuing treasury notes in exchange for the gold on hand as a form of currency. In 1934, we were taken off the gold standard by President Franklin Delano Roosevelt which eventually gave way to unrestrained money supply expansion, long term inflation and exorbitant credit revenues for banks allowing them to take advantage of huge profits. Over time, more money was put into circulation than the gold standard could support. This weakened the American Dollar to the point where now it's not "real" currency but rather legal tender or an I.O.U so-to-speak. At the rate in which the Feds are printing money, eventually the dollar will be equivalent to me writing out an I.O.U on standard notebook paper without any collateral. If there's nothing to back my "note," then it's just a worthless piece of paper.

Although we call it "Federal," the Federal Reserve System is privately owned by member banks, they make their own policies, and they are not subject to oversight by Congress or even the President. The American people were duped into thinking the Federal Reserve System was an official aspect of government that would strictly serve as a form of nonpartisan financial agency. Congressman Louis McFadden, House Committee on Banking and Currency Chairman (1920-31), stated: "When the Federal Reserve Act was passed, the people of these United States did not perceive that a world banking system was being set up here. A super-state controlled by international bankers and industrialists . . . acting together to enslave the world . . . Every effort has been made by the Fed to conceal its powers but the truth is—the Feds have usurped the US government." It is well enough that the people of the nation do not understand our banking and monetary system, for if they did, I believe there would be a revolution before tomorrow morning.—Henry Ford

Coincidentally, the Federal Reserve System logo bares the same eagle as the Great Seal of America holding the olive branch with the "13" leaves as well as the shield baring "13" stripes. As we were able to determine previously, the number "13" is indicative of the Illuminati. Therefore anytime we see that an organization is adhering to these Masonic symbols, we can only assume that they are somehow connected. That being the case, we can then postulate with good reason that the implementation of a "Central Bank" was orchestrated by the banking cartels in an effort to control the Nation's monetary system. Again, Baron M.A. Rothschild said: "Give me control over a nation's currency and I care not who makes its laws." This is because once you control a country's monetary system you have the ability to indebt that country and all of its citizens. Once this happens the country becomes enslaved while its tax paying citizens are illegally extorted by the IRS which is another Illuminati organization. As American Chronicler Thor H. Asgardson writes in *The Evil Doers—The Federal Reserve*: "This pattern of financial enslavement, ensures everlasting bondage to the central bank, as the public loses purchasing power, with the ultimate result being corporate consolidation over a free people. In short; it has taken two centuries to achieve, but the central bankers have finally consolidated their hold over the destiny of the United States of America."

The Central banking institutions have sought to gain control of the monetary systems as early as 1791 with the formation of the First Bank of The United States later followed by the Second Bank of The United States. But it wasn't until early November 1910, when Nelson Aldrich met with five well known members of the New York banking community to devise the central banking bill which was later accepted as the Federal Reserve Act. One of the attendees of the meeting was none other than Paul Warburg, long time advocate for central banking, and director of the Council on Foreign Relations (CFR). Coincidently, Warburg was appointed as member of the first Federal Reserve Board by President Woodrow Wilson, serving until 1918. Initially, Aldrich's plan to centralize banking was met with opposition by those understanding how this could affect the countries sovereignty and economic stability, not to mention how Aldrich was being influenced by wealthy bankers such as J. P. Morgan and John D. Rockefeller, Jr., who just so happened to be Aldrich's' son-in-law. Nevertheless, the Federal Reserve Act was still passed. You have to remember, whenever you have people like the Warburg's, Rothschilds or the Rockefellers involved all of which happen to be members of the Illuminati which is the "13" ruling families, one has to be concerned about their overall intentions which in this case happens to be global control through centralized banking. As Charles Dudley Warner put it; "politics make strange bedfellows," and these wealthy families have been in bed together for centuries working to bring about an oligarchic system of rule. This is a classic system of the "Golden Rule," where whoever has the "gold-rules." It is the wealthy "banksters" that manipulate governments in order to help implement policies that will further their global agendas. There are no bigger crooks than these guys trust me. Hence the International Banking Cartel *is* the New World Order.

What makes these guys so ruthless in their pursuit for world domination is that they lack compassion and have little or no regard for human life. Thomas Jefferson wrote:

> "The Central Bank is an institution of the most deadly hostility existing against the principles and form of our Constitution . . . if the American people allow private banks to control the issuance of their currency, first by inflation and then by deflation, the banks and corporations that will grow up around them will deprive the people of all their property until their children will wake up homeless on the continent their fathers conquered."

One of the ways the central bank is able to control nations is by inciting wars between two factions and in order to profit they will then fund both sides further indebting both parties where they eventually become ravaged and deeply indebted to their funders. This allows the controlling power behind the central banks to rewrite the policies and eventually take control of war torn nations. This was the case in both World Wars and continues to be the case to this very day. They've just become more sophisticated with time. Through their continued financing of both sides in a war, they have managed to put nation after nation into massive debt. And as a result, they can further manipulate and control governments and its citizens to further enact their goal of global government and a central banking system run—by them and for them—at the expense of all of humanity.

❖   *United Nations:* The "peace keeping ass-kicking," United Nations (UN) was founded in 1945 after WWII and it was by far one of the major achievements towards a one world government. Accordingly, the UN was founded after World War II to replace its predecessor in the "League of Nations." Its primary aim was to stop wars between countries, and to provide a platform for dialogue. However, as we can see from history, most of the major wars, political upheavals, and economic crisis of the last century, were masterfully orchestrated by the very same people. These wars include; The Spanish-American War (1898), World War I and World War II; The Great Depression; the Bolshevik Revolution of 1917; the Rise of Nazi Germany; the Korean War; the Vietnam War; the 1989-91 "fall" of Soviet Communism, the 1991 Gulf War; and the recent War in Kosovo. Even the French Revolution was orchestrated into existence by the Illuminati and the House of Rothschild.

The UN contains multiple subsidiary organizations with the North Atlantic Treaty Organization (NATO) serving as the military arm and the North American Free Trade Agreement (NAFTA) to help implement tariffs and embargos to prevent international uncensored trading. Other prominent UN system agencies include the World Health Organization (WHO), and the World Food Program (WFP). These two agencies make it possible for them to administer drugs like Fluoride and Aspartame into our food and water supplies in order to create a docile society that is unwilling and unintelligent enough to recognize what is being carried out against them.

At present, there are 192 member states of the United Nations. This includes practically every sovereign state in the world. On February 10, 1972, President Nixon announced the United States was to be divided into 10 Federal Regional Councils. Each council was to be controlled by an appointed official in an effort to control and coordinate the activities of all levels of government. The goal of creating these sub-regions was to eventually merge the U.S. into a one world government under the United Nations. This is currently being carried out without public scrutiny. Coincidentally, each of these 10 regions is funded through Federal revenues which makes them dependant on the Federal Reserve. This way, pressure can be applied to any level of state government that refuses to comply with the dictates of the regional government rulers. In keeping with the plan, all but 1 of the 10 federal regional capitals is either a Federal Reserve Bank or branch bank city. Following are just some of the policies of the United Nations:

> ➤ Control of all zoning matters in the United States and the control of our national parks, rivers and historical sites.
> ➤ Control over whether women are allowed to have babies.
> ➤ Control over the economic and judicial policies of all nations.
> ➤ Programs are being processed to create a tax on citizens of the United States as a permanent method of UN funding.
> ➤ The UN has its own Army and all United States soldiers must swear allegiance to this foreign government.

I understand how preposterous this must sound but after reviewing the facts of history and looking at the subsequent actions of our government over the past few centuries, it becomes painfully obvious how a few key players have covertly served as the puppet masters of nations by usurping control of all natural resources; by seizing control of the monetary system through the formation of central banking institutions; by instigating wars and funding both sides; by manufacturing recessions and the flow of currency through interest rates; by devaluing the American dollar by printing worthless paper unsupported by any real collateral; by borrowing inordinate amounts of money from the Central Banks and repaying these debts by imposing illegal taxes on American citizens; and by forming United Fronts such as the UN to maneuver all independent nations into a coup d'état.

One of the integral families involved in global governance has always been the Rockefellers. After instigating its formation, the Rockefellers donated 18 acres of land for the UN headquarters in New York and since then, they have virtually conceived and funded most of the destructive UN programs. The Rockefellers along with the Rothschilds are among the key supporters of a new world order. They believe 2/3 of the population is simply a waste of oxygen, food and natural resources and should therefore be eradicated while the remaining population should only be used to perform labor. The creators of the UN believe people are not smart enough to live on their own and should therefore be governed and controlled by them. Their goal is to have total sustainability in all aspects of our lives and to essentially reduce the world's population down to just two classes of people; the ruling elite and then everyone else. Consequently, you and I fall into the last category. The founders of the UN believe the individual must be sacrificed for the greater whole as they establish a socialist government. This is the same ideology of Nazi Germany only Hitler's understanding was more racially motivated rather than political.

After closer review, it becomes evident how the same coterie of people have always been instrumental in advancing the plans of the NWO. Time and time again, we are confronted with the same group  of people all of which stems from the Illuminati and its succeeding families, factions, clubs, orders and societies. Although they work in "secret" cleverly manipulating events and circumstances from behind the political scenes, they make it known to their respective membership how they are in control by utilizing signs and symbols as indicators of their existence. These people are initiates of secret rites, orders and covens so they are hell-bent on using key symbols and numbers as signs of allegiance to their group's overall plan. In *The Illustrated Encyclopaedia of Traditional Symbols* by J.C. Cooper it says of symbols how; "They are instruments of knowledge and the most ancient and fundamental method of expression, which reveals aspects of reality which escape other modes of expression." Cooper goes on to say; Symbols are external, or lower, expressions of the higher truth which is symbolized, and is a means of communicating realities which might otherwise be either obscured by the limitations of language or too complex for adequate expression." He finishes by saying; "The symbol is a key to a realm greater than itself and greater than the man who employs it."

One can always tell exactly who is behind most events throughout history by learning to recognize certain symbols. In looking at the flag of the United Nations as depicted here, once again we see the olive branch symbology of the Acropolis (highest city of ancient Rome) which held the life and fate of the people. What I also find to be interesting is that if you look closely, you will see there are 32 divisions on the globe with the center being the 33rd. Here again we find a number associated with the highest degree of the Masonic order. This is not coincidence.

The United Nations is a cabal of Illuminati factions, ranging from ultra wealthy banksters, specialized organizations, key players, and heads of states that are systematically and forcefully taking control of the world through every method possible. They control the Federal Reserve; therefore they control the nation's currency. They control the World Trade Organization (WTO), the World Health Organization (WHO) and the World Food Program (WFP), which means they pretty much control all the trading, pharmaceuticals and food and drug distribution worldwide. They have a world army which consist of (NATO) and all of our militaries and local law enforcements agencies. In short, the (UN) of the United Nations basically represents a tyrannical, oligarchic government that is essentially; (UN)-necessary, (UN)-fathomable, (UN)-civilized, (UN)-caring, (UN)-concerned, (UN)-scrupulous, (UN)-favorable and as it stands—(UN)-stoppable. What is more, we as a people are totally—(UN)-aware!

❖ *North Atlantic Treaty Organization*: The North Atlantic Treaty Organization (NATO) was signed on April 4, 1949 and is slowly becoming a "world army." Its original twelve nations included; the United States, Belgium, Canada, Denmark, France, Iceland, Italy, Luxembourg, the Netherlands, Norway, Portugal and the United Kingdom. Eventually, Greece, Turkey, West Germany, Spain, Czech Republic, Hungary, Poland, Bulgaria, Estonia, Latvia, Lithuania, Romania, Slovakia, Slovenia, Albania and Croatia each signed on as consenting nations. "One for all and all for one," describes the key section of the treaty in Article V which commits each member state to consider, *an armed attack against one state to be an armed attack against all states*:

"The Parties of NATO agreed that an armed attack against one or more of them in Europe or North America shall be considered an attack against them all. Consequently they agree that, if such an armed attack occurs, each of them, in exercise of the right of individual or collective self-defense will assist the Party or Parties being attacked, individually and in concert with the other Parties, such action as it deems necessary, including the use of armed force, to restore and maintain the security of the North Atlantic area."

The September 11, 2001 attacks against the World Trade Center and The Pentagon caused NATO to invoke Article V of the NATO Charter for the first time in its history in what was called; "Operation Eagle Assist" and "Operation Active Endeavor." Today based on numerous statements, witnesses, and factual data, it is very likely that the United States government did in fact orchestrate the attacks on 9/11 as a *"false flag"* operation which is a covert operation designed to deceive the public in such a way that the operations appear as though they are being carried out by other entities. The name "False Flag" is derived from the military concept of flying "false colors." or flying the flag of a country other than one's own. As a result, the Patriot Act was born of which we will discuss in greater detail in the coming pages. Essentially, the North Atlantic Treaty created a world "bully" or "superpower" that was poised to respond to any attacks against one of its treaty members. Just to give you an idea of how vast and far reaching this army actually is, the combined military spending of all NATO members constitutes over 70% of the world's defense spending with the United States accounting for 43% of that spending.

At the very outset, NATO was formed as a "super-national" power to help protect the people against dictatorial leaders, so we thought. However as we're beginning to see, it is actually being fashioned as the "World Police" that will eventually serve as a force against its own people. The wars in the Gulf, Bosnia and Kosovo have all served as stepping stones in this direction. NATO, says Icke in *The Biggest Secret*, ". . . was a creation of the Brotherhood (Illuminati) and is designed to evolve by stealth into a world army by encompassing more and more countries and by manipulating 'problems' which give it the opportunities to operate outside its designated areas." He supports this by pointing out how the last six Secretary Generals of NATO have all been members of the infamous Illuminati Bilderbergers.

Since NATO is quickly becoming a world army with many of the major nations as its members, who will be left to fight? The grim truth is . . . civilians, but not all civilians, only the ones that are rebellious and refuse to go along with the new structure of government. Anyone seeking to thwart or interfere with the plans of this elitist system will be subsequently dealt with by force. An example of this is the U.S. Patriot Act which allows the government to falsely imprison anyone deemed a "threat to national security," indefinitely and without due process.

The government has employed some of its top scientist, psychologists and experts to help them understand how to better control the thought processes of a population. They are highly sophisticated in understanding what it takes to subdue an entire planet of people into a state of docility. The plans in which they seek to carry out have been slowly instituted into the fabric of society for many years as a sudden change in the status quo would definitely give rise to suspicion and resistance. Much of what the "shadow government" is doing has been a slow yet deliberate implementation of policies, agencies, forces, tariffs and treaties over several decades in preparation for what is to come. I'm not a religious person, but some say this will be equivalent to the *"Revelations"* attributed to St. John in the bible. The planners of this new regime feel they can covertly achieve their aims without the use of force and subversion. Thus the United Nations (UN) and its world army is only a contingency plan in the event that anarchy ensues when the people finally wake up and realize what their own governments have been seeking to achieve.

When the final veil of secrecy is lifted and all the plots become known, the hidden hand behind all the world's crises, the wars, all the treachery, lies and deceit will finally be made visible. Marshall Law will be declared and all the exercises that are secretly being carried out by private and government law enforcement agencies on how to subdue a mob will finally be put to use. Extreme force will be exacted upon all civilians of all nations. Resistance will be futile. Many of us will be carted off to camps for slave labor while a great deal of us will be slaughtered like worthless cattle. The agency that is currently being groomed to carry out and manage an event of this magnitude is the Federal Emergency Management Agency (FEMA)!

❖ *Federal Emergency Management Agency*: The Federal Emergency Management Agency (FEMA) was created by Presidential order on April 1, 1979. Unfortunately, many people are clueless as to what FEMA actually is. In truth the Federal Emergency Management Agency is an arm of the government that would serve as the "National Police" in the event that Marshall Law was declared. Accordingly, Martial law can be declared during time of increased tension overseas, economic problems within the United States, such as a recession or depression and civil unrest to include; demonstrations or riots. Under such circumstances there are emergency plans which exist to suspend the Constitution and turn over the reigns of government to FEMA. Under Marshall Law, FEMA has the power to suspend all laws, relocate entire populations separating people from their families, arrest and detain citizens without cause or a warrant and hold them without due process. During times of Marshall Law, FEMA would have the right to order the detention of anyone whom they deemed a threat by engaging in, or conspiring to engage in acts of espionage or sabotage against the government. The plan also authorizes the establishment of concentration camps for detaining the accused without trial. They can seize all private property, food supplies, transportation systems, and they even possess the power to suspend the Constitution. Once the Constitution becomes annulled, all civil liberties including the right to bear arms, freedom of speech and the right to assemble would be instantly eradicated. The United States of America would virtually become a "prison nation" policed by a FEMA trained civilian army comprised of all law enforcement agencies, the military and privately trained civilian soldiers. And since FEMA was granted control of the State Defense Forces, they can also serve in the absence of our own military forces should they be deployed elsewhere.

FEMA is by far considered to be the most powerful and dreadful organization in the United States especially considering it was not created by Congress under Constitutional law which means, they don't answer to Congress. Essentially it was created in a series of Executive Orders which by-passed Congress and ultimately created a "Czar." Technically, FEMA's responsibility was primarily only for new disasters including urban forest fires, home heating emergencies, refugee situations, urban riots, and emergency planning for nuclear and toxic incidents. However, they have been preparing to serve a much more sinister purpose in the NWO agenda.

Over the course of its inception, FEMA first participated in the 1979 Hurricane Andres, the 1989 Loma Prieta earthquake in the San Francisco bay area, then again in the 1992 Los Angeles riots, as well as the aftermath of Hurricane Katrina in New Orleans in 2005. Certain sources now believe the U.S. government possesses the technology which allows them to alter certain weather conditions by utilizing what is called; "HIGH FREQUENCY ACTIVE AURORAL" equipment which they have stationed in Alaska (HAARP). Supposedly, this equipment can somehow affect the climate in a way that can trigger; massive Earth Quakes, Tsunamis, Tornadoes, Hurricanes, and other climactic disasters. The Katrina Hurricane was believed to be a colossal scale exercise carried out against the people of New Orleans for the sole purpose of preparing FEMA for insurgency methods. Hurricane Katrina caused the deaths of over 3,500 people, thousands of displaced families and an estimated $81 billion dollars of damage over 90,000 square miles of the United States. And yet to those who cleverly manipulated these events, this was nothing more than an "exercise in preparedness."

Ever since FEMA first began in 1979, reports indicate they have only spent about 6 percent of its budget on national emergencies while the bulk of their funding has been used for the construction of "secret" underground facilities to assure continuity of government in the event of a major emergency, foreign or domestic. After FEMA dropped the ball with Hurricane Andres in Florida, congress began to investigate them. What they discovered was that FEMA was spending 12 times more for "black operations" than for disaster relief. It spent $1.3 billion dollars building secret bunkers throughout the

United States in anticipation of government disruption by foreign or domestic upheaval. This was not known by many of the members of Congress. FEMA is apparently able to function covertly with some type of "black curtain" around its operations. Why would an agency designed to assist during natural calamities be spending the bulk of its resources on building "secret" underground facilities? What are they expecting that would warrant such a substantial push for underground facilities? Executive Order Number 12656 appointed the National Security Council as the principal body that should consider emergency powers. This has allowed the government to increase domestic intelligence and surveillance of U.S. citizens and restrict the freedom of movement within the United States and grant the government the right to isolate large groups of civilians. The National Guard could be federalized to seal all borders and take control of U.S. air space and all ports of entry. Therefore, when they say both "foreign and domestic threats," it seems to me that the threat for them would surely be "domestic" if they are planning to *"increase surveillance of U.S. citizens, isolate large groups of American civilians, and restrict the freedom of movement within U.S. borders."*

According to Harry V. Martin with research assistance from David Caul in an internet article titled *"FEMA—The Secret Government,"* These are just a few Executive Orders associated with FEMA that would suspend the Constitution and the Bill of Rights:

> ➢ EXECUTIVE ORDER 10990 allows the government to take over all modes of transportation and control of highways and seaports.
> ➢ EXECUTIVE ORDER 10995 allows the government to seize and control the communication media.
> ➢ EXECUTIVE ORDER 10997 allows the government to take over all electrical power, gas, petroleum, fuels and minerals.
> ➢ EXECUTIVE ORDER 10998 allows the government to take over all food resources and farms.
> ➢ EXECUTIVE ORDER 11000 allows the government to mobilize civilians into work brigades under government supervision.

- ➤ EXECUTIVE ORDER 11001 allows the government to take over all health, education and welfare functions.
- ➤ EXECUTIVE ORDER 11002 designates the Postmaster General to operate a national registration of all persons.
- ➤ EXECUTIVE ORDER 11003 allows the government to take over all airports and aircraft, including commercial aircraft.
- ➤ EXECUTIVE ORDER 11004 allows the Housing and Finance Authority to relocate communities, build new housing with public funds, designate areas to be abandoned, and establish new locations for populations.
- ➤ EXECUTIVE ORDER 11005 allows the government to take over railroads, inland waterways and public storage facilities.
- ➤ EXECUTIVE ORDER 11051 specifies the responsibility of the Office of Emergency Planning and gives authorization to put all Executive Orders into effect in times of increased international tensions and economic or financial crisis.
- ➤ EXECUTIVE ORDER 11310 grants authority to the Department of Justice to enforce the plans set out in Executive Orders, to institute industrial support, to establish judicial and legislative liaison, to control all aliens, to operate penal and correctional institutions, and to advise and assist the President.
- ➤ EXECUTIVE ORDER 11049 assigns emergency preparedness function to federal departments and agencies, consolidating 21 operative Executive Orders issued over a fifteen year period.
- ➤ EXECUTIVE ORDER 11921 allows the Federal Emergency Preparedness Agency to develop plans to establish control over the mechanisms of production and distribution, of energy sources, wages, salaries, credit and the flow of money in the U.S. financial institution in any undefined national emergency. It also provides that when a state of emergency is declared by the President, Congress cannot review the action for six months!

This sounds like Nazi-Germany all over again. All of this could possibly be carried out right under our noses in the cloak of darkness by a "secret" government who wishes to eliminate public freedoms and confine its populations. I didn't believe this until I saw for myself how the government is preparing and maintaining concentration camps all over the world for housing millions of people. I've seen exposes clearly showing concentration camps with barbed wired fences designed to incarcerate thousands of people. I've seen a proliferation of "make-shift" coffins stacked by the millions in preparation for use. These apparent "concentration camps" are so-called abandoned facilities which are still being maintained by government agencies and they are highly restricted areas. To go anywhere near these facilities would be grounds for being shot and killed or incarcerated indefinitely without trial. These are FEMA camps for the purpose of warehousing and managing large populations of people. FEMA . . . says Icke, ". . . is a major arm of the Brotherhood and is building concentration camps in the United States capable of holding thousands of people." He says, as I have seen, ". . . that they have railway lines running into them in classic Nazi fashion." One such facility he mentions is the Santa Rosa strip in Sonoma County, California which lies just along Route 101, approximately 55 miles north of San Francisco. While it is supposed to be closed, there are still planes coming and going each night under the cover of darkness. I'm sure the people of Sonoma County have no idea what is taking place right in their own back yard.

The NWO leaders would be hard pressed to get the entire country to submit to a new form of government and it would take an act of epic proportions before the people of the United States voluntarily surrendered its sovereignty to a dictatorship. To date, we have only come close to Marshall Law on three separate occasions. The first time was in 1984 under the Reagan administration. The second and third times were in 1990 and 1992 under the Bush administration.

The first time FEMA was poised to declare Marshall Law was in 1984 when President Reagan signed Presidential Directive Number 54 which allowed FEMA to engage in a secret national "Readiness Exercise" under the code name *REX 84*. This "Readiness Exercise" was a contingency plan developed by the United States federal government to suspend the United States Constitution, declare martial law, place military commanders in charge of state and local governments, and detain large numbers of American citizens who were deemed to be national security threats. The exercise was to test FEMA's readiness to assume military authority in the event of a "State of Domestic National Emergency." Under *REX 84*, all U.S. military and National Guard units would become the police of the government used solely for domestic law enforcement. The very same military in which we depend on for the protection of our civil rights would now wage war against its own friends, families and fellow Americans. They would have orders to carry out "sweeps" arresting all undocumented American immigrants in the United States. These immigrants would then be locked up at detention centers and military bases located throughout the country. *REX 84* was such a well guarded secret that anyone without a "need-to-know," or a high enough clearance was literally "locked" out of areas where *REX 84* was being discussed. Oddly enough, only personnel wearing a special red "Christian Cross" or "Crucifix" lapel pin was allowed into these discussions. What is more, this plan advocated the rounding up and transfer of a least 21 million African Americans in the event of massive rioting or disorder just like the rounding up of the Jews in Nazi Germany in the 1930s. This is classic "Eugenics" folks and so-called fear based "Ethnic-Cleansing" procedures on the part of the American Government.

In the round-up and arrest of all undocumented immigrants, a huge number of Spanish immigrants would also be detained. According to Harry V. Martin, the first targets in any FEMA emergency would be Hispanics and Blacks. He says the FEMA orders call for them to be rounded up and detained. He believes tax protesters, demonstrators against government military intervention outside U.S. borders, and people who maintain weapons in their homes would also become targets. "Operation Trojan Horse" he says; is a program designed to learn the identity of such people. The program lures potential protesters into public forums, conducted by a "hero" of the people who advocates survival training. The list of names gathered at such meetings and rallies are input into a data base and then targeted in case of an emergency.

The second and third times that FEMA was poised for action was in 1990 when project "Desert Storm" was enacted. During this time, FEMA drafted new laws which increased its formidable powers by setting up operations within any state or locality without the prior permission of local or state authorities. Prior to this new legislature, prior consent was always required by local and state authorities before establishing operations of any kind. During this time, the U.S. government feared an economic collapse and while the war with Iraq may have been conceived as a ploy to boost the bankrupt economy, it only pushed the West further into debt and deeper into the recession.

Finally, the third opportunity for FEMA to exert its force was when the Rodney King verdict was announced. And while the careless exoneration of the involved officers did generate a "riotous" effect, the rioting was contained to just the Los Angeles area, which curtailed FEMA's involvement. Had the rioting been wide-spread, perhaps FEMA would have become involved.

Although fortunately none of these occurrences was sufficient enough to warrant Marshall Law. In order for FEMA to declare Marshall Law, there would have to be a crisis dangerous enough for the people of the United States to willingly accept a complete government takeover. Some of these would include; the threat of imminent nuclear war, major rioting in several U.S. cities, a series of national disasters that would affect a widespread population, massive terrorist attacks, a major depression leaving several million people without a means to eat or provide food for their families, or a major environmental disaster.

Another scenario which I believe the government to be working towards would be a staged alien invasion. This would create a large scale panic allowing FEMA to go into action. In an interview on the radio talk show *Coast to Coast AM* hosted by George Noory, author Stewart A. Swerdlow describes how the government has the ability to project large scale holographic images (that appear life-like) into the skies. He believes the government plans to utilize this technology in order to create a *"War of The Worlds"* type scenario in order to justify the use of Marshall Law. I wouldn't put anything past the shadow government. As time draws closer to 2012, they have become more brazen in their attempts. Based on numerous testimonies and supporting evidence, it would appear that the 9/11 incident was just one of the many crimes of government carried out against the American people on its own soil. Paul Warburg a wealthy member of the banking cartel and reputed (CFR) member couldn't have stressed this point any better when he said: "We will have a world government whether we like it or not. The only question is whether that government will be achieved by conquest or consent."

What you need to know is that FEMA still wields the power to declare Marshall Law at any time which would render the United States a police state in the event of a real or manufactured crisis. Although these policies and procedures were never officially adopted, they were also never officially abandoned either. In fact, it is believed that FEMA still has a folder with 22 Executive Orders for the President to sign in the event of an emergency. If this were to ever happen (and many feel that it will in the coming years); unfortunately, according to Executive Order 11921, Congress cannot review a Martial Law action until six months after it has been declared. And whether we realize it or not, under the FEMA plan, there is no contingency by which Constitutional power can ever be restored.

❖ *The USA/Patriot Act*: The Patriot Act is an Act of the U.S. Congress signed into law by President George W. Bush on October 26, 2001 in the wake of 9/11. Very few people are aware of how the entire bombing incident that took place on September 11, 2001, was nothing more than a ploy in which to implement the USA/Patriot Act. You see, America would never knowingly or willingly volunteer its sovereignty but it would have to be obtained through some type of ruse. For centuries now, the powers behind world events to include wars, tariffs, embargoes, taxation, and the slow erosion of civil liberties has all been orchestrated through a clever methodology that David Icke calls; "*problem-reaction-solution.*" The way this works is; first the people seeking to implement new policies will create a "problem." Typically this problem will be manufactured by the very same people seeking to implement change. These problems are generally on a large scale, such as wars, depressions, recessions and threats to the national security and safety of the people. This in turn will generate the desired "reaction" from the people crying out that something must be done in which to rectify the situation. Then; the manipulators propose the "solution" of which they wanted from the very onset. According to Icke, this has been their modus operandi throughout history.

Such is the case with 9/11 which was considered to be the new "Pearl Harbor." The Shadow Government is seeking to usurp the civil liberties of the American people by leading us to believe that our freedom is at stake. "In the manipulation of people, one of the strongest weapons is to make people believe someone else did it." The U.S. government wants us to believe that Osama Bin Laden did it but did you know that just six weeks before the bombing of the World Trade Center towers, the owner of the towers had a new insurance policy made up insuring that he would receive $3.5 billion dollars per tower in the event of a terrorist attack. Apparently, he suspected something or he was made aware of this event well in advance.

These global elitist create public scares that threaten our very way of existence hoping to pull the wool over our eyes with the passage of the USA/Patriot Act which is a contrived acronym, which stands for *Uniting and Strengthening America by Providing Appropriate Tools Required to Intercept and Obstruct Terrorism Act of 2001*. (Poppycock!) This is nothing more than a case of surrendering freedom for safety albeit that very same safety is nothing more than a ruse to further imprison us. The vast majority of the American people are not even aware of what the USA/Patriot Act allows the U.S. government to do under certain provisions. First of all; they no longer need a search warrant to enter a person's home, vehicle or any other form of personal property. Prior to the Patriot Act, a search warrant was required before entering and searching a person's home. This is no longer the case. Not only this, but now a person can be unlawfully detained indefinitely without *habeas corpus* which used to be an important legal instrument safeguarding individual freedom against arbitrary state action. Before the inception, or should I say deception of the Patriot Act, a writ of *habeas corpus* which is a summons with the force of a court order, addressed to the custodian or prison official demanding that a prisoner be taken before the court, and that the custodian present proof of authority, allowing the court to determine if the custodian has lawful authority to detain the person. If the custodian does not have authority to detain the prisoner, then he must be released from custody. The prisoner, or another person acting on his or her behalf, may petition the court, or a judge, for a writ of *habeas corpus*. One reason for the writ to be sought by a person other than the prisoner is that the detainee might be held in solitary confinement where they are denied contact with any other persons outside of prison authorities. This means we no longer possess the right to be tried in a court of law. There have been countless cases of the local authorities in conjunction with Federal authorities, detaining individuals without due process on the suspicion of them being a "threat to national security."

Today, Homeland Security has the ability to detain anyone they deem as a "threat to national security" and the only form of evidence they need is a suspicion. Often times, with the help of the media and falsified evidence, things can be manufactured or manipulated in such a way that the accused appear to be guilty of "terrorists" acts. In fact, the very act of me writing this could be deemed as a "terrorist act" simply for speaking out against the government in which they are seeking to impose on us? Did you know that today, according to Wikipedia that the USA/Patriot Act:

> ". . . dramatically reduced restrictions on law enforcement agencies' ability to search telephone, e-mail communications, medical, financial, and other records; eased restrictions on foreign intelligence gathering within the United States; expanded the Secretary of the Treasury's authority to regulate financial transactions, particularly those involving foreign individuals and entities; and broadened the discretion of law enforcement and immigration authorities in detaining and deporting immigrants suspected of terrorism-related acts. The act also expanded the definition of terrorism to include domestic terrorism, thus enlarging the number of activities to which the USA PATRIOT Act's expanded law enforcement powers could be applied."

This means Homeland Security can monitor all financial records and activities, phone conversations, emails, text messages and internet activity. They are currently working on a new software program that can read and decipher a ridiculous amount of data in a very short period of time. This allows them to monitor all internet activity for any "buzz" words that would imply a threat to national security. The United States of America is slowly acquiescing into a prison state and all of our civil liberties are being eroded from the inside out. The United States Constitution was designed to protect civil liberties and provide equal rights to all citizens of this great nation. Our Constitutional way of life is quickly becoming a thing of the past as we move closer to a complete "Orwellian" scenario. In his novel *1984*, which was a glimpse into what we could expect from our government in the years to come, Eric Arthur Blair (1903-1950) better known by his pen name, George Orwell depicts a scenario where our every move is watched and monitored by what he calls "Big Brother." Whether you knew this or not, George Orwell was a member of the Fabian Society which is another Illuminati organization. According to David Icke in his new book *Human Race Get Off Your Knees: The Lion Sleeps No More*, the Fabians utilized the "drip, drip, drip" method of change over long periods of time. He says it was adopted from the roman general Quintus "Fabius" (Fabian) Maximus Verrucosus who employed carefully planned strategies to wear down the enemy over long periods of time and avoided battles that could prove decisive either way. As a member of this organization, Orwell was made privy to certain information which is how he was able to know in advance what was to come.

Today, Big Brother is a reality in what is code named *"Echelon,"* which is the world's largest espionage system consisting of a vast network of listening posts, extremely advanced computers and an enormous number of people, satellite dishes and wire taps. Echelon computers are said to capture every communication via, internet, GSM, UMTS, landlines, television and radio broadcast satellite communications, private, military and diplomatic and listens to every word for key words and phrases of which they flag for further examination. With this technology, the NSA can plug into every telephone call or message entering, leaving or transiting the country. There are cameras and monitoring devices everywhere you look. Our every move is being scrutinized and categorized as a "threat" or "non-threat," this is Big Brother's only concern. Who will comply and who will not? For several years, the NWO has sought to gain control of the world through covert activities; this is because you can control people for much longer if they are not aware they are being controlled. However, once they discover that they've been duped, you can definitely expect an uprising. This is why all of these security measures are being implemented because once the people of the world finally discovers that they've been "hood-winked" into believing in a lie, there will be bedlam in the streets. There will be wide-spread discord and public outcries from the people but it will be too late.

There is absolutely nothing Patriotic about the Patriot Act. In fact, the people who consider themselves to be patriotic and supporters of a "free" America are the very people that will be targeted for suppression. Anyone wishing to maintain our Constitutional way of existence will pose a national threat to the new regime. Once Marshall Law gets declared, the Constitution becomes null and void and there are no provisions which allows for it to be reinstated. The Constitution was established to be the framework for the organization of the United States government and for the relationship of the federal government with the states, citizens, and all people within the United States. It was designed to be the supreme law of the United States but it will be superseded by FEMA law and everything the Constitution once stood for in the way of freedom, liberty and justice for all will become nonexistent. The relationship of the federal government including the states will be antagonistic towards its citizens. There will be no place for patriotism in the new world, only servitude. Serfdom will replace patriotism and the Patriot Act provides the means for them to do this.

Radio Frequency Identification (RFID: The Radio Frequency Identification or (RFID) for short, is a technology that uses communication via electromagnetic waves to exchange data between a terminal and an object such as a product, animal, or person for the purpose of identification and tracking. It was first developed in 1945 by Russian inventor Léon Theremin. This is a passage taken from the King James Bible in revelations chapter 13 verses 16 through 18:

> "And he causeth all, both small and great, rich and poor,
> free and bond, to receive a mark in their right hand, or in

their foreheads: And that no man might buy or sell, save he
that had the mark, or the name of the beast, or the number of
his name. Here is wisdom. Let him that hath understanding
count the number of a man; and his number is Six hundred
threescore and six." (666)

In India as well as many other countries, the government is
actively in the process of providing 600 million people with what
is called a "Unique Identification Number" consisting of 16-digits.
This number would then serve as that person's total identity
world-wide. These bar-codes so-to-speak, will be interfaced with a
global computer bank housing every bit of information about every
person on the planet to include; name, social security number, health
information, credit information, military information, criminal
records and financial accessibility. Essentially, this world computer
is the epitome of the "Zion Mainframe," as depicted in the *Matrix
Trilogy* of which Neo, Morpheus, Trinity, Cypher, Tank, Dozer,
Mouse, Apoc, Switch the Oracle and all those who chose to be freed
from the deceptive illusions of the governmental matrix fought to
preserve. However, once they gain access to the mainframe and
assign everyone a virtual Electronic Product Code number (EPC)
which is what they're using to track practically every product in the
world, then we too will become nothing more than an inventoried
and tracked commodity. This is not the future people this is now and
it's happening at this very moment with the implementation of RFID
technology.

Basically, what the fascist elite would like to have is everyone
on the planet tagged and tracked. An entire network of readers,
terminals, satellites, databases and scanning equipment is being
blanketed all over the planet to act as check-points for monitoring the
whereabouts and activities of global citizens and it's all being done
in a neo-Nazi type fashion where every living person is being issued
a "RealID" number as a license and ultimately as a subcutaneous
microchip. This microchip is nothing more than a small cylindrical
device no bigger than a grain of rice that doesn't require power
and functions off the electromagnetic field of the Earth. One study
showed where these devices can be so miniscule that they virtually
become undetectable. In fact researchers recently mounted such a

device on ants in order to monitor their behaviors. I've even read where these RFID chips can be so tiny that it could virtually be concealed in a period mark.

Currently the smallest RFID chip measuring only 0.15mm x 0.15mm is manufactured by Hitachi. However, the world's largest manufacturer of implantable chips by far, is a company called Allied Digital Solutions of which we will discuss shortly. Right now, this method of tracking goods, animals and eventually all people via Radio Frequency Identification (RFID) is progressing at a feverish pitch. According to one industry analyst, in 2004 there were already sixty thousand companies operating under RFID mandates and scrambling to get with the spychip program as quickly as possible. One can only imagine the progress they've made over the last 6 years. Practically every company including companies like Wal-Mart, Dairy Queen, 7-Eleven, MasterCard, American Express, Nokia, Albertsons, Target and Best Buy are all following suit. In fact, practically all the major grocery store chains are implementing this method of tracking not only to inventory goods but also as a means to determine how and when we shop and what our methods and shopping habits are in order to further solicit us to other purveyors of goods and services.

In their book *Spychips: How Major Corporations and Government Plan to Track Your Every Move with RFID*, Katherine Albrecht and Liz McIntyre clearly delineates how there has been a widespread plot perpetrated against the entire planet by their very own governments to place them under a microscope. We see it happening everywhere and yet we haven't been able to piece it all together. We think it's really just technology made to simplify our lives when in reality it's systematically causing us to surrender any and all traces of independence and privacy. According to an article titled *"Human chips more than skin deep"* on zdnet.com in August 23, 2004 by Michael Kanellos, "Critics, say such technologies would make it easier for government agencies to track a person's every movement and allow widespread invasion of privacy."

We currently see how RFID technology is being used in our vehicles, at toll roads, for branding cattle, in hospitals, it's even been mandated by the Wal-Mart conglomerate and the Department of Defense that all vendors must use RFID coding. It is even believed that Facebook recently had a conference suggesting that RFID would be used in the coming future for logging in purposes giving anyone savvy enough access to profile pages and other forms of private information. But wait because it gets worse. This technology is soon to be in every product on the planet including human beings. It's everywhere, Fed-Ex, UPS, GPS, USPS, Libraries, schools. I thought to myself, why would they want RFID in libraries and then it dawned on me, the global elite are frightened to death of educated people who are aware so they want to monitor everything we're reading and who's reading it. One thing you might find interesting or coincidental depending on how you look at it, is that the very first library to implement RFID tracking was the Rockefeller University in New York back in 1999. You have got to be shitting me! And yet people still find it hard to believe there's a plot being carried out by certain families to monitor and control people but yet the same names of these key players continue to show up time-and-time-again!

We are beginning to see RFID implementation more so in the United States because of its massive volume of people with over 300 million people not to mention undocumented people. However, there is also a wide-scale push to inundate the UK as well as Japan with RFID tracking mechanisms. The NWO has the entire world in their sights and no part of the civilized world will be left outside of their roving eye.

In 1998, Malaysia began using RFID in passports to monitor all movement to and from the country. Norway followed the same policy in 2005, which was then followed by Japan, the United States, Spain, Ireland, UK, Australia, Hong Kong and most of the countries of the European Union (EU) in 2006. Two years later in 2008 Serbia adopted this practice as well as the Republic of Korea and Taiwan. Finally in 2009, Albania implemented the chipped passport as well as the Philippines. This means that all the passport carrying citizens of these countries have tracking and monitoring devices in which their governments can monitor their coming and going and travel activities. But if you think that's unusual, schools in Osaka, Japan just recently started chipping the children's clothing along with their back-packs and student ID cards. This is also being done in certain parts of England where the children's uniforms are being chipped. There's a club in Spain where its VIP patrons have agreed to be chipped in order to gain faster access to the club as well as a means to pay for their drinks. This implies that their RFID chip actually has financial accessibility that serves as a link to either a checking account of some sort or a credit card . . . *"and that no man might buy or sell, save he that had the mark, or the name of the beast, or the number of his name . . ."*

In the pursuit for global control, one of the key components to achieving this would be to completely digitize money. This would allow governments to debit accounts as it sees fit, monitor all spending and shopping habits and even seize or freeze all assets by essentially disabling ones RFID chip. Paper money is becoming a thing of the past as we are slowly beginning to see now with the inception of "Point Of Sale" (POS), transactions with ATM/Debit cards, credit cards, speedpasses, wands, and self-help check-out services. Fewer and fewer people are utilizing cash or checks to make purchases. In fact, when someone does use one of these methods of payment, they are almost made to feel unusual by either the waiting patrons or the checkers themselves. Paper money is becoming archaic and electronic methods are made to appear faster and more convenient to the consumer. This mind-set has conditioned us into a digitized state which is exactly how they designed it. This way, all of our spending gets monitored as we slowly acquiesce into using electronic methods of payment rather than actual currency. This makes us more susceptible to having an implant with purchasing ability so we no longer have to carry money or credit cards and run the risk of losing them or even worse, being robbed of them. At some point, the goal is to make the RFID chip appear en vogue touting it as the "thing to do" when in reality, it's probably the worst thing we can ever do if we are to protect our privacy and civil liberties. Ultimately, I'm told we will no longer have a choice in the matter. That is, if we choose to live among society according to its cleverly mandated guidelines.

Supposedly, there are over a million people who have knowingly or unknowingly been implanted with the RFID chip since it was approved by the FDA in October of 2004. This was done even after certain studies have shown where the RFID implant was responsible for causing cancer in lab rats. Other serious health issues related to the RFID chip according to the FDA included; electrical hazards, MRI incompatibility, adverse tissue reaction, and migration of the implanted transponder. This was based on an October 12, 2004 letter issued by the Food and Drug Administration (FDA). Be that as it may, the RFID chip is still being implanted into human beings at an alarming rate.

There are all types of discussions on how RFID implants are a good thing because they will allow medical facilities to know the medical history of an individual because their history will be associated with the 16-digit code on the chip. Some are saying that by chipping children at birth, we can reduce the number missing children by locating them with their chip transponder. Also, they believe moving forward with implanting people will provide for a much safer society in the generations to come because fugitives, parole violators, and violent felons can be located and jailed much quicker. While I agree these are all laudable reasons for wanting a means to locate those among us that are causing such problems, I also know that these are only ploys utilized by the "spin-masters" to get us to comply to a controlled and monitored lifestyle. Essentially they are asking us to trade our freedom in for safety. One of the test families who agreed to be chipped shortly after the 9/11 incident was so convinced that this was the right thing to do that they actually said they would rather be safe and that they would worry about the privacy part later. This is exactly what the NWO would like us to think. They continue to create public threats claiming them to be acts of terrorism so that eventually we will all be in such a state of alarm and panic that we'll relinquish control to the very agencies that have been terrorizing us all along.

As I mentioned earlier, one of the primary providers of the human RFID "Verichip" is manufactured by a company called Applied Digital Solutions and when they first started providing these chips for human implantation, their funding came from none other than computer giant, IBM which is a known Illuminati organization. In their book *Spychips*, the authors cleverly use the letters (IBM) to stand for; "[I]'ve [B]een [M]onitored." As such; IBM generously provided $30 million dollars for the funding of the RFID technology stating that, ". . . it was to ensure that micro-chipping was in place for future generations." IBM has supported the monitoring and tracking of human beings and a one world government for quite some time. Their contribution to a fascist regime dates back to the early part of the twentieth century when they created a system called the Hollerith Card Punching System which they leased to the Nazis and Hitler's regime to track non-compliant persons so they could be removed from society.

In 1976, IBM launched its release of the Apple I computer selling it for $666. If you'll refer back to the scripture in Revelations 13: 16-18, it clearly cites the mark of the beast as being [666]. In addition to this, on May 3, 2001, IBM filed patent application #20020165758 under "IDENTIFICATION AND TRACKING OF PERSONS USING RFID-TAGGED ITEMS." Now I know this may all seem like one big coincidence but when you trace it back and discover who the key people are in these major corporations, you will find that most, if not all of them are members of the same cabal. Their ideas, loyalties and agendas hover around those of the central power structures which are the world banks and its controllers. If you'll recall according to the biblical version of genesis, it was Satan or the snake which tempted the proverbial Adam and Eve into biting from the "Apple." Today the trademark representing Apple computers is none other than the bitten from apple . . . How utterly apropos. IBM is a part of the Illuminati organization which is behind the world agenda for a one world government with one central bank and a few major corporations and nothing in between.

But wait, because it gets even more complicated. Oddly enough, the manufacturer for the Verichip happens to be a company called Raytheon which is a large scale weapons manufacturer and the 5th largest government defense contractor in the world. But that's not all; Verichip was formed by a merger between the Verichip Corporation and a company called Steelvault which was in the business of security and identity theft protection. Now if that doesn't take the cake I'm not sure what else will. These people are in the business of manufacturing weapons and identification management and yet here they are making RFID chips in which to insert into humans so that they can monitor and control everyone on the planet.

We have all been deceived into thinking the government has our best interest at heart when in truth; they are the very ones seeking to commandeer our sovereignty by introducing shit like this. Their hope is that we will reach a point where we will eventually see the usefulness in being chipped but if by chance that doesn't happen, perhaps they will impose a law making it mandatory and anyone not having the "mark of the beast" will be deemed a threat to society and an outcast. Soon, our very way of existence will be usurped by a select group of corporations, banks, and governmental agencies and we will be led to believe that it's for the betterment of our societies. But this is the furthest thing from the truth. In reality, we have been led to the slaughter like unsuspecting sheep trusting the guidance of the dastardly sheepherder.

I'm not a conspiracy theorist or an investigative journalist and I'm certainly not a politician. So why is it that I'm even concerned with such matters? I ask myself, how does any of this global elitism or the New World Order, pertain to me as a spiritual and metaphysical person. And the truth is; I didn't ask to be privy to any of this stuff. All I ever asked for was wisdom, understanding and truth. And as a result, my studies led me to these conclusions. With each book I read and with every documentary I watch, I become more and more enthralled by this plot to take over the world. I wanted to know more, so I began to seek out the truth which led me to discover how spirituality is at the core of all of this whether we can see it or not. Everything in which happens during the course of evolution, happens according to cyclical occurrences, cycles throughout the ages that have always been about the struggle between two forces be it "light" and "dark" "good" and "evil" or basically "God" against the "devil." Whatever the case, these types of struggles have raged on for as long as we can remember. Systems rise and fall and governments succeed and fail because the people either embraced them or revolted against them. History portrays a repetitive phenomenon . . . enslavement-revolt-freedom-apathy-enslavement. Enslavement frequently followed revolution because the people did not realize that socialism was slavery, not freedom. But in the wake of it all, time has always proven that no matter how formidable the foe, eventually the people decided they were not to be subdued by the tyranny and dictatorship that was being foisted upon them by their ruthless governments.

Chapter Four

Cosmic Truth

Cosmic Truth

"All truth passes through three stages: First it is ridiculed; second, it is violently opposed; and third, it is accepted as self-evident."
—Arthur Schopenhauer (1788-1860)

What is the truth of the Cosmos? In its most basic sense, the Cosmos is an orderly or harmonious system. It is divine order. I can certainly relate with the definition provided by Webster's Online Dictionary which says the Cosmos is the; *"extraterrestrial vastness or the Universe in contrast to the Earth alone where it is concerned with abstract spiritual or metaphysical ideas."* However, the more accurate description is given by philosopher Ken Wilber who defines it as *"all of manifest existence, including various realms of consciousness."* In looking at the vastness and the multidimensional aspects of the Universe, it is almost mind boggling to fathom all of its complexities, possibilities and unknown realities. One must truly have an open mind when dealing with the Cosmos and its wondrous diversity. In my first book *Ultimate Truth: Book 1* I write:

> "If a library consisting of thousands upon thousands of volumes of books were the Cosmos, our Milky Way galaxy (which is one of billions of galaxies in the observable Universe), would comfortably fit within the size of a period mark in one of the many books."

Believe it or not, our Sun is presumably only one of a 100 billion stars in this galaxy alone. In fact; notable Physicist and Nobel Prize winner Francis Crick believed there to be roughly 100 billion galaxies in our Universe postulating there are at least one million planets in our galaxy which could support life as we know it. Therefore, it is appropriate for us to know that ours is not the only form of intelligence in this vast Cosmological existence we call the Universe. There are far more beings than humans which have populated the Cosmos for eons. According to Hindu scriptures, there are inestimable Universes created by God to facilitate the implementation of the separated desires of countless living entities. Aside from the numerous Universes which are material, there is also the unlimited spiritual world, where the purified living entities live with perfect conception about life and ultimate reality. With our planet being roughly 4.5 billion years old, we are essentially infants in the cosmic realm. Our Universe is so rich and diverse with ranges, dimensions and vibrational octaves that we have only begun to experience life as intelligent beings.

You should know that there are layers upon layers of different realities and forms of existence happening simultaneously all around us at this very moment. Our minds cannot even begin to fathom the vast amount of possibilities that abound. In measurement, the Cosmos are considered to be at least 93 billion light years in diameter. That means it would take light traveling at 186,000 miles per second roughly 93 billion years to traverse it. Typically, the diameter of a galaxy is about 30,000 light-years, and the average distance between two neighboring galaxies is roughly 3 million light-years. In comparison, our Milky Way Galaxy is about 100,000 light years in diameter, and our nearest sister galaxy, the Andromeda Galaxy, is located nearly 2.5 million light years away. There are probably more than 100 billion of these galaxies in the observable Universe. The average galaxy ranges anywhere from ten million stars up to one trillion stars. An overall calculation from these numbers would suggest there are around one sextillion stars in the observable Universe; although a 2003 study by Australian National University astronomers resulted in a figure of 70 sextillion. But this is only the "observable" Universe. Science has determined that not only is there a Universe but a "Multiverse" meaning that ours is just one of countless unconnected Universes all of which are just as vast and diverse as the next. The ramifications of this are so far reaching, that we can't even begin to understand just how minuscule our perception of reality actually is. I'm just talking about the physical aspects on the 3rd density but I'm not taking into consideration the fact that there are other dimensions, each consisting of intricate and more elaborate forms of existence that we couldn't possibly be aware of. The adept truly knows that life and truth are not confined solely to this physical realm and planet.

Metaphysically speaking, there are actually 12 possible dimensions (science believes there are 11) each of which has 12 overtones. This means there are possibly 144 levels of reality of which we are only on the higher octaves of the 3rd level. How trivial we are to think that ours is the only intelligent life form. This is entirely presumptuous on the part of human beings. David Icke believes that the number of life forms in this galaxy alone is beyond imagination and that if we judge the possibilities only by what we see on this one little planet, in this one little solar system, our range of perception, imagination and vision will be so microscopic, that an understanding of what is really happening would be far too impossible to grasp. The truth is; the Cosmos encompasses the totality of everything that exists, including all physical matter and energy, the planets, stars, galaxies, and the contents of intergalactic space. Therefore, in discussing some of these cosmic truths, we will be looking at various topics that expand beyond our typical everyday understanding. Some of these topics will touch upon things many consider to be science-fiction but I have come to label them as science-fact. Much of what we may consider to be bizarre or too far-fetched for reality is actually truth disguised as fiction. Unfortunately, our conditioning will not allow us to accept this information and so we've become cut-off from this esoteric type of information. Over time, our sense of awareness has atrophied to the point where we've become deadened to this form of understanding. It is only when we begin to allow this type of information back into our consciousness that we are able to jolt the memory codes imbedded within our DNA. I'm not just referring to the two-stranded coding but rather the additional strands that we're equipped with but have not been able to utilize. These missing strands, once reactivated, enable us to tap into the other 90% of our brains capacity. It's there; we just have to utilize it in order for it to become stimulated.

So, in an effort to stimulate the all knowing awareness, in this chapter I will be speaking in depth about the planet called *Maldek* which is where many people believe extraterrestrials traveled from to visit Earth during the Atlantean times. *Panspermia* which postulates how the "seeds" of life existed throughout the Cosmos long before there was life on Earth. I will also be discussing the *Logos* or the "order and knowledge of the Cosmos" as well as the

Oversoul, Walk-Ins, Starseeds, Light-Workers, Cosmic Laws and the *Cosmic Mind* and its implications on our spiritual transition.

It takes a great deal of courage to entertain the notion that life as we know it is really just a fraction of what is happening in the Universe. In order to fully embrace the wisdom of these writings which requires a great deal of study and introspection, one must be open-minded to the degree that all forms of prior conditioning becomes openly challenged thus enabling us to reevaluate what we know about truth. One will come to find (just as I did) that our truth is minuscule in terms of "Cosmic Truth" and the vast amount of information that has been sequestered and hoarded by a select few in an effort to keep us ignorant and unaware.

There are billions of stars, millions of planets and countless levels of reality which we've never stopped to take notice of. Things are constantly occurring on different levels and degrees to include the mental realm, the astral realm and the physical realm. The mental realm alone expands as far as the imagination's span. But even this realm has become limited by what we perceive as possible or impossible. The astral realm reaches beyond our scope of reality and as humans we have been reduced to a tangible world where we believe only in what we can see with our physical eyes. And so our sight has become near-sighted to say the least because it's only based upon human experience. If our scope of awareness is limited only to human experience on the physical realm, then we're completely ignorant to a panorama of circumstances that continually happen all around us. We have become blinded for all intent and purposes. We have eyes but yet we do not see and ears yet we do not hear. Only 10% of the Universe is physical or knowable while the other 90% remains unseen. It is this 90% that actually governs controls and determines what happens to the other 10%. And since the cosmos are indicative of the human body with the Universe being the macrocosm and the human vehicle being the microcosm, we are similar to the Universe in that our brains only utilize 10% of its capacity if that. Imagine what possibilities would abound to those of us that were better able to access the far reaches of the invisible Universe and in so doing, tap into the unchartered areas of the vacuum which we call "Mind."

There is a far greater truth to be told by venturing into the unknown recesses of Mind. By Mind I mean the "Cosmic Mind" which is the Universal brain. Within this brain lie all the answers that we've been seeking but have not yet been able to acquire. Our failure to obtain these precious gems of wisdom has been hindered by our inability to see beyond what is presented to us. We've been taught only to believe in what can be experienced through the five essential senses. Not to mention how we've become docile and conditioned through various means of mental control. These avenues are masquerading as truth in the form of organized religions, dogmas, doctrines, creeds and false and unfounded beliefs being promulgated by adherents of clandestine activities. But the greatest of these is religion which continues to imprison the hearts and minds of anyone that would dare to venture out into unchartered regions of thought and mental independence. It is for this reason that I write so that anyone who dares to escape the strong-holds of mental enslavement can find solace in knowing that knowledge is power and that power alone will serve to help humanity free itself from the tyranny of ignorance. *"For you shall know the (real) truth and this truth shall set you free."*

Planet Maldek

In my previous book *Ultimate Truth: Book I*, I write about a celestial battle that took place between two planetary bodies called *"Tiamat"* and *"Marduk"* in what is known as *"The tale of the celestial battle and the cleaving of Tiamat,"* where Tiamat destroys Marduk leaving the asteroid belt as remnants of this battle. When I wrote about this proverbial *"battle of the gods,"* I unwittingly believed it was the infamous planet known as *"Nibiru/Marduk"* that was destroyed although further research has led me to recant that statement. My understanding of this event was derived from the work of Zecharia Sitchin whose theory was based on the planets *"Tiamat"* and *"Nibiru"* or the Babylonian *"Marduk."* According to Sitchin, Tiamat supposedly existed between Mars and Jupiter. He postulated that it was a thriving world in a very different solar system, with jungles and oceans, whose orbit was disrupted by the arrival of a large planet or very small star which passed through the solar system between 65 million and four billion years ago. The new orbits caused Tiamat to collide with one of the moons of this object, which is known as Nibiru. The debris from this collision is thought to have formed the asteroid belt, the Moon, and the current inclination of planet Earth. What I have come to discover is that the planet that was destroyed during this cosmic collision was actually planet "*Maldek*." I also discovered that what was left of Maldek eventually became our Earth and its Moon which was later established as a strategic outpost for some of Maldek's remaining survivors. On the website www. cosmologycorner.com; it suggests that the Earth's Moon is heavily cratered because it was originally Maldek's moon which received the brunt of the explosion. Supposedly, the Moon served as a kind of Noah's ark for Maldek's survivors before it was blasted away and captured by our Earth's orbit. Based on recent findings, science is certain that the Moon's composition is entirely different than that of the Earth's so it couldn't possibly be derived from the Earth. Also, the Moon has been determined to be "hollowed" out. This would make it possible for it to harbor its inhabitants in its inner surface. For more on this please read David Icke's *Human Race Get off Your Knees: The Lion Sleeps No More.*

Here recently, the planet that used to orbit between Mars and Jupiter is referred to by many names to include; *Maldek, Malona, Nibiru/Marduk, The Twelfth Planet, Lucifer, Phaeton, Tiamat,* and the original *Atlantis.* Whatever the case, they are essentially one-in-the-same planet whose destruction was the greatest catastrophic event to occur in the history of this solar system. Scientist refer to this event as the "disruption theory," which states that there was once a major planetary member of the solar system circulating in the present gap between Mars and Jupiter between 8800 BCE and 1500 BCE, which was variously destroyed thus changing our solar system and all life in it forever. It was this explosion and the resulting debris that cratered the planets and moons and produced their rings, disrupted the planetary orbits and rotations, and gave birth to the meteors and comets. The destruction of Maldek caused incredible chaos and disruption across the entire solar system from the razing and cratering of nearby planets to the orbital and axial displacement of planets as far away as Uranus. Consequently, Earth and Mars were especially affected, with Earth acquiring much of Maldek's water and Mars losing most of its own. Much of the debris of Maldek settled into what are now known as the asteroid belts, while other parts of it became the meteors and comets and stray moons and small planets of our solar system. No one can know for certain what actually brought on Maldek's destruction but here are some very interesting versions of what could have caused such a devastating event:

> ➤ It veered too close to Jupiter and was torn apart by the gas giant's powerful gravity.
> ➤ It was struck by another large celestial body.
> ➤ It was destroyed by a hypothetical brown dwarf, the companion star to the Sun known as Nemesis.
> ➤ It was shattered by some internal catastrophe.

Maldek was also known as "Lucifer" to certain people and to them its destruction was referred to as the "Lucifer Rebellion," where the being known as Lucifer was the embodiment of this planet. In ancient times, planets where named after the governing deities of those planets. During this time, Lucifer was a perfect and beautiful being and his planet was one of ten in the solar system of that time. The Sun's reflection on the watery surface of Lucifer/Maldek caused it to shine brightly like a second sun, and like a brilliant star from afar. Some of this can be gleaned from scriptural versions only much of what we read in the scriptures is fragmented and based on allegory so it's hard to actually decipher between myth and facts. In the bible's version; Isaiah refers to Lucifer/Maldek by admonishing the king of Babylon for his pride by saying:

> *"How art thou fallen from heaven, O Lucifer, son of the morning! how art thou cut down to the ground, which didst weaken the nations!" For thou hast said in thine heart, I will ascend into heaven, I will exalt my throne above the stars of God: I will sit also upon the mount of the congregation, in*

the sides of the north: I will ascend above the heights of the
clouds; I will be like the most High." (Isaiah 14: 12-14)

In the Jewish Encyclopedia it says; "it is obvious that the prophet (in attributing to the Babylonian king boastful pride, followed by a fall), borrowed the idea from a popular legend connected with the morning star." We see this falling-star image again in John's revelation but without a name. However, in the 4th century, Christian priest St. Jerome translates the "morning star" to mean "Lucifer" which carried the fallen-star myth-element into Christian mythology. In any event, it is believed that planet Lucifer/Maldek was full of splendor and so it rivaled the Sun for its brilliance and set out to prevail over it.

In Greek Mythology, Maldek is called "Phaeton" which means the "shining," and it is also an epithet of Clymenus by Merope or Clymene and Lucifer the Morning Star Venus. But, in an attempt to become ruler of the solar system, it is believed that Lucifer/Maldek along with a third of the entire solar system was defeated and destroyed. Conversely, at the time of this great rebellion, the inhabitants of Maldek were very spiritual in nature but their planetary leader caused them to fall from grace. This version is very similar to Greek mythology where this hypothetical planet Phaeton/Maldek, the son of the Sun god Helios attempted to drive his father's solar chariot for a day with disastrous results and was ultimately destroyed by Zeus. According to the legend, Phaeton/Maldek was the son of Helios where Phaeton seeks assurance that his mother, Clymene, is telling the truth that his father is the Sun god Helios. When Phaeton obtains his father's promise to drive the Sun chariot as proof, he fails to control it and the Earth is in danger of burning up when Phaeton/Maldek is killed by a thunderbolt from Zeus to prevent further disaster.

In Astrological terms, the purpose of the downfall of Lucifer/Maldek was because:

"Lucifer/Maldek was of the combined nature of Virgo, Libra, and Scorpio, which according to esoteric tradition were then one sign (and one planet). Virgo was Lucifer's purity and dedication. Libra was Lucifer's perfect beauty and wisdom, and Scorpio was Lucifer's dark or extreme side. These three qualities made Lucifer too powerful or gifted for his own good and led to his conceit, rebellion, and downfall. Before Lucifer's unruly power got out of hand, he was supernaturally cut down and changed forever. His essence was literally divided into three separate parts so that he was greatly weakened and no longer posed a threat. Lucifer became the new signs of Virgo, Libra, and Scorpio, increasing the zodiac from ten to twelve signs. There were now also twelve major planets instead of ten."

Author William Lester Blessing talks about the downfall of Maldek/Lucifer in his book *Inner Earth People and Outer Space People*. Blessing postulates how the planet Lucifer/Maldek was in fact planet Earth in its previous incarnation. He says the Earth was then as large if not larger than our Sun making ours a binary solar system which was populated by "Luciferians" named after its leader Lucifer; although others referred to them as "Maldekians." Accordingly, many planets and moons revolved around this planet including Lilith named after Lucifer's wife but are now scattered across the solar system after it was destroyed or went nova. Blessings describe the people on Lucifer/Maldek as being giants that lived to be at least a thousand years old. Perhaps, says Blessings, this is where the original creation story of Genesis in the Christian bible comes from which is nothing more than a description of the rebirth, reconstruction, or partial restoration of a former and greater Earth.

Another version of how Maldek was destroyed comes from the website: cosmologycorner.com where they postulate how an event took place somewhere between 68 and 80 million years ago when an advanced race of evil grey beings called the Zetans (from the constellation Reticulum which is a binary star system located about 39 light years from Earth), began to colonize Maldek and upon its completion, it became inhabited by the Drakars from the Drakarian Empire who then set out to launch three asteroids to the hominid civilizations; one for Venus, one for Earth, and one for Mars. According to this information, the first one struck Mars' atmosphere about 65.5 million years ago, wiping off over two-thirds of the Oxygen rich atmosphere. The one that hit Earth didn't wipe off the atmosphere, but ended many species of life and set off some massive ice ages on Earth. The third one hit Venus also, but never reached the surface much less beneath it because the Drakars underestimated how violent the atmosphere really was. The Galactic Alliance responded quickly and with an iron fist by sending Erran and Scenarian warships, which destroyed Maldek killing all of its inhabitants.

Something about all of this appeals to a greater part of me that knows this to be true. Whether or not planet Maldek was destroyed by a collision or through a calculated assault by planetary warships is of little importance to me. What is important is the fact that our science is either wrong or they know something in which they are not telling us. Half truths are still mistruths and until we are able to know the *whole* truth, we will forever be at the mercy of those withholding the information. "Truth-or pieces of Truth revealed to any one of us are part of a larger mosaic, and thus it is up to each of us to arrive at our own conclusions concerning the Truth that others have to share with us," says Rick Martin in a 1999 interview with Zulu Shaman Credo Mutwa on the website; librarising.com. For years I have maintained that everyone on Earth is not of the Earth. I've had this sense of knowing that has favored this mindset. When I look at all the varying cultures and languages that humans have on this planet alone, I'm led to believe we are all not from the same origins. Granted we are all *"humanoid"* for the most part, many of us come from various parts of the cosmos. In the destruction of Maldek, billions of lives were lost, and the Maldekians (who were a mix of human and reptillian) had to reincarnate on other planets. Many of them came to Earth for a new start and have been here ever since.

Panspermia

For years I have maintained that "human" biological life did not begin here on planet Earth but rather it was started perhaps in a distant place far, far from our galaxy. The principle of *Panspermia* states that life originated someplace else and was deposited on Earth's surface by means of a collision with some other object that already harbored intelligent life. In some of Zecharia Sitchin's work, he speaks of an ancient Sumerian account where Earth/Tiamat, collided with Nibiru/Marduk in a celestial battle. Accordingly, Earth became "seeded" by this collision thus making life on Earth possible. That being the case, the life forms that existed on Nibiru/Marduk were already well into existence on other planets throughout the Universe. Nobel Prize winner Professor Francis Crick suggested that the seeds of life may have been purposely spread by an advanced extraterrestrial civilization facing catastrophic annihilation, or hoping to terra-form planets for later colonization. But exactly where and how did life begin on these other planets? Well, as we begin to see just how far back life actually goes, we can better understand that human life didn't actually begin here on planet Earth but based upon the most accepted understanding, life for humans originated in the Lyran constellation and was then deposited here on Earth to evolve into greater aspects of itself.

Science suggests that many of the organic compounds which are components of life on Earth were already present in the early solar system. The theory of "exogenesis" puts forth the idea that life on Earth was transferred from elsewhere in the Universe. Given the fact that life existed in the Cosmos long before arriving here on Earth, we must still take into consideration how human evolution cannot be explained among single-celled organisms; hence the programs for higher evolution must have therefore come from an intelligent genealogy.

Unfortunately, most people find the concept of life existing elsewhere hard to believe. This may be due to a religious foundation or one based upon a biblical understanding. But, it's no secret that biblical accounts of creation are solely based upon Sumerian and Babylonian texts (among other prior civilizations) which deals primarily with the creation of the first "*Adammu*" or human-reptilian hybrid by the Nefilim visitors. However, humanoid forms have existed for eons in various parts of the Universe only not in primate form as we now do. Accordingly, prior to a spontaneous genetic upgrade by these highly advanced visitors (so-to-speak), Man had only progressed to the point of *Cro-Magnon* which was a very primitive form of being. As a result of genetic in-breeding and cross-breeding, a newer more advanced and intelligent form of Man was created in what we now call *"Homo Sapien"* or "Thinking Man." This advanced human evolution by millions of years and even scientists today still can't seem to understand how this could have taken place without factoring this possibility into their scenario. I know for some of us this might be a far stretch for the imagination, but understand this; life did not begin here on this planet a mere 6,000 years ago in the so-called "Garden of Eden." That's absurd. There were ancient civilizations such as Lemuria, Mu and Atlantis which date as far back as 10,000 to 12,000 years. In fact, Sitchin's account alone dates as far back as 300,000 to 400,000 years.

Today, science has discovered human remains dating as far back as a million years and yet some people still hold the Genesis account to be accurate. In some of Edgar Cayce's readings, he was able to go as far back as 10 million years where ancient civilizations existed on this planet. One has to wonder, if this planet was formed some 4.5 billion years ago, why would life on this planet be limited to such a short period of time when the earliest possible emergence of life in the Universe was about 12.7 billion years ago? I know we have to allow for the cooling off of the planets and the proper conditions to support life through evolution. However, the "Precambrian" fossil record indicates that life appeared soon after the Earth was formed. This would imply that life appeared within several hundred million years when conditions became favorable. On May 11, 2001, Geologist Bruno D'Argenio and molecular biologist Giuseppe Geraci from the University of Naples announced the finding of extraterrestrial bacteria inside a meteorite estimated to be over 4.5 billion years old. Needless to say, the Universe, as well as planet Earth, has been inhabited by intelligent beings far longer than the bible's Adam and Eve.

Panspermia actually means "seeds everywhere" and it has quickly become a viable theory which postulates how humans were parented through a celestial lineage that I believe has continued to monitor the growth and progress of its progeny as indicated by this statement:

"Today, the Panspermia hypothesis has finally achieved some measure of scientific respectability. Although it remains the orthodox view that life evolved in situ (naturally) on this world and, possibly, many others, there is mounting evidence of at least some extraterrestrial input to the formative stages of planet-based biology."

These Cosmic parents of ours consisted of many different forms of intelligence ranging from Bird-like beings, to Reptiles, Felines, Amphibians and many other forms some of which are non-physical. Many of these advanced races were from various constellations throughout the Universe but primarily humanoid beings were first created in the Lyran constellation with the help of advanced races such as the Orions, the Sirians, and the Pleiadians. All total there were about twelve different types of beings that took part in our creation each of which provided a particular code within our genetic make-up. This might be why the number 12 has had such a huge significance for us. In truth, we were designed to be multidimensional beings with the ability to communicate with our various lines of Ascendants. And since we know how life can only descend from ancestors at least as highly evolved as itself, our evolution to higher forms depends on our genetic programs that come from our celestial parentage. Human beings were originally designed to have a 12-stranded DNA structure which would enable galactic communication, but through genetic tampering and manipulation, this system has been decoded preventing us from becoming our true intergalactic selves. Nevertheless, it is known that intelligent life can only come from prior intelligent life. Therefore, this intelligent life must have always existed in some form or another and what we have thought of as "evolution" is actually humans naturally developing into their original form as highly evolved beings.

The theory of Panspermia was first advocated by the Greek philosopher Anaxagoras, who also influenced Socrates. In the 1870s, British physicist Lord Kelvin and German physicist Hermann von Helmholtz also agreed that life could have very well come from the outer reaches of space. Later, in the first decade of the 1900s, Swedish chemist Svante Arrhenius theorized that bacterial spores propelled through space by light pressure were the seeds of life here on Earth. However, some people such as Aristotle argued in favor of "spontaneous generation" which postulated that life was a spontaneous occurrence. This hypothesis was later supported by American chemists Stanley Miller and Harold Urey who proved that some amino acids can be chemically produced from ammonia and methane. But, to further support the claim of Panspermia, British astronomers Fred Hoyle and Chandra Wickramasinghe observed light from distant stars with traces of life, in the intervening dust. In either event, none of these hypotheses supports the idea of the biblical genesis or any other religious version of creation here on Earth and yet countless people still hold this to be true. Contrary to religious belief, it is now widely accepted that space actually contains the ingredients for life. And while Panspermia does not attempt to provide an explanation for evolution or where and how life itself began, it does however; attempt to solve the mysteries of the origin of life on planet Earth.

Life itself is eternal and we are just one expression of a vast and magnificent Intelligence. This Intelligence is creation, it is life and it is manifest throughout the millions of galaxies all of which harbor life in the most diverse forms. Life doesn't have to be physical to exist. This might be the reason why we have had such a difficult time discovering other "life forms." It is because we lack the means to do so. Or perhaps it is because we are seeking something possessing physical "form" when in reality, higher forms of existence can be "formless." God exists in all forms, shapes and variations to include creations we have yet to discover. The human eye can only see ultra-violet lights and anything beyond that spectrum, we fail to see. Because we can't see it, we deem it non-existent. But in reality, there is far more to this multitude of galaxies and Universes than we will ever know. God is life, but exactly when and how life came to be escapes human logic. All I know is that we have limited ourselves to the belief that human beings are the only life forms to exist. It is utterly pompous of us to think such a thing for to do so would render God limited to this one form of dynamic expression. We pride ourselves on being created in the "*image and likeness of God*," when in truth this could never be for God is the unmanifest energy of the Cosmos ever expanding into greater aspects of itself. The idea that we were to be created in the "*image and likeness of the gods"* was uttered by Enki (Nefilim) in his attempts to create a primitive slave race through invitrofertillization methods in ancient Africa which later became intelligent, thinking humans. These were the human-reptilian crossbreed of Sumer. But even these visitors themselves are expressions of the One and eternal stream of God that permeates all life forms. This life force courses through the veins of every living creature and it is eternal. It is God and we are its expression. Therefore, we are God made manifest in human form. But we are not the totality of its design nor of its expression for we are just a single microbe in the grand scheme of life.

Starseeds

Not everyone on Earth is from Earth. Scientists in the United States, China and Mexico are studying a new type of children who are appearing in ever-increasing numbers throughout the world. They are commonly referred to as *"Starseeds."* They are called Starseeds because they are believed to be from other worlds and have come to assist the planet during its ascension process. (I explain this in detail in the chapter on Ascension). In his book *The Ancient Secret of The Flower of Life: Volume 1*, Drunvalo Melchizedek gives a very fascinating scenario about a baby born with AIDS in California during the early 1990's. Doctors at UCLA began examining a boy when he was first born. They examined him again at six months and then again when he was a year old. Each time, the boy tested positive for the AIDS virus. Doctors decided to follow up again when he turned five and what they found was that the boy didn't show any traces of the AIDS virus. It was like he had never contracted AIDS. The Doctors were bewildered at how his system had somehow become immune to the AIDS virus. They set out to do a complete diagnostic on the boy checking everything including his DNA. They soon discovered that the young boy did not have *"human"* DNA. I'll explain; as human beings we typically have 64 codons in our DNA. These are the codes in which the body utilizes to build proteins and amino acids which are the building blocks for our bodies. In typical human beings, only 20 of these codons are activated. The rest are inert or just simply not functioning. This means that our instructions for full development are shut off or not fully functional. (See the chapter on DNA for a thorough explanation). What doctors found was that this young boy actually had 24 codons that were fully functional which allowed his system to create "new codes" thus allowing him to become immune to AIDS. And get this; not only was he immune to the AIDS virus but he was also immune to all viruses. His immune system was 3000 times stronger than that of a normal human being. Later they found another child with the same situation. So they started a clinical trial testing several other people. First they found a 100 people with this type of DNA and then 10,000 people with the same genetic make-up. Scientists now believe that at least 1% of the planet has made this genetic mutation. There are an estimated 6.5 billion people on the planet therefore this would imply that at least 65 million children and adults are no longer human by definition. Scientists now believe that a "*new*" human race is being spawned from these new genetics.

Starseeds are now entering this phase of existence because they have elected to assist planet Earth during its ascension to the fourth dimension. This planet we live on was often referred to as "the planet of the children," by many advanced civilizations. Apparently, this is why so many off-planet civilizations have ships orbiting this Earth. These celestial visitors are part of our lineage and therefore, they have a vested interest in seeing the planet succeed. These Starseeds actually are monadic "sparks" of the One soul having multidimensional experiences that have just recently begun inhabiting human bodies over the last one or two life-spans. They chose Earth as a place to learn and grow into the full awareness of who they actually are until the time comes when they will assist in helping to raise the planets vibration to that of the fourth dimension. Many people believe these Starseeds are ancient souls from Mu and Atlantis who have returned to help humanity find its way during this difficult time. This is not unusual when you take into consideration that we are all Starseeds who have lived in many realities in many planetary systems and in higher realms as other life forms during the days of Atlantis and Lemuria but have become trapped in this physical experience.

In his book *Awakening To Zero Point: The Collective Initiation*, Gregg Braden talks about how these Starseeds have incarnated relatively recently into the memory-pool of human awareness in an effort to infuse a renewed understanding into the conscious matrix. Braden points out how biblical texts mentions there were originally 12,000 "seeds" that incarnated into each of the original 12 tribes of Israel. This would mean 144,000 individual seeds anchoring a unique expression of light and information. Braden feels that because these Starseeds have very little experience within the Earth incarnation loop for lifetime upon lifetime, that they are less likely to incur heavy karmic debts.

The actual purpose of a Starseed is to "seed" planets with information and spiritual frequencies when one cycle of time is about to end and another begin. As our planetary frequency increases, so too does the Starseed's level of awareness. This activates their dormant purpose which is to help others, and return to their natural state of being as a soul spark of light. This is made possible through the genes of the Starseed which are encoded with a "wake-up call" designed to "activate" them at a pre-determined moment in life. Braden describes this by saying, "They will feel the call as a series of pulsed vibrational tones that will be recognized on a level beyond that of conscious knowing. Through a harmonic resonance achieved as the result of the life experience, their bodies will be "tuned" to come into harmony with these tones." This awakening process can be gentle and gradual for some or quite dramatic and abrupt for others. In any event, their memory is restored to varying degrees, which allows them to consciously take up their missions. When this happens, their connections to the Higher Self are strengthened permitting them to be largely guided by their inner sense of knowing.

Accordingly, many of the souls that have entered this life stream since 1968 are potential Starseeds. They are souls whose previous incarnations were on more advanced planets but have volunteered to incarnate on Earth in an effort to help facilitate the spiritual evolution of this planet. Based on an internet description, Starseeds have great charisma, compelling eyes, a nagging sense of being from somewhere else, an urgent need to find and fulfill their mission, a chronic dull pain in the back of their neck, and chronically congested sinuses which are caused by a difference in monadic frequency between their home planet and Earth. Starseeds have willingly volunteered for these Earthly missions because they are able to gain further ascension for doing so. This 3-dimensional experience greatly accelerates their cosmic evolution. It is for this reason that Starseeds must face and overcome many more obstacles and challenges than a normal person would. Does this sound like you? On her website (www.nibiruiancounsil.com), Jelaila Starr provides a list of traits that are common among all Starseeds:

> They have an intense sense of loneliness.
> They feel like they don't belong in their Earth families.
> They have a fascination with the stars and feel as though their home is out there, but they can't remember where.
> They begin to question the ways of Earth at an early age. Many are the black sheep of their family.
> They are drawn to Metaphysics seeking answers to why they feel so alone and why they don't seem to fit in on Earth.
> Many have an adversarial relationship with the parent of the opposite sex.
> The majority of Starseeds have the facial shape of their mother but the remainder of their physical body is like that of their fathers, or the other way around depending on which parent is the Starseed parent from off planet. This is done for a reason.
> Lower than normal body temperature and inability to handle heat.
> The majority of Starseeds carry the Crystal Gene for DNA Recoding/Ascension. Once activated, the crystal gene allows for clearer guidance with beings on other dimensions. It acts as a guidance system of sorts, keeping the individual on course in their respective mission. It allows for quicker understanding of the emotional blocks that must be cleared in order to recompile DNA via DNA Recoding.
> Many feel drawn to do grid and vortex work.

When we incarnate on this planet, we do so as willing souls in an effort to grow and learn from the karma of past experiences. As such; our world is set aside as a place where we can work out our differences free of the memories that created the conflicts. When we enter into this realm, we forget from whence we came and a veil of amnesia keeps us from remembering our soul's purpose. Few beings would volunteer to do such work at the risk of forgetting who they are and losing their connection with their divine Higher Selves. Starr believes that many of the Starseeds from other worlds have come to Earth for this very purpose and they are here on Earth as representatives of their off-planet civilizations. She says their sole purpose is to create templates that can be used by the members of their home world to overcome some problem that hinders their spiritual evolution as a soul group. Starr also believes that Starseeds commonly have three parents, two Earth parents and one off-world parent. For example there can be an off-world father. In this case the Earth father will be the surrogate. There are also instances when a child has two or more off-world parents, each one contributing DNA to create the Starseeded child. Starr says there is a contract made between the Earth parent and the off-world parent, for the Earth parent to love and rear the Starseed child. Often times the Earth parent is a Starseed as well. This scenario adds credence to the upgraded DNA being found in 1% of the world's population.

I know much of this information may seem a bit strange but we have to understand that there is so much more to us as spiritual beings than we could ever imagine. It's really unfortunate that we have such a limited per view when it comes to things of this nature. We're taught only to believe in what can be observed through the five physical senses while 90% of the Universe remains invisible or unknowable to the person hell-bent on only believing what they can see, touch, hear, taste or smell. We are multidimensional beings yet we only utilize 10% of our capabilities at best. I find it very interesting that we only utilize 10% of our brains potential while the other 90% remains a mystery. The microcosm of the human body emulates the macrocosm of the Universe and once we are able to harness the full potential of our minds, we will then be able to experience the full potential of the Universe. The unknowable would suddenly become knowable and what we once thought of as imaginary would suddenly become a reality. Imagine what would happen once we learned to utilize all 64 codons of our DNA. There would be no sickness, no limitations and we would be reunited with our true, higher selves. We would become *"as the gods,"* knowing all things. Interdimensional travel would be possible, and we would have the ability to travel the distant stars rediscovering our divine heritage. We are all Starseeds who have willingly chosen planet Earth as our learning ground for growth, expansion and ascension.

Walk-Ins

Aside from Starseeds, there is also what is called a "Walk-In," whereby a pre-arranged agreement is made between two souls to occupy the same physical body during the life of the vehicle. A Walk-in is thought to be a person whose original soul has departed his or her body and been replaced with a new soul either temporarily or permanently. The term "Walk-in" is an ancient concept first described in Hinduism whose modern name originated in the Spiritualist faith and was popularized by the New Age movement. It later became a popular theme through the writings of Ruth Montgomery.

When the individuated, embodied part of Spirit, the Soul, has completed what it set out to accomplish in a lifetime, it has three basic options: take on a new life goal (Reincarnation-in-Same-Body), die, or walk-out. If the Soul chooses to walk-out, an agreement is made with another Soul to walk-in and continue the physical embodiment. This is not to be confused with soul possession. It is not a requirement that a person be a Walk-in to ascend. It is simply an individual agreement and another way of entering onto the planet. In most cases a Walk-in is not two lives in conjunction but rather it occurs simultaneously in a synchronistic type of way. Upon completion of one life's journey in that particular incarnation, another soul enters it at an agreed upon time. In some cases though, the original soul is said to remain present, coexisting or integrating with the new one. Typically this exchange can happen without notice because on a mental level we are unconscious of the "when" and "how" this is to take place. Often times the soul contracts we make prior to incarnating are forgotten until we are able to fully interpret and understand our soul-mission. In most cases, neither soul knows exactly what has taken place only that something has occurred. In some rare situations, a Walk-in can be fully conscious of his/her mission upon coming into a physical vehicle and sometimes, the person walking out will also be aware of the transition. Nevertheless, the transition between two souls often referred to as "*soul-braiding*" is never easy to say the least. What will typically occur for an exiting soul are feelings or longings of moving on. This deeply rooted sense of longing creates a vibrational frequency around the individual that attracts or magnetizes the appropriate circumstance for a traumatic or near death experience where the transition can be made. At the precise moment, the departing soul exhales and takes its last physical breath while the entering soul inhales taking its first physical breath. And from that point on, for the purpose of evolution, the leaving soul moves on to its next form, thus allowing for the agreed upon soul to occupy its physical vessel in order to carry out its Earthly mission.

"Walking-in" seems like a strange concept but in truth it's actually not. In fact, we are all Walk-ins to some degree and we have all had some type of soul agreement to take on human form at some point throughout our journey. The concept of a Walk-in is sometimes hard for people to believe. If you think about it, everyone is a Walk-in in the sense that everyone walks into or becomes fused in a baby's body in its early stages of development. The only difference here is that the Walk-in moves into an adult body rather than an infant body. The term "Walk-in" is differentiated from being born because typically in order to come through the birth canal one would have to lose all awareness of why they have come here in order to further learn from new experiences. This is the primary reason for incarnating, which is to experience the density of human form with all the nuances, emotions, and feelings associated with having a physical body. Our physical bodies help with the learning process because our soul (which is our divine aspect) now has a physical constitution in which to experience the result of its choices through free will and the law of cause and effect. These choices begin to form the "*karmic cycle*" for that physical form to endure, integrate and ultimately transcend. One of the prerequisites for "Walking-in" to a pre-existing form is to take on the "*karma*" associated with the vehicle of which it is attached.

If we look at the concept of "Walking-in" from a different perspective, perhaps it will help us understand how the body is merely a vehicle for transporting the actual soul or essence of an individual. When a fetus is formed through conception, it is only a developing form of life. In its early stages, perhaps for the first 4 to 5 months, the fetus is nothing more than a physical form lacking the soul or spirit which quickens the fetus. Perhaps this is the reason why the Quran, for example, forbids abortion after 120 days, once the soul is formed. Prior to that time, the soul (psyche or consciousness) "hovers" until the physical fetal brain is sufficiently matured to accept such an energy fusion or transference safely. At the precise moment of quickening prior to the fifth month, a certain type of an electrical jolt or psychic-physical significance fuses soul and body and produces self-awareness. In that instant, miraculously, a human being is created. So it's safe to say that the developing fetus is really nothing more than a shell or a casing in which the soul enters. It is merely a living human form, matter, separate, with as yet no separate identity or self-consciousness of its own. At the moment of quickening which is when the designated soul enters the fetus, it becomes conscious and self-aware.

We are all spiritual beings inhabiting physical bodies in order to experience life on Earth. We are each spiritual beings having a human experience by way of physical incarnation. In Hindu beliefs, each person is comprised of several bodies, including the physical, astral, mental, refined, and so on. So a Walk-in can take one or many of these bodies. At the time of the Walk-in, the old spiritual, mental and emotional bodies are released with the original occupant as the total life experience and the new spiritual, mental and emotional bodies of the incoming soul are attached to the physical body. New patterns and emotions are brought into the etheric body and the old patterns are released. It is the etheric and physical bodies that sustain continuity.

A new Walk-in is like a newborn baby. In most cases this is an advantage because the Walk-in has not been indoctrinated into any false sense of understanding by having gone through the developing patterns and learning stages of the previous soul. And since the emotional and mental bodies are "new" they have not yet been imprinted from the environment. Souls normally come into bodies of infants, and spend many years growing, learning and being educated, but a Walk-in comes into an older body and takes over the memories of the body, bypassing all of the enculturation and educational learning. This is a favorable condition because at times it can become very difficult to overcome what we were previously taught in order to fully understand the vastness of who and what we truly are as spiritual beings. Walk-ins are afforded the opportunity to bypass the process of childhood maturation and Earth socialization which increases the likelihood of their awakening and remembering their soul purpose much faster. It was Albert Einstein who said "The only thing that gets in the way of my learning is my education."

Similar to a baby, a Walk-in is a sponge for the emotions, traits and beliefs of the people around them so it is vitally important that a new Walk-in carefully chooses the people they spend time with for they will be imprinted with those people's qualities and biases whether they are enlightened or not. This allows them to stay very much in tune with their mission and the reality of their nature which is eternal. This can be somewhat awkward for the relationships that have already been developed with the parting soul because many of its immediate friends, family and loved ones will not be able to accept the fact that the person they once knew has moved on and the person occupying the body is not the same personality they are familiar with. This is usually why many marriages of Walk-ins typically don't last very long.

All souls come to this planet in order to accomplish missions of cosmic significance and the Earth plane is a wonderful way to expedite that spiritual learning process particularly now during our ascension to the higher dimensions. Based on recent studies, the number of Walk-ins and Starseeds has increased exponentially in recent times because many of them have volunteered to assist the Earth during this time of ascension. This is the reason why the waiting list to occupy a human body is so immensely long at this time. As a means to circumvent this process and enter the Earth plane a lot sooner, agreements have been made for two souls to occupy one body which makes perfect sense when you think about it. If I came here on a spiritual journey of evolution, (as I have), and I was able to experience the lessons in which I sought to have prior to my physical body expiring, why would I still need the vessel? I wouldn't. Therefore, in knowing before hand exactly which lessons I would need to experience, upon completing those lessons I would allow another soul to occupy my earthly body and make use of it for the sole purpose of their spiritual journey. Sound crazy . . . ? I'm sure it does, in fact I struggled with this one for some time until I was finally able to free my mind from the confines of what I thought was normal. From what I understand, one of the reasons why a "Walk-out" would volunteer the use of their body vessel is because they are somehow propelled along in their own ascension. I've come to understand now that anything is possible and just because I've never heard of a concept or because something appears to be unimaginable, doesn't necessarily mean it's untrue. Once I was able to adopt the idea that everything is simply energy and that energy can change and transform as often as it likes, I was finally able to start accepting the full aspect of metaphysical concepts and how nothing is what it seems and therefore anything is possible.

My first introduction to this concept came in 2004 when I read an interview from the author and founder of the Flower of Life teachings, Drunvalo Melchizedek. In that interview, he talked about having been a "Walk-in," a term of which I had not heard up to that point but for some reason the truth of which he spoke resonated within my being. Here is a full account of that interview where he discusses how another person actually occupied his body until he was ready to utilize it. He says that person undertook certain training and schooling that he was later able to use. This was all done through prior agreement because it is illegal, according to Universal Law at the highest level, to take over a body without having prior consent. Taking over a body without having prior consent would constitute a "possession" which is entirely different from being a soul agreement. However, in Drunvalo's case, his walk-in experience was somewhat unique in that he actually remembered everything that took place. He says he can remember almost every minute of coming through the dimensional levels, from the thirteenth all the way down to the third dimension. He says he purposely placed a veil over his memory of the thirteenth dimension because to have any memory of life on that level would be far too painful to bear. He says there is no way we could exist here on the third dimension and maintain full memory of what the thirteenth dimension is like. He does remember being on the thirteenth dimension and being asked by his father to come here, and he also recalls being given a movement pattern to move inside the "Great Void," which is what he had to go through to get here.

This information was fascinating to me especially since I was completely unaware of there ever being a thirteenth dimension. Drunvalo goes on to say he moved in this pattern through the "Great Void" for a long time. He doesn't know how long it was in Earth time, but it was a long time, perhaps millions of years or so. From there, he continued to move until light reappeared, and at that time and place he was met by a being called Machiavinda. He then went through the center of a Nebula, the middle star in the belt of Orion. Supposedly, this is one of the primary Stargates to other dimensional levels. There are believed to be thirteen different Stargates in our galaxy with the Halls of Amenti being one, but the middle star in the belt of Orion is considered to be a very special one. At this Stargate, great light and great darkness operate very close together and it is from this Stargate that many of the interdimensional beings such as the Greys or Reptilians emanate. Drunvalo goes on to say that after going through the belt of Orion, he headed for the Pleiades with his destiny being a particular fourth-dimensional planet with a green atmosphere. While on this planet he had no actual dense form but he was conscious of his form being a ball of light. There, he says he gestated in a baby's body and kept it for about fifteen Earth years. He discovered that the Pleiades contained a Galactic University where all its inhabitants dwell on the higher overtones of the fourth dimension and all learning is accomplished through pleasure and joy and all teachings utilize games. Upon gaining the knowledge he needed on the Pleiades, he then transported to the third planet out from Sirius B which was a water world. The Sirians he says are also on the fourth dimension but on a lower overtone than the Pleiadians where they do not experience joy and pleasure to the same degree. On this marine planet, Drunvalo says he had no body and he was just consciousness. Here he existed by attaching himself to a very large being, a female orca whale. He swam with this whale for about one year, and while he swam with her, she told him the history of the Earth. She had the total memory pattern of Earth encoded inside of her. Drunvalo says his joyous interlude ended when three fourteen-to-sixteen-foot-tall humanoid Pleiadians came to him and said it was time to go. They took him to the land mass of the planet he was on and gave him an already-made adult male Sirian body at which time he discovered how other beings in most places of the Galaxy don't waste bodies the way Earth humans do. The body he was given contained the memory patterns of how to run the Sirian ship he was provided. He, along with 350 crew members, took this Sirian ship with a prepared flight pattern for Earth. This involved flying from Sirius B right through the middle of Sirius A. He says you can pass through successfully simply by tuning to the same vibration as the Sun so that hot is no longer hot in the sense of the word. Ninety seconds later, they came out through our Sun. This is made possible because of our intimate connection with Sirius. Using this maneuver, he and the crew reached the orbital field of Venus, the world containing the Hathor race which is considered to be the most advanced beings in this solar system. After some adventures in dimensional reality on Venus, they transited to Earth and came in one overtone higher than our own dimensional level. Drunvalo says he left his Sirian body and ignited into a ball of light. He describes it as a "Shift in Consciousness" before his rude introduction to polarity consciousness. He shifted upward into the Earth's fourth dimensional level and from there kept climbing dimensional levels looking for a trace of life but found none on the fourth or fifth dimension. Finally, he was able to find the Ascended Masters on the tenth, eleventh and twelfth overtones of the sixth dimension where he joined them and learned from them from 1819 to 1850. In 1850, Drunvalo was born as a female into the Taos tribe in New Mexico where he maintained this woman's body for forty years but in 1890 he left it consciously by holding her breath. He returned to the sixth dimensional level and stayed this time until 1972 where on April 10, 1972, he "walked into" his current body in one breath. The spirit leaving breathed out while he breathed in. That was it, clean and legal. He says he communicated with the departing spirit for almost nine years prior to making his transition as a Walk-in. This is a very fascinating account of one soul's journey as a Walk-in. At first brush it almost sounds like an epic tale of science-fiction but upon opening up to a higher understanding of things, truth always sounds like fiction. In fact, real truth in most cases *is* stranger than fiction.

Another detailed account of a walk-in situation was given by Jelaila Starr author of *We are The Nibiruans: Return of The 12ᵗʰ Planet* and *The Mission Remembered*, where she discusses a soul arrangement where she agreed to walk-out as Jocelyn and allow Jelaila Starr her ninth-dimensional oversoul to walk-in. In her accounting, Starr talks about the many differences between her and her soul-cohort where it took her a long period of time before she actually became aware of what happened. She says in her case, she agreed to complete Jocelyn's soul contract before beginning her own work. This became a bit confusing to her because she thought she was still Jocelyn yet she was acting from both her "tapes" or pre-conditioning. This, she says, is the reason for the confusion many Walk-ins have. She says everything about her changed from her clothes, her appetite and her personality. This is not uncommon for most Walk-ins which is why many people who have undergone this transition without knowing it can sometimes feel as if they are losing a grasp on life. Not only does this pose a problem for the individual undergoing the transition but also for the people that have become accustomed to the person being a certain way.

What I would like for you to understand here is that there are all sorts of things that occur beyond human logic. Many of us are so conditioned by our parents, society, the church and many other institutions to believe only in what our logic tells us. But in truth, there is far more to be learned by letting go of what is considered to be logical or practical according to modern day standards and learn to embrace the unimaginable and the unknown. We each might be members of these special soul groups that have elected to Walk-in in order to help raise planetary consciousness but unless and until we embrace this possibility, our awakening will only be prolonged. We have all chosen to "Walk-in" during this unique time in Earth's history and it is up to each of us to remember our soul purpose for being here which is to help usher in the higher dimensional frequencies of the fourth and fifth densities.

Light Worker

In addition to the many Starseeds, Indigos and Walk-Ins, there are also Light-Workers which are highly enlightened beings that have chosen to bring more light to this planet. Light-workers are not Starseeds or Walk-ins but both can become Light-workers once they make a conscious choice to begin their spiritual path and assist others. Unlike Starseeds who have existed in human form for only one or two life-cycles or Walk-ins who have just recently acquired a physical body, Light-Workers have continued to evolve on different planes over a series of countless existences until finally reaching a point of awakened enlightenment. Accordingly, some of us have been with the Earth for millennia, some of us only since Lemuria, some of us only since Atlantis, and some of us only since the end of the "dark ages." By recognizing the divine presence within all beings, the Light-worker is better able to serve humanity.

Light-workers are constantly active in enlightenment or in cultivating enlightenment in others and have taken it upon themselves to help bring others to a more heightened state of awareness. A true Light-worker is any being who is aware of their eternal nature which is the "I Am" presence and acts in accordance with it. Hence, anyone can become a Light-worker after coming into balance and raising their consciousness. Additionally; Light-workers are souls who have a strong inner desire to spread Light, knowledge, freedom and Self-Love on Earth. They are often attracted to spirituality and to therapeutic work of some kind. This often makes them feel different or isolated from other people. By experiencing different kinds of obstacles throughout their journey, they are provoked into finding their own unique path. As a result, Light-workers are usually always solitary individuals, not fitting into fixed societal structures.

The term "Light-Worker" can be a misconception because it suggests that some of us are superior or more enlightened than others. This is not the case because eventually, we all become awakened or enlightened. However, some of us have evolved to a greater degree and have already reached a critical point in our evolution because we are older than most souls presently incarnate on Earth. According to Pamela Kribe who channels the being known as "Jeshua," "We must understand that a Light-worker is not something we simply are or aren't, it is something we become, once we go through the journey of experience: experiencing light and dark, actually being light and dark." As such; Light-workers possess the ability to attain spiritual awakening much faster than others because they carry within them certain coding for a more rapid spiritual awakening. At the designated time, the individual becomes activated thus allowing them to receive Light in the form of information. It's an awakening of the spirit which caters to a rapid progression. Because of this, Light-workers appear to be on a faster track than most people. In fact, many of us have lived many, many lives on other planes and reached a particular stage of enlightenment long prior to ever incarnating on Earth. This is what distinguishes us from the rest of Earth's population. Earth souls are believed to have incarnated in physical bodies here on Earth relatively early in their development. As a result, they started their Earthly journey when their souls were yet in the infant stage while the Light-workers soul had already matured. Below is a description (taken from Pamela Kribe at www. jeshua.net) of some of the psychological traits of a Light-worker.

Psychological characteristics of Light-workers:

From early on in their life, they feel they are different. More often than not they feel isolated from others, lonely and misunderstood. They will often become individualists who will have to find their own unique ways in life.

They have trouble feeling at home within traditional jobs and/or organization structures. Light-workers are naturally anti-authoritarian which means they naturally resist decisions or values based solely on power or hierarchy. This anti-authoritarian trait is present even if they seem timid and shy. It is connected to the very essence of their mission here on Earth.

Light-workers feel drawn to helping people as a therapist or as a teacher. They may be psychologists, healers, teachers, nurses, etc. Even if their profession is not about helping people in a direct manner, the intent to contribute to the higher good of humanity is clearly present.

Their vision of life is colored by a spiritual sense of how all things are co-related. They consciously or subconsciously carry memories within them of non-Earthly spheres of light. They may occasionally feel homesick for these spheres and feel like a stranger on Earth.

They deeply honor and respect life which often manifests as a fondness for animals and a concern for the environment. The destruction of parts of the animal and vegetable kingdoms on Earth by human doing invokes deep feelings of loss and grief in them.

They are kind-hearted, sensitive and empathetic. They may have trouble dealing with aggressive behavior and they generally experience difficulties in standing up for themselves. They can be dreamy, naive or highly idealistic, as well as insufficiently grounded, i.e. down-to-Earth. Because they easily pick up negative feelings and moods of people around them, it is important for them to spend time alone on a regular basis. This enables them to distinguish between their own feelings and those of others. They need solitary time to touch base with themselves and with mother Earth.

They have lived many lives on Earth in which they were deeply involved with spirituality. They were present in overwhelming numbers in the old religious orders of the past as monks, nuns, hermits, psychics, witches, shamans, priests, priestesses, etc. They were the ones providing a bridge between the visible and the invisible, between the daily context of Earth life and the mysterious realms of the afterlife, realms of God and the spirits of good and evil. For fulfilling this role, they were often rejected and persecuted. Many of them were sentenced to the stake for the gifts they possessed. The traumas of persecution left deep traces within their soul's memory. This may presently manifest as a fear of being fully grounded, i.e. a fear to be really present, because they remember being brutally attacked for who they were.

At present, there are literally millions of self proclaimed Light-Workers active on planet Earth all operating at different levels of consciousness. In fact, if you are reading this, more than likely, you are a Light-worker and you are here to help uplift the vibration of Love and Light on this planet. My spiritual awakening started some twenty years ago during a time in my life when I was at the lowest point of my existence. It was the quintessential "Dark night of the soul." But, like always, it was in the depths of the darkest regions of human nature that this blossoming occurred for me. It's usually at these times when we realize there has to be something more to life than what we've been taught by society, the church, especially the church, our parents, the schools, the media etc . . . I started on a path of true self discovery by seeking to understand (for myself) exactly why I was here on this planet and what purpose I was to serve. It was in that instant that I began to awaken from the illusion (Maya) of my life. I stopped using drugs and alcohol and set out on a course of total recovery including mind, body and spirit. That was in 1990 and from that day to this very moment as I write these words; I have continued to pursue the truth and knowledge of which I freely divulge here in this book. Although I've had what I would consider to be "set-backs," I've also come to understand how every situation in my life is simply a time of enlightenment and some how or another, these "set-backs" can also be "set-ups" for greater opportunities. My deepest lessons and the truest test of my character have all come during times when I faltered.

Therefore, it is incumbent upon me to continuously give back in the form of wisdom and knowledge so that others might be enlightened by not only my experiences but also by my countless years of study and research into esoteric matters. It is not my purpose to keep this knowledge for myself for where much is given much is required. It is my goal to make that which is "esoteric," (hidden, secret) into an "exoteric," (open, exposed) knowledge that is available to us all. I intend to "shed light" in the world by openly talking about the mind control of organized institutional systems such as the governments, churches, religions and false mass conceptions. My purpose on this planet is to help change the paradigm of false belief systems through; writing, lecturing, counseling, teaching, workshops and any other venues that will allow me a platform in which to be heard.

It is for this reason that I consider myself to be among the many Light-workers of our time.

Cosmic Law

Much of what I discuss here on Cosmic Law is extrapolated from various authors some of which I cannot name as a huge portion of this chapter was derived from various sources. Some of it has been extracted, copied verbatim (quoted), or revised. I do not fully understand these laws, for there is much that I personally do not know. Nevertheless, I remain indebted to these various authors for their contribution on this subject as my scope of understanding is rudimentary at best. This work is thus solely not my own but the result of a collective mind inspired by the Universal intelligence that is us all. I am merely regurgitating and interpreting this information. Therefore, you should not accept everything that I put forth here. Having said that; you should always refer to your own inner sense of awareness and you should trust your inner-guide as your teacher. As such; what is revealed in this book should merely be considered as a guideline for your own research, study, and application.

❖ *Cosmic Law*: Cosmic Law is the attribute of Divine Intelligence in operation throughout the Universe. What we call *Logos*, is merely the nature and behavior of the One Universal being, expressing through its many facets. Greek philosopher Heraclitus described the *Logos* as ". . . the principle of order and knowledge in the Universe." He believed that ". . . all things come to be in accordance with this Logos." This implies that everything happens for a particular reason and although the reasons may not be apparent, we can rest assured in knowing that something is definitely governing the outcome to all of lifes situations. Nothing happens by chance and there are no coincidences. To speak in terms of chance or coincidence would suggests that our Universe is a random set of events and therefore nothing upon nothing can be predicted with any degree of accuracy or certainty. I tend to disagree. If you believe in an intelligent Universe, there's no way possible not to believe in order. Although we tend to differ on what labels we ascribe to this intelligence, Its existence is indisputable. Some call this intelligence God while others call it Divine Mind. In Stoicism, *Logos* is the active principle of the Cosmos usually identified with God. Stoics believe it to be the source of all activity and generation which is the power of reason residing in the human soul. For them, *Logos* is merely Cosmic Laws which are the rational principles that govern and develops the Universe. On this I can agree.

The Cosmos would be chaotic without some form of intelligence governing and overseeing it's multitude of laws. Behind all occurrences, there is a form of intelligence masterfully weaving a thread of consistency and continuity. We refer to this as "synchronicity." Although we can't see this Intelligence, we know it exist simply by recognizing the precision and ease with which the Universe is synchronized. There is a divine and unknown purpose to everything. The planetary bodies move and function according to this divine purpose. This decree is the mind of God being executed on all levels of existence and there is no place, dimension, solar system, or galaxy where it does not function or operate as the administrative organ of the Cosmos. Every event from the largest to the smallest is superseded by Cosmic Law or the expression of Universal Intelligence. Every manifested thing, from atom to solar system is but a thought in the mind of God.

Everything takes place according to a grand and what appears to be a miraculous way. But our criteria for evaluating and judging these natural expressions are subjective and faulty from the spiritual point of view. We witness these laws in physics all the time but much of what we don't see is also governed by the very same Intelligence. Life and truth are not confined solely to this physical realm and planet. We should understand that what Cosmic Law produces in the physical world, also has its source in higher dimensions. Although some Cosmic Laws may be confined to certain dimensions, these laws, in and of themselves are living potentials on every dimension. In fact; they exist in the Mind or Beingness of God which eventually become manifested on the physical plane. That being the case, it's easy to understand how becoming aware of these laws, can change or determine the outcome of an event. For example; we know that based upon the Law of Gravity, what goes up, must come down. Therefore by knowing this, we can expect with a degree of certainty exactly what the outcome will be whenever the Law of Gravity is in effect.

❖ *Law of Gravity*: The Law of Gravity has existed long before its discovery and non-belief in this law does not affect its being or cause it to be non-existent. Cosmic Laws are impartial. If a highly spiritual person were to fall off a building, gravity would force them to the ground just as it would an immoral person simply because it's the law and the law is immutable and no *"respecter of persons."* It simply is.

You don't have to be aware of Cosmic Laws in order for them to work, they are always working. Back of every situation, there is always a force at work adhering to a strict set of principles. Once we become aware of the rules, we can learn to predict with a certain degree of accuracy what the outcome will be. Those who are ignorant to Cosmic Laws simply go through life lamenting their fate which no being, God or otherwise has predetermined except for those individuals themselves, whether consciously or unconsciously. Ignorance or denial of Cosmic Laws does not abrogate their existence. The first thing we must do is to become aware of these laws and in doing so, we can learn to align ourselves with them in order to create a more fluid-like existence with each occurrence being predicted with precision and ease.

Knowledge of Cosmic Laws can help us overcome or avoid the many unnecessary, excessive hardships and struggles in our lives. Easier said than done?—Of course. However, by learning to recognize the rules, we can better function in the game. By knowing, understanding, and applying Cosmic Laws in a positive, constructive, and creative manner we automatically promote our spiritual growth and evolution. But we don't want to wait until we're on the battle field to put on our armor. It's best to arm ourselves prior to going into the skirmish. We have to know the rules of the game in order to succeed and whether we realize it or not, life *is* the game. The ones who have taken the time to learn the rules become better equipped because they know what to expect based upon Cosmic order. We commit an act and we get a certain result based upon our actions, it never fails. By knowing the causes of certain effects and by tracing the causation of life's various situations, we can begin to learn the nature of certain Cosmic Laws and learn to abide by them by utilizing them for our own benefit. Some of these laws have already been discussed at length in the chapter on Hermetic Wisdom. Nevertheless, I feel it necessary to include further discussion on some of the other key laws. Hopefully by knowing this information, it will encourage us to learn the rules so that we can become better players in the game of life? Agreed . . . so, let's take a look at some of the rules and hopefully, this will allow us to become more skillful in life by learning to align ourselves with the Universe. This knowingness will enable us to become conscious co-creators with God and thus masters of life. *We* determine our reality and *we* are the sole cause of everything that transpires in our lives whether we're consciousness of it or not. By knowing the cause of our situations through a better understanding of Cosmic Laws and the principles involved, we can each take proper control and direction of our own lives. This approach helps eliminate suffering which allows for peace, health, abundance, and greater prosperity to be attained.

One way to create a life free of chance and uncertainty is to understand the Cosmic *"Law of Causality,"* otherwise known as *"Cause and Effect."* Words like; "chance," "coincidence," or "accident" are names of the functions of the unrecognized influence of the *Law of Karma*. In *Ultimate Truth: Book I*, I write:

> "The Random House unabridged dictionary suggests that Causality is *'the relationship between one event called "Cause" and another event called "Effect" which is the direct consequence of the first.'* Our life is a series of overlapping events one giving rise to the other through the mechanics of Causality and ignorance. We must awaken from our ancient slumber so that we may redirect our purpose with the full awareness of our being. Then, we will no longer live a hapless existence full of unsuspecting events but rather one of purpose and intent."

Simply put; every action will bring about an equal reaction and every occurrence has a cause. In order to best understand an outcome, we would have to trace each situation back to its beginning which generally has its origin in the mind which culminates into thoughts. For we know all too well that thought is energy and it can create just as well. Thoughts are things which ultimately become our reality. Therefore; Mind or Consciousness is the primal cause of all things. As such, everything we experience today is actually the result of a prior thought which manifested on the physical plane through a series of events which have been orchestrated by Divine Intelligence. Our thoughts are then carried out as deeds which ultimately design our lives and the experiences we are to have through the Cosmic Law of Karma.

❖ *Law of Karma*: There's an old adage which says; "Sew a thought; reap an action. Sew an action; reap a habit. Sew a habit; reap a character. Sew a character; reap a destiny." This series of actions begins with the thought as the original cause and what typically follows are the results of our own doing. Karma is the result of our own past actions and our own present doings. The Law of Karma is neutral and therefore, impersonal. *Karma* is not punitive. It does not punish. It is designed to assist us with our evolutionary process. It is educative in nature and is the task-master that sometimes makes us learn harsh lessons. What we put out, returns unto us or "*as ye sow so shall ye reap.*" It's a known fact that whatever we put into motion with our thoughts, words and deeds have their effects and consequences, and they always rebound back to us. This is the boomerang effect of the Law of Karma. This is why it is so imperative that we "*do until others as we would have them do unto us.*" All actions have their equal reaction. So, in being kind to others, we essentially receive that in return. Energy returns to its source whether instantly, later in life, or in later lifetimes. This is why it is necessary for the Law of Reincarnation to exist. In general, *Reincarnation* as a law refers to the periodical incarnation of a divine spark of God into the physical realm for the purpose of evolution, for the purpose of spiritual growth, discipline, learning, and remembrance; although in the process of incarnation, the soul, or divine spark often creates *Karma* which binds it to the law and prolongs its needless stay in the realm of matter. This karmic bondage is also one of the factors causing the soul to forget its true purpose of being.

❖   *Law of One*: Another one of nature's crucial Cosmic Laws is the Law of One or the Law of Unity which says; absolutely everything is inextricably linked together in one way or another. This is the blending of one's consciousness with all Mind and all Life in all space and dimensions. It is to become one with that which we already are and to realize and have awareness that we are God in essence. In the movie Avatar released in 2009, James Cameron depicts this truth by showing how an indigenous tribe of sapient humanoids, called the Na'vi are able to co-exist in harmony with nature, while worshiping a mother goddess called *Eywa* which is the life force that maintains all existence. Although many of us hold movies such as Avatar, Star Wars, and the Matrix to be "science fiction," in truth they are derived from a higher form of understanding making them "science fact."

Everything throughout all time and space is inextricably linked either directly or indirectly to everything else. Everything is connected at the core. This implies that what happens on one level of existence, affects everything else on all levels. What we think affects others on a mental level; what we feel affects others on an emotional level; and what we do physically affects others on the material level. We're all One and underlying all manifestations there is only one ever evolving essence which we call God, the Creator or the Universe. Every manifestation in the Universe may be reduced to its common denominator which is energy. Everything is composed of energy vibrating at varying frequencies. Energy possesses characteristics attributed to God: omnipresence, omnipotence, omniscience. This would indicate that energy is identical to God or at least a part of divine expression. That being the case, every manifestation in the Universe is but God's expression, or God's being. Sometimes I don't like to use the word "God." This isn't because I don't honor, love and cherish the All but because it has become synonymous with religion and all the atrocities associated with the wide-spread destruction of doctrine and dogma. What I'm referring to here in using the word "God," is the essence and life of all things being expressed as the One Universal Energy that permeates all forms, the reality of the manifested and non-manifested Universe in its totality. Almost all religions (in their most pristine forms) are aware of the truth of the One Essence in all and the Unity of Being through the Law of One.

While there are many Cosmic Laws, some of which are known and many of which are not, it would take far too much time to fully delineate each law here in the breadth of this book. Having said this, from here on out rather than providing you with a lengthy analysis of each law, a basic description and explanation will be provided.

❖ *Law of Labeling/Judgment*: Another Cosmic Law is the Law of Labeling or Judgment. This law basically says; when we label anything, we exclude true information concerning it. This closes us off from further inquiry because the thing becomes obscured by other information stored under the label for that particular thing. One such way is by labeling things as "good" or "bad," "right" and "wrong." Labeling is related to opinions and opinions seldom reflect truth; if they were, they would be deemed as facts. When we label something, we impose the deep structure of the label system used on the way we perceive the thing being labeled.

❖ *Law of Energy Conservation*: There's also the Law of Energy Conservation which says; nothing in nature is ever wasted or destroyed it merely transforms in a continuous flux. Isaac Newton postulated that "energy is never destroyed, it merely transforms from one form to the next." Truth is; the potential energy of this Universe has always remained constant. In Rhonda Byrne's book *The Secret*, one of the writers postulates how energy is the essence of God because it shares the same attributes by it; "*always being present, always is and always was and it can never be destroyed.*" Such is the case to this very day. There is nothing new under the Sun which means the same energy has continually perpetuated itself throughout the ages. Since nature functions in a manner that conserves energy, we must also reflect on its processes in order to fulfill our sense of oneness and harmony with it.

❖   *Law of Association*: We have the Law of Association which says; if two things have something in common, that thing in common can be used to influence both. They also have a mutual influence on each other because of their similarity and the more they have in common, the more influence they exert upon one another. This is very similar to the "Law of Contagion" which says; once things come into contact with one another, they continue to interact at subtle levels after physical separation. More appropriately; this law asserts that once anything comes in contact with a substance, person, or object, it may then be used as a witness or an etheric link for that substance, a person, or an object; and through that link, influence them in certain ways.

❖   *Law of Intelligence*: There's the Law of Intelligence which says; any energy pattern of sufficient complexity will act intelligently when treated as an entity. The more complex an energy-structure, the more intelligence it possesses. The Universe is composed of energy-structures within a greater structural energy-pattern. This is clearly visible when we closely observe the molecular structure of all things. We know that electrons are contained within atoms and atoms are an integral part of a molecule but molecules are only a part of a greater structure called cells and a structure of cells ultimately forms higher living organisms. But this is only the beginning. Human Beings are only a minute part of something much larger. What is important to know here is that at every level, some sort of intelligence is evident and displayed. There is nothing that we can touch, feel, see, or interact with on any level that does not have an intelligence of some kind.

❖   *Law of Self-Preservation*: A law I happen to be particularly fond of is the Law of Self-Preservation which implies how every life-unit is striving to sustain its existence at some level by attempting to exist on a higher spiral of being. We call this, evolution. Fundamentally, all life-units have a right to exist so long as they do not encroach upon the existence of other life-units and disturb the harmony of the Universe. Self-preservation also implies preserving or maintaining the awareness of one's real Self, one's true identity, and one's divine spark at the level of one's mundane consciousness.

❖   *Law of Harmony*: This brings us to the Law of Harmony which says; each life-unit has to be in harmony with its surroundings, with itself, and with the entire Universe in order to evolve and maintain its integrity at every level. Harmony is a direct result of right relationships, which should be ingrained in our behavior and attitude towards our environment, towards others, and towards our higher selves. It is a natural and simple way of life without the indulgence of any excess or shortages. The Buddha spoke of the "Middle-Path" or non-extremes because too much or too little of one thing causes imbalance. Harmony may also be defined as the submission of one's will to Cosmic Laws, to God's unfolding plan and to the Cosmic Intelligences that cooperate with Cosmic Laws in bringing God's Plan into manifestation. Harmony means peace, contentment, and spiritual awareness. Living in attunement and alignment with the laws governing one's being results in harmony. Disharmony with the Universe and with our natural being only results in pain, illness, suffering, misery and "dis-ease." Whenever we find ourselves out-of-harmony with the Universe, divine law always has a way of bringing us back into alignment. The ways and means for this to take place are strictly contingent upon the severity of our disharmony. Some situations demand that we be removed from our environment entirely through incarceration or other forms of institutions, while others simply require a minor readjustment in our approach to how we are living. Our Universe is designed for order and balance, as such; it will not tolerate disruption of its design for any extended period of time. However, it will allow us to correct the injustice before it exacts its retribution.

❖   *Law of Love*: Another very important aspect of Cosmic Law is the Law of Love and everything in the Universe is directed by this decree. Divine Love is the highest vibration known to man and it is the active expression of God-Consciousness. Love gives us access to spiritual and divine energies thus our spiritual growth is dependent upon the unfoldment of Love within our hearts. The greater our unconditional and impersonal Love, directed by wisdom and understanding, the greater our spirituality. Subsequently, Love must first be generated within if we are to experience it coming from without. Before sending Love out to the world, we must first possess it within ourselves, for we cannot give what we do not possess and we cannot transmit something that we do not have.

❖ *Law of Liberty*: The Law of Liberty says all humanity has been given freedom of choice. The gift of freedom of choice should not be misused or abused as they result in negative consequences. Since the divine does not impose its will upon us, likewise we should not impose our will upon others. Every creature enjoys its freedom. It is an instinct implanted in all life-units. Therefore, tyranny and oppression in any form is a crime against liberty. The Law of Liberty declares that all beings are free to express their pristine, innate nature so long as it does not harm anyone or anything; and anyone or anything that interferes with that expression violates this law.

❖ *Law of Circulation*: There's the Law of Circulation which says; whatever resources, energies, abilities and time we possess must be used to promote the welfare of all beings. By circulating our energy, we have it returned to us manifold. But by the same token, when we hold up our energies, possessions, or resources for selfish reasons, this can result in a lifeless conscious state. This is the reason why money is also referred to as "currency." Therefore, it is our privilege to direct this "current" and not to control, possess or own it. All things have been given to us on consignment and this law is associated with the Law of Tithing and is generally applied for prosperity. Tithing doesn't always entail the giving of one's money. We can also tithe our time, energy, knowledge, or earthly goods. By giving away a portion of our earnings or that which we have been blessed with, we ensure their continual supply in abundance. What we give returns to us multiplied. I used to think tithing only meant giving 10% of my earnings and I used to have a real problem with that because I didn't necessarily like contributing to the continued growth and wealth of another while I could barely pay for my own necessities. Today I understand that I can give of my time and my energy and this too is a form of circulating currency. I've come to understand how the vital attitude behind the whole Law of Tithing is that of sincerity. The law works truly if we give in all sincerity without actually expecting anything in return. Today I know that currency is energy and it doesn't necessarily have to be in the form of money that I expend it.

❖ *Law of Discernment*: The Law of Discernment is the law governing the evolutionary progress of life-units possessing human consciousness. This allows us to discern or discriminate between what is real and what is unreal; what is illusory and false, and what is true. The real is immutable, it does not change. Forms are related to illusions, whereas the essence that brought forms into existence is the part of nature that is real. Identifying with what is unreal is ignorance and prolongs our consciousness in a state of slumber. The awakening liberates us from the mortal state. By exercising the Law of Discernment we eventually transcend the lower planes and reach the spiritual dimensions.

❖ *Law of Immortality*: The Law of Immortality says; God is eternal and immortal; and that which contains the essence of God in its inner core is also eternal and immortal even though its outward form, vehicle or expression is subjected to change. Energy is immortal. It cannot be destroyed, only transformed. Forms composing of energy may appear to die or vanish but, scientifically speaking, there is only a molecular or atomic mutation. In actuality, there *is* no death; there is only the transition from one dimensional phase to the other.

❖ *Law of Power*: The Law of Power says; everything is energy, therefore everything has power—the power to influence, the power to create, the power to manifest, the power to sustain, the power to destroy. Though everything has power, no power external to us has control over us unless we allow it. We give our power away by fearing or having negative feelings over a thing. Power or energy may be received through external sources and also shared; however, all of our power comes from within. Power is the result of energy, force, intelligence, and consciousness. The more we acquire or increase the degree or ratio of any of those four principles, the more powerful we become.

❖   *Law of Now*: The Law of Now says; all events; past, present and future are illusory phenomena conceived by the conscious mind. They do not exist in an eternal Universe where there is no real framework or reference point where time may be based. Everything is occurring in the Universe right now. All power, happiness, joy, peace, etc., that we seek should be sought now, not in the abyss of the future. For we have no power in the past or in the future and now is the moment to implement change. Now is the only time we can act. Why should we worry over a future problem that has not occurred and has the probability of not occurring? 90% of everything I've ever worried about in life, never came to pass. Why should we relive traumatic experiences of the past when we should be focusing on the now moment with its many opportunities and possibilities of expansion, understanding and growth? Ancient sages tell us to live a day at a time. 12-step programs implore the individual to live one-day-at-a-time, that is, not to live in the past or in the future, for by dwelling in those two states, we miss the opportunities that are before us. Someone once said to me; "If I spread my legs by putting one foot in the past and the other in the future, I'll end up pissing on today." How painfully true this is.

❖   *Law of Infinity*: The Law of Infinity says; the Universe is infinite and eternal. In actuality, there is no limit to anything and there is always room for growth on the evolutionary path. There is no limit to anything unless we believe that there are limits. There are no limits to what we can do. We manifest limitation by utilizing our creative minds in a narrow, negative sense. In order to properly conceive and apprehend the nature of infinity and eternity, we would have to utilize the higher abstract mind and the higher faculties of the Soul.

❖ *Law of Duality*: The Law of Duality says; any concept or force may be divided into two totally opposite concepts or forces, each of which contains the essence of the other. Every manifestation is an effect of two causes, one primary, the other secondary; one active, the other passive; one positive, the other negative, one electric, the other magnetic. Every magnetic-field possesses a dual quality. We call these qualities, "Polarity." In a general sense, polarity refers to positive and negative poles. This is symbolized by the Tai Chi symbol, the Yin and Yang. Opposites can be defined only in relation to each other. Duality is the sense and perception of our Universe as other than who we are; the seperative "You and I" concept. It defines the world we realize. This law represents the oppositional poles to be found in all planes of manifestation, all levels of becoming. For instance: attraction-repulsion; cold-hot; contraction-expansion; darkness-light; destruction-construction; evil-good; love-fear; night-day; nothing-everything; noumena-phenomena; spirit-matter, etc. However, duality is an illusion of the senses, an illusion perceived by life-units of human and animal consciousness levels. In truth, the absolute state knows only Oneness called "the void."

❖ *Law of Attraction*: The Law of Attraction says; at the atomic or electronic level: like attracts unlike, like repels like. Paradoxically, at the spiritual and psychological levels this is reversed: like attracts like, unlike repels unlike. More simply put: we attract what we are. Whatever the case, the nature of our magnetism attracts to us things that resonate with our radiation. For instance, if we fear a thing and radiate fear, that thing shall be part of our experience for we would attract it to us. Subsequently, this law may be usefully applied to becoming prosperous and wealthy. We can create the conditions we wish to manifest within our consciousness through magnetism. This, along with the proper action and belief, will allow us to create the lives we desire. But we have to start by removing any negative fixations and complexes we have about money or anything related to wealth. Next, the subconscious mind will have to be reprogrammed with new patterns of thought. Often times we are programmed from childhood to have certain ideas about money which can ultimately contradict us later in life. For me, I grew up hearing my mother say things like, "*I'm not made of money,*" or "*Money doesn't grow on trees.*" Consequently, I started to feel as though money was this elusive thing that very few people were able to acquire. This became a part of my subconscious conditioning which would later become a huge disservice to me in my desire for wealth. We ourselves are responsible for our own happiness and misery. We create our own Heaven as well as our own Hell. We are the architects of our own fate and we each are responsible for our own outcomes be it just for today or throughout eternity. Up to this point, we may have believed that life simply happens *to* us. However, our lives do not proceed inward from outside accidental causes toward effects, but rather our thoughts proceed outward from our causative mental desires toward reactive external physical effects. This makes each of us responsible for everything in our lives today whether we label it good, bad or indifferent.

It is very important to fully understand the Law of Attraction because it brings our world into perspective when we understand how everything we have experienced or will ever experience in life, is merely a reflection of how we think and feel on the inside. Struggles, suffering and strife in life are basically expressions of reality that we ourselves create. We participate in creating the world by the way we perceive it. In order for us to change our reality, we must first change what we think.

❖   *Law of Perspective*: which says; our conception, interpretations and beliefs concerning outer reality plays a definite role in determining the reality we are to experience. Subsequently, by changing our perspective of reality, we can also change the perceived world or the reality we see. This is crucial because our inner world has a tremendous impact on the world we touch, see, and act upon and if that reality is shared collectively by many individuals comprising a group-consciousness, then the whole group can effectively bring about change on a larger scale by establishing a collective thought form. I firmly believe most of the world's problems can be solved by simply changing our world view, our attitudes, perspectives, feelings, and beliefs. Needless to say, this method of changing our view of the world internally is how we will create the outer reality we desire.

Much of what we believe to be true is based solely upon where we place our attention. In other words, we tend to believe in what we focus our attention on. In short, we perceive what we wish to perceive. We interpret things in accord with our beliefs. We change facts to fit our conceptions. Our behavior and reactions or responsive actions to the world are dependent upon what world-views we constantly keep alive in our minds by our conscious or subconscious attention. This is made true through the Law of Attention which says; the more evidence we look for to support a given law, conclusion, or world-view the more we will find. Wherever we focus our attention, we broadcast vast amounts of energy. "Energy flows where attention goes" and what we focus on will generally expand. By focusing our attention on an object or situation with a certain thought or feeling, we impress our thought-feeling force upon that object or situation, thus influencing it.

By knowing and understanding these Cosmic Laws, we can help bring about a more harmonious existence for all. And while each individual has the power to transform his or her own personal reality, conversely, a group of individuals possesses the power to transform a collective reality by working together for a common purpose. This is called the Law of Group Conscious. Everyone knows there is more power working in numbers than when working alone. A single person can hardly save the planet from catastrophe but collectively, a shared belief can definitely bring about change on a global scale. The prayers of one individual may have the power to affect two persons and the prayers of two individuals may have the power to affect 4 people and so on. Each time the power is multiplied by two it grows in momentum. This is what will enable us to create Heaven here on Earth. By holding the vision of a Utopian existence, this vibration will become a shared Group-Consciousness thus adding to its efficacy. And in time, this vision will become the "perceived" reality for all.

Cosmic Mind

Cosmic Mind is the unadulterated Mind of God. In Theosophy, it is the sum total of all Divine and spiritual intelligences. It is the essence from which all things manifest. Hence, nothing can exist without being an aspect of Divine Mind. In his writing on *"Cosmic Mind in the Microcosm,"* Rudi Jansma says:

> "In the creation story of the Vishnu Purana, the first thing to manifest at the beginning of our cosmic cycle is Cosmic Intelligence (Mind). From this Cosmic Intelligence emanates the individual intelligences of all existing entities in the Universe. In men and women it manifests as human intelligence, the human mind. But it also appears as the intelligent influence in all of nature's kingdoms, visible and invisible."

All universal order, laws and designs emanate from this Cosmic Intelligence. In terms of creation, first the thought exists within the Mind and given the right set of circumstances, manifestation occurs. This is the basic process for bringing anything into creation on any level. The Cosmic Mind of God first desires to know itself in the form of a Galaxy, a Star, a Planet or a Human embodiment and from that inclination, it simply becomes that in which it desires. This creative process is the express design of all consciousness and we are the unique individuated expression of this all encompassing Mind. It is spirit manifested in human form. The entire Multiverse consisting of untold diversity and countless hues and shades of dimensionality all happen in the Cosmic Mind of God. But, the Cosmic Mind entails so much more than this. It is also, the sum total of all things, all energies and manifestations, all forms, subtle and unpleasant, sacred and ordinary. It is the prevailing condition which in its subtlest form is undifferentiated pure consciousness which is the primordial substance from which the myriad forms of existence emerge. Simply put; all is Mind and Mind is all.

The notion of a Cosmic Mind or an intelligent *universal* principle that unites into a harmonized *whole* is a difficult concept for the average person to understand. Truth is, not only is this concept difficult for the average person but it is also difficult for the philosopher and scientist alike.

Consciousness is universal and within every organism there is a vital principle or intelligence which leads one to confirm the existence of this Cosmic Mind. For example; take the human body with its multitude of functions all of which are governed by a form of intelligence beyond our individual perception. While there are some functions such as those orchestrated by the conscious mind through the five senses, there are also other functions being carried out systematically on a subconscious level without the help of the conscious mind. The vital organs of the body are able to carry out their designated tasks and yet we have no direct control over these bodily functions. Trillions of cells perform without being instructed because every cell in the human body is furnished with its own brain, with a memory of its own, and therefore with the experience and power to discriminate between things. And since discrimination is the basis of consciousness, the intelligence of Cosmic Mind is also represented within each cell. Madame Helena. P. Blavatsky tells us in *Kosmic Mind* that; "Every atom is a little Universe in itself; and every organ and cell in the human body is endowed with a brain of its own, with memory, therefore, experience and discriminative powers." Thomas Edison believed that even atoms possess a certain measure of intelligence and this same intelligence is governing the vital processes within the body of which without, it would cease to perform in the way that it does. This Cosmic intelligence or consciousness is what governs large bodies such as planets, solar systems, galaxies and universes. In other words, the macrocosmic intelligence which guides the processes of the Universe is also reflected on a microcosmic scale in each individual being. It is the Cosmic Mind in action on all levels of existence from the diminutive to the magnificent.

Cosmic Mind is eternal, immutable, impersonal, ever active, not only on the plane of physical matter, but also on the invisible inner planes. Hence, this intelligence is no respecter of persons and thus all things are subject to its precepts as Cosmic Laws. The Universe is not a chaotic place and to suggest that chaos exists in the Universe would be suggesting there is no intelligence. This would imply there is no order behind every occurrence or that there is no "plan" or direction involved in the evolutionary process. Progress or evolution in and of itself implies a *plan,* and a plan would therefore have to imply a *"Planner"* of a cosmic nature. The Cosmic or Universal Mind serves as this planner and the plan is the intelligent design which underlies, interpenetrates and sustains all forms as the Universal Life-Force. It is this cosmic plan which provides for the unity and evolution of all sentient and conscious life. Conversely, the mind of man is capable of apprehending and reflecting this Cosmic Mind. The spiritual aspect in every individual is one with Cosmic Mind and it is up to each individual to cultivate the "Higher" aspects of ones self or the Divine Mind within in order to align with the *Atman* or Higher Self. As I stated earlier, there is a Cosmic Mind or one stream of consciousness permeating all existence and this consciousness stream has been the same energy manifesting over and over again in countless forms throughout the ages.

There is no "new" energy. The energy today is the same primordial energy which created and maintained the Universe we know of as well as the innumerable ones that we do not. The energy being animated throughout our continuous life streams is the same energy which can never be destroyed. It is immortal. Hence; so are we. The pure essence of our being *is* the Higher Self which is one with the Cosmic Mind. They are essentially "one-and-the-same" with the only difference being one of degree. The "I" that we see when we look in the mirror is really not the totality of our being it is only one small aspect of whom and what we truly are. Our Soul or Essence is one with Divine Mind which is being carried out during this particular version of our awareness. And, considering our limited per view when it comes to previous life streams, it is virtually impossible for us to remember let alone understand the purpose of our prior incarnations. However, the Cosmic Mind functions as a continual unbroken form of the Higher Self which is the plane of eternal wisdom. From this vantage point, it is able to survey the past, the present and the future with the power of its time-less awareness and it is from this knowingness that our incarnated personal consciousness is able to retain the limited memories of each manifestation. Our physical mind simply serves as the emissary in the field of incarnation in gross matter with the higher Cosmic Mind overshadowing each incarnation. There is but one common source of all beings; one common root of all life and consciousness; and one common goal of evolution. In other words, there is only One Mind, One Life and One Consciousness of which each of us is a mere expression. The supreme realization is that all things are interdependent and essentially One. It is the Cosmic Mind which connects, compiles and computes all life streams as its own. We are simply giving expression to the one Cosmic Mind in the way that we do through our unique personalities and evolution in nature is no more and no less than the ever continuing cycle of consciousness unfolding as the Cosmic Mind.

The Over-Soul

"The soul looks steadily forward, creating a world before her, leaving worlds behind her. She has no dates, nor rites, nor persons, nor specialties, nor men. The soul knows only the soul; the web of events is the flowing robe in which she is clothed."
—*Ralph Waldo Emerson*

As I have said, the Cosmic Mind also known as the "Over-Soul," functions as a continual unbroken form of the Higher Self which is the plane of eternal wisdom. It is the collective indivisible Soul of which all individual souls and identities are included. This Over-Soul is able to survey the past, the present and the future with the power of its timeless awareness. It is from this knowing that incarnated personal consciousness is able to retain the limited memories of each physical manifestation. For this reason, the Over-Soul serves as the repository or collective aspect of all experiences. "It is the absolute reality and basis of all existences conceived as a spiritual being in which the ideal nature imperfectly manifested in human beings is perfectly realized."—Webster's Dictionary

The term "Over-soul" has more recently been associated with the concept of *Paramatman* where (*param*) means "Supreme" and (*atman*) means "Soul." Thus, *Paramatman* literally means; "Supreme-Soul." In this context, the term "Over-soul" is understood as the experience of this underlying reality of the indivisible "I am Consciousness." If you understand the concept of One Mind, One Spirit and One Consciousness, then you can understand the Over-Soul. According to Ralph Waldo Emerson's essay *IX*; "The Over-Soul is the celebration of the mystery of the human soul in matter and its mysterious existence as 'part and particle' with the eternal One." In truth, there is really only One Life of which everything else is merely a representation. The Over-Soul is the ever abiding presence i.e., the Creator. All manifestation is simply the Oneness of being, re-presented in various forms, all forms. There is only one consciousness from which the entire Multiverse is spawned. Awareness or consciousness happens on multiple levels many of which are unfathomable to the human mind. What we perceive as life on the third dimension is really just a minute form of the vastness of creation striving evermore to achieve the highest aspects of its being. All are consciously or unconsciously seeking to attain higher self-awareness.

There is an evolutionary progression constantly being carried out on all levels of existence and this progression is constantly being managed by the Over-Soul much like our own individual life experiences. The Over-Soul (being the source from which all things originate) is essentially the collective repository of creation on every level from the very fundamental to the extremely complex. This is not to be mistaken with the Cosmic Hall of Records or the Akashic Record which is the collective memory but rather the Over-Soul is the immaterial essence, the animating principle, or actuating cause of each individual life. It is the spiritual principle embodied not only in human beings but all rational and spiritual beings. It is the intelligence of all existence both great and small.

There is nothing new under the Sun. All life is from one essence. As such; life is continual or eternal I should say. Nothing that is created is new. It is only the ever expanding consciousness of divine intelligence seeking newer and fresher expressions of the One life. All experience is simply the creative aspect of this intelligence seeking knowledge in which to continually expand from. Because it is fractal in nature, it continually fragments itself into counterparts of itself with each part still containing the essence of the whole. We are all one eternal family and the Over-Soul is merely a large fragmentation of all that is which contains all the fragmentations of all the various physical lives that we understand ourselves to be. Your life stream and my life stream are essentially one in the same. Our countless streams of existence are generated through the ever expanding consciousness that is seeking to experience life as the individuals that we are right now, on this day, in this age. We are each minute aspects of the All, creating and experiencing human awareness in the form of life. Emerson attests to this by saying, "That Unity, that Over-Soul, within which every man's particular being is contained and made one with all other; that it is the common heart shared by all." Throughout each of our life experiences, our collection of lessons gets stored in the Over-Soul of which our overall life purpose is stored. The divine plan of our lives is known only through this massive mind and the individual mind always mingles with the Universal mind.

The lives we are now living are one of many in an un-broken stream of consciousness that is being played out on various densities and realities. And again, each aspect and counterpart of the Over-Soul has its unique, individual personality construct which contains portions of the whole. Referring once again to Emerson he says, "We live in succession, in division, in parts, in particles. Meantime within man is the Soul of the whole; the wise silence; the Universal beauty, to which every part and particle is equally related; the eternal ONE." This consciousness stream is in everything as everything has a certain degree of awareness. The level of awareness depends upon the type of intelligence. Human Beings are simply one aspect of this intelligence while there are far more examples of it on various levels of existence some of which are lower in consciousness and some of which are much more highly evolved. Be that as it may; everything is constantly evolving and the Over-Soul acts as the cosmic administrator of all evolution.

In the bible and countless other places, the Over-Soul is considered to be an on-going repository or account of all deeds; hence, the "Book of Life." Every experience is being recorded not so much for an impending judgment but rather for the sole purpose of keeping track of our evolutionary progress. Upon completing each life-stream, it is my belief that we return to our source which is the Over-Soul where we undergo a life review of sorts. This synopsis enables us to know and understand first hand the type of existence we carried out. During this soul-review, it is decided which experiences we are to have in our on-going process of spiritual development. These experiences are then introduced to us in a future incarnation by those particular individuals that have agreed to assist us along our path of discovery and spiritual development. These lessons come in the form of experiences being carried out by everyone within our particular soul-group. Parents, siblings, close friends, loved ones and other members of our soul-groups have all agreed to be a part of our journey, as we have agreed to be a part of theirs. We show up in each other's lives to present the experiences that we have decided to have in order to expand our unique sense of awareness. And as I have said, there is no new creation, only different forms. Therefore; the people we encounter throughout our many life cycles are the same people or spirits recurring in different bodies, different aspects and differing roles. A parent for us in this life may have been our sibling in a previous life. Conversely, we may have been the parent. Oftentimes we interchange roles within our soul group to better serve one another. The point here is that we ourselves are not capable of keeping track of our soul lessons because the Over-soul is said to be veiled from the human mind by "*sanskaras*," or impressions, acquired over the course of evolution and reincarnation. These past impressions form a barrier between the Over-Soul and its true identity. However, the Over-Soul *is* aware and therefore able to keep track of each and every occurrence throughout our many levels of existence. Thus the world, as perceived through the impressions of the past appears plural, while reality experienced in the present, unencumbered by past impressions, perceives itself as the one indivisible totality, i.e. the Over-Soul.

Finally Emerson says: "Man is a stream whose source is hidden." He goes on to say . . . "Our being is descending into us from we know not whence. The most exact calculator has no prescience that somewhat incalculable may not balk the very next moment. I am constrained every moment to acknowledge a higher origin for events than the will I call mine." This adds credence to the fact that we are continual streams of awareness which the source is of a higher origin:

> "So come I to live in thoughts, and act with energies, which are immortal. Thus revering the Soul, and learning, as the ancient said, that 'its beauty is immense,' man will come to see that the world is the perennial miracle which the Soul worketh, and be less astonished at particular wonders; he will learn that there is no profane history; that all history is sacred; that the Universe is represented in an atom, in a moment of time. He will weave no longer a spotted life of shreds and patches, but he will live with a divine unity. He will cease from what is base and frivolous in his life, and be content with all places and with any service he can render. He will calmly front the morrow in the negligence of that trust which carries God with it, and so hath already the whole future in the bottom of the heart."—Emerson

Chapter Five

Transcendental Truth

Transcendental Truth

"I know not any crime so great that a man could contrive to commit as poisoning the source of eternal truth."
—*Samuel Johnson (1709-1784)*

The word "Transcendental" is derived from Latin and it means; "climbing or going beyond." Thus, "Transcendence" is to go "beyond" the normal standard. Transcendentalism deals with an ideal spiritual state that "transcends" the physical and empirical and is realized only through the individual's intuition, rather than through the doctrines of established religions. In dealing with truth, Wikipedia says; ". . . it can have a variety of meanings, from the state of being the case; being in accord with a particular fact or reality; being in accord with the body of real things, events, actuality; or, fidelity to an original or to a standard truth behind everything, the ontological truth based on existence." Agreeably, we can say that "truth" involves both the quality of faithfulness, fidelity, loyalty, sincerity, veracity and that of "agreement with fact or reality."

Therefore, in dealing with this chapter, I will be discussing that which goes beyond the normal standard of thinking by engaging in intuition which is an "inner knowing." This inner knowing transcends the physical or knowable and is based solely upon one's unique sense of understanding. As such, transcendental truth is not based on doctrines or established religions, hence it is considered to be "out of the norms." It is however, based upon the standards of truth by staying in accordance with fact and reality. And while many may argue with the verity of this statement, I still hold these truths to be self evident.

Many of us today wouldn't know the truth if it were staring us in the face. This is because our idea of truth has been shaped and molded by years and years of conditioning and false programming not to mention false teachings and indoctrination. For many years people thought the Earth was flat. This concept was arduously held by the Church fathers and anyone not believing in such an idea was considered a heretic and tried for heresy which was punishable by death. This was the accepted truth until the ignorance of the Church was dispelled by scientific proof which showed the Earth was in fact globular. The Church argued this could not be so because; "In the day of judgment men on the other side of the globe could not see the Lord descending through the air." Seriously . . . ? Fortunately, in the early part of the sixth century, Pythagoras taught that the Earth was not only round but also that it circled the Sun. But, St Augustine argued this fact by saying; "It is impossible there should be inhabitants on the opposite side of the Earth, since no such race is recorded by scripture among the descendants of Adam." Father Inchofer adds to this by saying; "The opinion of the Earth's motion is of all heresies the most abominable, the most pernicious, the most scandalous; the immobility of the Earth is thrice sacred." Lactanius concludes with; "It is impossible that men can be so absurd as to believe that the crops and trees on the other side of the Earth hang downward and that men have their feet higher than their heads." (You've got to be kidding me!) By the third century, Aristarchus outlined the true heliocentric theory that was further developed by Copernicus some nineteen centuries later. But again, the Church had this to say; "This fool wishes to reverse the entire system of astronomy; but sacred scripture tells us that Joshua commanded the Sun to stand still and not the Earth." Prior to this knowledge, many people credulously thought and believed in the flat Earth theory without ever questioning the Church's position. And just as Will Durant, one of Americas most prolific philosophers stated; "The great snare of thought is uncritical acceptance of irrational assumptions."

The same holds true of our solar system. The Church's belief at the time was that the Earth was at the center of the Solar System and the Sun revolved around the Earth. How else could they explain the Sun moving from one part of the sky to the other? In their ignorance, they simply postulated that the Sun revolved around the Earth rather than vice versa. They held this belief because it suited their notion of the Earth being God's primary focus. But this was not the only inaccurate belief held by the Church. In fact, they also believed there were only seven, yes you heard me, seven planets in the entire Solar System where today we know there are billions of planets throughout a myriad of Solar Systems. However, this is why today we have seven days of the week all of which were named after these seven celestial bodies. Sunday was named after the Sun; Monday or *"Lunes/Lunar"* was named after the Moon; Tuesday *"Martes"* was named after Mars; Wednesday *"Miercoles"* was named after Mercury; Thursday *"Jueves"* was named after Jupiter; Friday *"Viernes"* was named after Venus and Saturday, *"Sababo"* which was the original *"Sabath,"* was named after Saturn. That was it. Imagine if they knew then what we know now just how much our lives would have been affected. Would there have been ten, twelve or even fifteen days of the week based on todays understanding of our Solar System? Who's to say? These are just a few examples of the Church's ignorance at the time. Sadly though, the Church was our primary source for truth and we looked to them for answers concerning our existence. But instead, they foolishly and sometimes deliberately mislead us into believing many mistruths.

This same type of falsehood still holds true to this very day but we fail to realize it because we cannot muster the courage or the ability to challenge these beliefs. So we accept without question all of what the Church and its fabricated bible purports. For example; Lloyd M. Graham cites a person in his book *Deceptions and Myths of The Bible* as saying, "I'd believe the Bible even if it said that Jonah swallowed the whale." Oddly enough, this is the general consensus among most Christians. However, Science has done its part to disprove many of the fallacies postulated by the earlier Church fathers. But, had it not been for someone to come along and disprove the Earth being the center of the Solar System theory, we would still be deceived by the Church's lack of understanding. Unfortunately, many of us still hold fast to the misinformation offered up by ignorant priests whether it pertains to the Earth and its relation to other celestial bodies or the fairytales of creation. For some unknown reason, we can't seem to bring ourselves to the point where logic and common sense outweighs credulity. In the future, we will all look back on the things we now hold to be true and laugh at ourselves for our immaturity in such matters. Such was the case with the flat Earth theory.

The truth of what I offer here in this chapter is comparable to the globular Earth theory of today as it would have been presented during the "dark ages." This is a transcendental truth that may appear strange at first but over time will gradually be accepted as the norm.

What is strange today will be widely accepted come tomorrow. If you told the average person fifty or a hundred years ago that everyone would someday be able to communicate wirelessly via text, internet, cell-phone etc, you would have been considered strange. If you uttered these things a thousand years ago, you would have been considered a heretic or a sorcerer and consequently stoned to death. And yet here we are, living in the modern age where all of these things have been made possible through the advent of modern technology. It never ceases to amaze me how technology can continue to evolve and progress and yet when it comes to religion, many of us are proverbially still stuck in the "dark ages" believing the World is flat and that there are only seven planets in the whole entire Universe. Or that God created the World in six days and there was a talking snake in a make believe paradisiacal garden where Man was fashioned out of clay and the Woman was fashioned from his rib. Why is it that we can gradually come to accept a modern and changing world but yet somehow we can't relinquish an antiquated belief system based on biblical fallacies? Is it fear? Or is it plain old obstinacy? "The time will come when our posterity (future generations) will wonder at our ignorance of things so plain."—Seneca

In this chapter I want to address a few topics that have intrigued me for many years. One of which is the subject of *Dimensionality* and the various stages at which to understand it. I would also like to discuss the concept of *Stargates* and how utilizing these portals can allow us to venture not only into the past but also into the distant future since there really is no such thing as a "time continuum." Furthermore, I would like to discuss one of these Stargates in particular in the *Halls of Amenti*. Later in this chapter, we will discuss the concept of *Hyperspace* and its implication on inter-stellar travel and the concept of anti-electrons in the form of *Antimatter*.

I know at first brush, transcendental truth can appear to be strange and unusual, as it is. However, just because something seems strange and unusual doesn't necessarily mean it's not based on truth. All cutting-edge technology once sounded futuristic until years later it became common place. Today, not to have a cell phone or to utilize the computer is considered abnormal where before it was quite the opposite. The same holds true with our beliefs. Today what sounds strange and unusual is nothing more than evolution happening. What we believed yesterday about the world, the Universe and God is antiquated and cannot be supported by any real truth. A new paradigm is emerging, one in which space ships, time travel and inter-stellar travel will be the order of the day. A time when off-planet beings are more widely accepted by not only those of us who know they exist but also by the Vatican itself with its recent admission of possible extraterrestrial existence. This is a new day and the beginning of a whole new era. Hence the deceptions of the past can no longer prevail over the changing paradigm. What we once knew about God, ourselves and existence is a dying belief system. We must usher in a new way of thinking and more importantly a new way of viewing what we hold to be true of ourselves and the Universe. There is much to be learned, or should I say "re-learned," for the ways of old have hindered us for far too long. It is time for evolution to happen as it can only happen in its time. Far be it for us to be held captive any longer by the vices of organized thought processes in the form of religion and tyrannical government systems. It is our destiny to evolve and evolve we must.

Dimensionality

Whether we realize it or not, at this very moment, there is a multitude of worlds and realities operating on different vibrational frequencies all around us. We refer to these various densities as "Dimensions." Each dimension has its own particular variance or nuance associated with its vibratory wavelength, although each dimensional level is somehow inextricably linked. The only thing separating dimensions from one another is the wavelengths or the rate at which they are vibrating. This is akin to notes on a musical scale where each tone on the scale sounds different because of its wavelength. Sound becomes inaudible to the human ear as it increases because the sound waves are imperceptible at certain ranges. However, this doesn't mean the sound doesn't exist, it simply means whatever exists on these higher octaves is undetectable to human sense.

Sound travels in waves through the air, the ground, and various other substances. And although sound cannot be seen, it can be felt by its vibrations. The number of vibrations produced per second is called a frequency and frequencies vary for each sound and are measured in hertz (Hz). One hertz is equal to one vibration per second and so on. A sound with a low frequency will have a lower density, while sounds with higher frequencies will be less dense. So, as the rate or cycle of vibration increases in frequency, the density lessens to the point where objects are no longer audible to the human ear. Humans cannot hear sounds of every frequency although certain animals have a much higher range of hearing than we humans. In fact, the range of hearing for an average human being is only about 20 to 20,000 hertz or cycles per second. Anything below 20 cycles per second or beyond 20,000 cycles per second is outside our normal hearing range but very perceptible to other types of animals. A frequency that is below the human range of hearing is known as "infrasound." This type of sound is so low it can only be detected with a special device or by a creature with large ears such as an Elephant. Research indicates that elephants actually communicate with infrasound. "Ultrasound," on the other hand, is above the range of human hearing. Animals such as bats, whales, porpoises, and dolphins use ultrasound or sound navigation and ranging (sonar) for navigation. Incredibly most bats can detect frequencies as high as 100,000 Hz.

Right now, at this very moment, there are different colors and sound waves happening all around us of which we are not privy to. Things are happening in the airwaves that only certain instruments can pick up. And yet without these devices, we wouldn't even know about the unseen world of sound waves or things happening beyond the visible light spectrum. At this very moment although I can't actually hear music playing, there is still a multitude of sound waves being broadcasted on various channels and frequencies. If I were to turn on a radio which is a receiver for certain high pitch frequencies, I would be able to hear these sounds or tones coming from the receiver. As I move the dial from one end of the spectrum to the next, I'm able to pick up or receive different sounds being broadcasted at certain frequencies. The call sign for most radio stations is generally the frequency at which they are broadcasting from and by tuning my dial to these designated frequency bands; I'm able to pick up signals or sound waves. The same holds true for a television and whenever we change the channel, we are actually tuning in to different wavelengths. But without the proper device, this wouldn't be possible. This is just one example of how there are many levels or dimensions in which things can exist; many of which are not discernable by human senses. However, this does not mean that they don't exist.

So what does all this mean and how does it pertain to dimensionality? Well, it has everything to do with it because octaves are dimensions which determine the overtones on every level. In actuality, there is far more happening on levels that we cannot see or hear than those happening on the physical plane. In reality, everything that appears on the physical plane, originated on one of these other planes prior to becoming form or matter in the physical. Planes of reality or dimensions always originate from inner needs or desires. Like all creations, they are the manifestation of inner visions and ponderings. Earth itself was created from an inner desire to bring together elements from different realities. Earth was intended to be a melting pot for a great array of influences. For now, suffice it to say that the Earth was a relative late-comer on the cosmic stage and that many souls lived many lives of exploration and development on other planes of reality (planets, dimensions, star systems, etc.), long before the Earth was even born.

The 3rd dimension is the physical plane where matter forms and the physical world makes up the three dimensions we observe. As such, we are held here, bound by the physical world. We can move left, right, north, south, east, west, up, down, and back and forth, but we are still stuck in a three dimensional existence. But what makes the physical world solid? Well, through a slowing down of molecules, that which is invisible eventually becomes materialized as dense matter. Once this occurs, it becomes a part of the 3rd dimension of which physical matter resides. But there are countless other non material worlds and realities co-existing all around us. In the Universe, there are many levels or dimensions of existence. One planet or star may exist in various dimensions, ranging from the material to the more ethereal dimensions such as 5th dimensional Venus. I believe the reason why we haven't been able to discover life on other planets is because they're non-physical beings existing on dimensions beyond what we can perceive. They're functioning outside the parameters of sight and sound of which we are capable of detecting. Their frequency range is far too high for human observation. In general, all of the galactic communities that influenced the Earth souls currently exist on much higher frequencies than we now exist. This is why these advanced beings are able to pop in and out of certain realities. They have learned to slow down their vibration to the point where they can materialize and dematerialize at will.

So then why are we only privy to the physical world? Well, by using the analogy of the dial on the radio or tuning the channel on the television, our consciousness dial is tuned only to the 3rd dimension making it our primary reality. On the 4th dimension, thought manifests instantaneously whereas here on the 3rd dimension there is a time-delay where the energy from our thoughts has to first coagulate into form. Thank god for time-delays because all thoughts are not pure and need to be resolved on other dimensions before manifesting into form. Each varying level or dimension is associated with a different gradation so to speak. In Kiara Windrider's *Doorway to Eternity: A Guide to Planetary Ascension*, he describes the differences on some of the higher dimensions thusly:

> ➤ 3-D—characterized by duality, and separation from soul where our experience of time is linear and our physical and planetary bodies are governed by the law of entropy or increasing chaos.
> ➤ 4-D—a transitional dimension, in which 3-D density is being loosened up and where time is increasingly experienced as synchronistic.
> ➤ 5-D—characterized by a more unified consciousness within and without, reflected in an "Age of Light" where many parallel realities can exist and interdimensional travel becomes possible. On this level, "Syntropy," the law of increasing order replaces entropy thus facilitating greater possibilities for the soul's expression.
> ➤ 6-D—ascension mastery becomes possible on both personal and planetary levels.

This helps broaden our perspective because what we can understand about dimensionality depends a great deal on how many dimensions we have in which to perceive something. Our Universe is so rich and diverse with ranges, dimensions and vibrational octaves that we have only begun to experience life as intelligent beings. There are virtually layers upon layers of different realities and forms of existence happening simultaneously all around us at this very moment. Our minds cannot even begin to fathom the vast amount of possibilities that abound. We exist in a multiverse and according to string theory or M-theory in science; there are actually 11 possible dimensions each having a higher tone or vibratory frequency. I happen to believe there are 12 levels each having 12 overtones totaling 144 octaves. Bob Frissell attests to this in his book *Something in This Book is True*, where he says we are just beginning to experience a paradigm shift into the third level of consciousness where he explains the five levels of consciousness we undergo as human beings. He writes:

> "There are five levels of consciousness associated with life. These levels are not the same as the 144 dimensions and overtones of the octave. For instance, it is impossible to exist on the higher overtones of the fourth dimension and be on the first level of consciousness. This was actually the case with the inhabitants of Atlantis and Lemuria. The higher overtones of the fourth dimension are also where we will be when we complete our own evolution to the next dimensional level. Where we are now, and where we have been for the past 13,000 years, is the second level. Where we are headed is the third level."

This understanding incorporates the dictionary definition of dimension which is "a level of existence or consciousness."

We need to understand that as human beings we are multidimensional beings having multiple experiences throughout the galaxy simultaneously. A good depiction of this was the 2001 movie *"The One"* starring Jet Li who plays a sheriff deputy fighting alternate Universe versions of himself and grows stronger with each alternate self he kills. Ultimately, we are spiritual beings subsisting in a multidimensional Universe with all sorts of probabilities in which to experience reality. As human beings, we are experiencing reality on a very basic three dimensional level. Our carbon bodies are merely the human outfit which is necessary in order for us to survive on this carbon based planet. It is only a housing mechanism necessary to exist here. Unfortunately, this means we are limited by our physical bodies and thus unable to experience the realms of pure spirit or energy. These other dimensions are vibrating at a much faster rate than we are capable of experiencing. Yet it is very naïve of us to assume that in such a vast, expansive and creative Universe, that human beings are the only form of existence. Dimensions subsist one within the other and there are parallel Universes happening all around us only our physical being is not capable of experiencing these other realities. We are separated by different wavelengths and we exist on one station while others exist on another. But these other stations still exist nonetheless. Within the Universe, there are countless planes of reality in which to explore and 3-Dimensional Earth is only one of them.

Stargates

This information is very intriguing to say the least and before you get the notion that what I'm referring to here is some fictional theme from the television series "*Stargate Atlantis*," you should think again. In order to make light of my findings, I want to give you a bit of history as well as educate you on how dimensionality is also a factor of time and therefore relevant to this topic.

Firstly, it is imperative that we understand how time works. Time is often referred to as the "fourth dimension" but not necessarily a spatial dimension but rather a temporal dimension to measure physical change. The equations used in physics to represent reality do not treat time in the same ways that we commonly perceive it. Time is not linear as we suppose it to be. This means time does not happen in a linear fashion where there's a past, present and future but rather all time is essentially happening simultaneously or at the same time. We have been misled into believing time starts and stops at certain points and that it travels along a line with one point being the beginning and the latter part being the end. The beginning signifies a starting point or *past*; now signifies where we are on this time-line which is represented as the *present*; and the end signifies the *future*. Anything outside this thought process seems fictional because we don't truly understand the nature of space-time.

Essentially, everything is happening simultaneously. This means there is no past, present or future but only awareness. Logically we think there has to be a past because we remember experiencing it. Or the future has to be happening at some later date because we have yet to experience it. In truth, time is an unbroken chain of events all occurring collectively but we only experience what we focus our attention on. This means our awareness determines where we find ourselves on the time continuum. If we focus our attention on the third dimension which is only just a degree of development and evolution according to where we are in our planetary advancement, then all further degrees or dimensions would be considered higher up or further along on the evolutionary plane.

Since we know all things evolve with time, or should I say with progression, then in truth, the higher dimensions such as the fourth, fifth, sixth and so on, are merely consciousness evolved to different degrees. And since we too are consciousness, then it's safe to say then that these higher dimensions are actually human consciousness further along in development. So the fourth dimension for instance, is nothing more than existence at a different point on the space-time continuum. According to Bob Frissell in his book *Nothing In This Book Is True, But It's Exactly How Things Are*, different dimensional realities are essentially divided by 90-degree angles. Upon making this 90-degree shift, we appear in a different reality on a different dimensional level. With that being said, other Universes or planes of existence are just a small distance away from our own, but the distance is in a fourth or higher spatial dimension. Therefore, if we were somehow able to "bend time," as Einstein stated, then we would be able to experience not only our future selves but other forms of beings which are further along on this time-continuum. I use the word "further" suggestively here and not to imply a future aspect but rather a more evolved aspect. So, once again, if we could somehow learn to breach the barriers that separate these other realities, chances are, we could visit our more advanced selves further along on this time-continuum.

Secondly, I want to point out an incident called the *"Philadelphia Experiment"* which took place around 67 years ago. In case you're not familiar with this event, I'll give you a quick overview. In 1943, an experiment was carried out at a U.S. Naval base in Philadelphia Pennsylvania referred to as *"Project Rainbow."* During this experiment, scientists were attempting to manipulate the magnetic field around the U.S. Navy destroyer escort *USS Eldridge* in order to render it invisible. Their understanding of how this would work was based on Albert Einstein's *"Unified Field Theory."* It was believed that some version of this theory would enable the Navy to use large electrical generators to bend light around an object in order to make it invisible. In one account the *USS Eldridge* was rendered almost completely invisible, with some witnesses reporting a greenish fog appearing in its place. However, crew members supposedly complained of severe nausea afterwards. Also, it is said that when the ship reappeared, some sailors were embedded in the metal structures of the ship, including one sailor who ended up on a deck level below where he began, and had his hand embedded in the steel hull of the ship according to *The Philadelphia Experiment from A-Z* written by Alex H. Hochheimer. Other accounts say the *USS Eldridge* actually disappeared out of the Philadelphia Naval yard for about four hours and upon reappearing, some of the crew members were literally imbedded in the deck, some were in bulkheads, some were on fire, some didn't come back at all while others were repeatedly materializing and dematerializing. The only thing that would cause this to happen would be if all the matter had somehow dematerialized and then rematerialized again. Many people argue that any such phenomenon could safely transport a human being. But in actuality it could transport a human being by transporting them through as an energy signature, and reintegrating them at the other end much like the transporters in Gene Roddenberry's *Star Trek*.

The film *Stargate* briefly describes how a Stargate actually works but we find a more detailed explanation in the subsequent television show. In the series *SG-1*, they explain how a Stargate's destination is not fixed, but is singled out by a process known as "dialing." Once a destination is selected by the traveler, the Stargate generates a "wormhole" between itself and a complementary device at the destination by being supplied with a threshold amount of raw energy. Objects in transit between gates are broken down into their *"individual elemental components,"* (energy signature) and then into energy as they pass through the event horizon, and then travel through a wormhole before being reconstructed (rematerializing) on the other side. This can be explained by the hypothesis that the diameter of the wormhole is very small, possibly microscopic in size. Energy would have no problem passing through on its own but matter would need to be converted into energy and then reintegrated at the other side. This would require an extremely advanced technology that would allow for the breaking down of physical matter and allow it to rematerialize at some other point as with the *Philadelphia Experiment*. Unfortunately, the proper techniques were not used thus resulting in the amalgamation of energy and the transfusing of matter. Nevertheless the experiment was altered at the request of the Navy, with the new objective being solely to render the *USS Eldridge* invisible to radar. Supposedly, the equipment was not properly re-calibrated, but in spite of this, the experiment was repeated again. However this time, the *USS Eldridge* not only became invisible, but it physically vanished from the area in a flash of blue light and teleported to Norfolk, Virginia, over 200 miles away. According to eye witness accounts, the *USS Eldridge* sat for some time in full view of men aboard the ship *SS Andrew Furuseth*, whereupon the *USS Eldridge* vanished from their sight, and then reappeared in Philadelphia at the site where it had originally occupied. Here's the part I want you to be aware of. It was believed by many that the *USS Eldridge* actually travelled into the future. This brings us to the topic at hand where we will discuss the possibility of utilizing certain "portals" and "wormholes" or in this case "Stargates" to manipulate the space time-continuum.

Accordingly, a Stargate is a portal device within the Universe that allows practical, rapid travel between two distant locations. Not distant as in length but distant as in time. These Stargates are often used to create shortcuts through space and time. In *The Ancient Secret Of The Flower Of Life: Volume 1*, Drunvalo Melchizedek says there are certain sacred places in the geometries of our reality here on

Earth where it's easier to become aware of the various dimensions and overtones—sacred sites, which are nodal points connected to the Earth and the heavens. He goes on to say, there are also specific places in space that are tied to the geometries of space which are referred to as "Stargates" or openings to other dimensional levels where it's easier to get through. The overall premise of a Stargate is drawn heavily from theoretical astrophysics particularly that of black holes and wormholes which happens to be a staple of science fiction. Although I maintain there's more truth in science fiction than we're led to believe. As long as Man can imagine a thing, then at some point in time, that conception becomes real through the creative principle of thought. So imagine then how highly advanced the future aspects of ourselves would be 1 million or 10 million years from now. Time travel would be nothing more than childs-play for us.

In the chapter on the Merkaba, we talked about the electromagnetic field that surrounds the body. This "field," so-to-speak, is what makes interdimensional travel possible. So in the case of the *USS Eldridge*, what scientists were attempting to do was activate the field around the vessel in order to render it invisible. The basic principle behind this is fairly simple when you consider matter and how it forms. As we all know, matter is nothing more than atoms or molecules that are attracted to one another through electricity. These atoms are essentially vibrating balls of energy which comprises physical matter. If we increase the speed at which these molecules are vibrating, eventually they transcend the visible light spectrum and become invisible. In reality, the object is no longer visible to someone on the dimension where solid particles are formed but rather this object would only be visible on an elevated dimension where objects are functioning according to that dimensional reality, hence the fourth, fifth, sixth and higher dimensional frequencies. This entire process is made possible by creating counter-rotating fields of energy moving at very specific speeds. Consequently, we know that whenever an object travels beyond the speed of light, time somehow becomes affected. This is the whole basis for time-travel via portals or wormholes.

The Stargate is what serves as the counter rotating device which makes time-travel possible. One other thing I discovered about the

Philadelphia Experiment was that apparently two of the experimental participants jumped off during the middle of the test and tried to swim away, but when they arrived on shore they realized they were on Long Island, New York. And get this . . . it was now "1983." They had somehow ended up 40 years into the future where a similar experiment called the "Montauk Project" was being conducted. Frissell explains this by saying there are four bio-fields of the planet and all four peaks out every twenty years on a particular day during certain years; "1943," "1963," "1983," "2003" and so forth. He says this creates a peak of magnetic energies sufficient enough to create a hyperspace field which caused the *USS Eldridge* to slip into hyperspace. What amazes me about this experiment and what Frissell says is that in actuality, the 1983 Montauk Project came after the 1943 Philadelphia Experiment, but this experiment created a "time-loop" in which the way we conceive linear time chronologically no longer applies. I'm almost certain this technology has now been perfected some 67 years later.

In some of my research I've learned how the U.S. Government has been in constant communication with higher forms of intelligence through some type of Earth/Extraterrestrial alliance or treaty whereby technology is being provided to the Government in exchange for biological research on human beings. From what I understand, these other beings have been trying to genetically manufacture organic human bodies in which to inhabit here on Earth. Needless to say, our technology has increased exponentially over the past 100 years. As a matter of fact, according to a recent study, our technology has advanced more in the past ten years than it has over the past thousand years. I attribute this to the aforementioned treaty. That being the case, time-travel via Stargates is nothing more than modern technology being provided to humans as a means of intergalactic travel. Again, we're talking about technology from our "future," that only appears unreal but in reality it's very real. Imagine if we were to travel back in our own time and provide some our technology of today to a civilization of a thousand years ago. To them Television, the Internet, Cellular Phones, Automobiles, Airplanes and Space Shuttles would seem far fetched but to us it's nothing more than modern technology. The same holds true for us today compared to our future counter-parts. We have come to a changing point in humanity where what once seemed impossible is now becoming possible. What I'm speaking of here is not science fiction. Much of what we think of as fiction is really just our ignorance to what is real. It only seems strange to us because we haven't entertained the possibility of such a thing. All it takes is for science to introduce a concept and suddenly that which we thought to be impossible suddenly becomes reality. It's just a matter of our intellect catching up with technology.

Today it is believed by many that there are actual Stargates buried in the sands of Iraq which was originally Mesopotamia the home of the ancient Sumerians who held strong extraterrestrial beliefs relating to interdimensional travel. The supposed location of this Stargate was in Uruk a city that also possessed airstrips for the landing of Alien space craft. This doesn't seem too far fetched especially considering the work of author and historian Zecharia Sitchin who has been studying ancient Sumerian text for many years. According to Sitchin's studies, a superior race of beings once inhabited this planet some 300,000 years ago which led to the genetic enhancements of *Homo sapiens* thus advancing humanity by millions of years. These beings were the Annunaki or the "Watchers" from the sky which later led to the creation of the biblical *Nefilim* which were the offspring of the "*sons of God*" and the "*daughters of men.*"(Gen: 6:2) These gods so-to-speak, are believed to have placed a Stargate on our planet for instantaneous transportation of humans to communicate peacefully with other worlds. They believed our intentions were pure so they left us with this device. Accordingly, these beings were utilizing space-travel, advanced forms of in vitro fertilization, genetic splicing and other forms of sophisticated technology eons ago. Therefore, the possibility of Stargates is a definite possibility today.

There have been several claims made suggesting that the U.S. Government is aware of these Iraqi Stargates and have been in pursuit of them for several years now. Dan Burisch, an area 51 (S4) worker, claims that a Stargate in Iraq actually does exist, and confirms the accusations that the Iraq war is a cover for the "fight for the Stargate." Some suggest the 911 attacks on the World Trade Towers were orchestrated by the U.S. Government and the Bush administration for the prime purpose of acquiring these Stargates.

Our involvement with Iraq has nothing to do with the oil as we proclaim or the ousting of Saddam Hussein for if this were the case, why are we still there? Iraq has never attacked America, and they've shown never shown any violence towards our nation, and no weapons of mass destruction have ever been found there that could harm America in any way.

It's a well known fact that the U.S. Government has conducted various projects involving advanced technology such as time travel, Stargates, Teleportation and Invisibility, all of which have been classified as "Top Secret." Our government knows for a fact that much of this technology does exist and they know for certain that whoever wins the arms race and masters this technology first; will ultimately rule the world. Renowned physicists Dr. Michio Kaku attests to this by saying the civilization that masters this theory will ultimately become lord of the Universe.

The Halls of Amenti

One such Stargate that cannot go without mention is the *Halls of Amenti* which serves as a school, Stargate, and cosmic energy vortex located in the exact center of the Earth on the Astral Plane. Aside from being a portal to other dimensions, it also serves as an extreme energy vortex which sustains, upholds, and repairs the planet in every way. Within the Halls of Amenti, there is a great assortment of Ascended Masters and energy beings teaching and tutoring the ultimate mysteries of time, space, alchemy, and the higher dimensions. One such teacher was Thoth of whom we discussed in the previous chapters. In *The Emerald Tablets*, Dr. M. Doreal translates the words of Thoth as he describes the Halls of Amenti as such:

> "Deep in Earth's heart lie the Halls of Amenti, far 'neath
> the islands of sunken Atlantis, Halls of the Dead and halls
> of the living, bathed in the fire of the infinite ALL. Far in
> a past time, lost in the space time, the Children of Light

looked down on the world seeing the children of men in their bondage, bound by the force that came from beyond. Knew they that only by freedom from bondage could man ever rise from the Earth to the Sun. Down they descended and created bodies, taking the semblance of men as their own. The Masters of everything said after their forming: 'We are they who were formed from the space-dust, partaking of life from the infinite ALL; living in the world as children of men, like and yet unlike the children of men.'

Then for a dwelling place, far 'neath the Earth crust, blasted great spaces they by their power, spaces apart from the children of men. Surrounded them by forces and power, shielded from harm they the Halls of the Dead. Side by side then, placed they other spaces filled them with Life and with Light from above. Builded they then the Halls of Amenti, that they might dwell eternally there, living with life to eternity's end.

Thirty and two were there of the children, sons of Lights who had come among men, seeking to free from the bondage of darkness those who were bound by the force from beyond. Deep in the Halls of Life grew a flower, flaming, expanding and driving backward the night. Placed in the centre, a ray of great potence, Life giving, Light giving, filling with power all who came near it. Placed they around it thrones, two and thirty, places for each of the Children of Light, placed so that they were bathed in the radiance, filled with the Life from the eternal Light. There time after time placed they their first created bodies so that they might be filled with the Spirit of Life. One hundred years out of each thousand must the Life-giving Light flame forth on their bodies; quickening, awakening the Spirit of Life.

There in the circle from aeon to aeon, sit the Great Masters, living a life not known among men. There in the Halls of Life they lie sleeping; free flows their Soul through the bodies of men. Time after time, while their bodies lie sleeping, incarnate they in the bodies of men. Teaching and guiding onward and upward, out of the darkness into the light.

There in the Hall of Life, filled with their wisdom, known not to the races of man, living forever 'neath the cold fire of life, sit the Children of Light. Times there are when they awaken, come from the depths to be lights among men, infinite they among finite men. He who by progress has grown from the darkness, lifted himself from the night into light, free is he made of the Halls of Amenti, free of the Flower of Light and of Life. Guided he then, by wisdom and knowledge, passes from men, to the Master of Life.

There he may dwell as one with the Masters, free from the bonds of the darkness of night, seated within the flower of radiance sit seven Lords from the Space-Times above us, helping and guiding through infinite Wisdom, the pathway through time of the children of men. Mighty and strange, they, veiled with their power, silent, all-knowing, drawing the Life force, different yet one with the children of men; aye, different, and yet One with the Children of Light. Custodians and watchers of the force of man's bondage, ready to loose when the light has been reached. First and most mighty, sits the Veiled Presence, Lord of Lords, the infinite Nine, over the other from each the Lords of the Cycles; Three, Four, Five, and Six, Seven, Eight, each with his mission, each with his powers, guiding, directing the destiny of man.

There sit they, mighty and potent, free of all time and space. Not of this world they, yet akin to it, Elder Brothers they, of the children of men; judging and weighing, they with their wisdom, watching the progress of Light among men. There before them was I led by the Dweller, watched him blend with ONE from above.

Then from HE came forth a voice saying: 'Great art thou, Thoth, among children of men. Free henceforth of the Halls of Amenti, Master of Life among children of men.

Taste not of death except as thou will it, drink thou of Life to Eternity's end, Henceforth forever is Life, thine for the taking. Henceforth is death at the call of thy hand. Dwell here or leave here when thou desireth, free is Amenti to the Sun of man. Take thou up Life in what form thou desireth, Child of the Light that has grown among men. Choose thou thy work, for all should must labor, never be free from the pathway of Light. One step thou hast gained on the long pathway upward, infinite now is the mountain of Light. Each step thou taketh but heightens the mountain; all of thy progress but lengthens the goal. Approach ye ever the infinite Wisdom, ever before thee recedes the goal. Free are ye made now of the Halls of Amenti to walk hand in hand with the Lords of the world, one in one purpose, working together, bringer of Light to the children of men.'

Then from his throne came one of the Masters, taking my hand and leading me onward, through all the Halls of the deep hidden land; led he me through the Halls of Amenti, showing the mysteries that are known not to man. Through the dark passage, downward he led me, into the Hall where sat the dark Death. Vast as space lay the great Hall before me, walled by darkness but yet filled with Light. Before me arose a great throne of darkness, veiled on it seated a figure of night; darker than darkness sat the great figure, dark with a darkness not of the night. Before it then paused the Master, speaking the Word that brings about Life, saying; 'Oh, master of darkness, guide of the way from Life unto Life, before thee I bring a Sun of the morning. Touch him not ever with the power of night. Call not his flame to the darkness of night. Know him, and see him, one of our brothers, lifted from darkness into the Light. Release thou his flame from its bondage, free let it flame through the darkness of night.' Raised then the hand of the figure, forth came a flame that grew clear and bright. Rolled back swiftly the curtain of darkness, unveiled the Hall from the darkness of night.

Then grew in the great space before me, flame after flame, from the veil of the night. Uncounted millions leaped they before me, some flaming forth as flowers of fire. Others there were that shed a dim radiance, flowing but faintly from out of the night. Some there were that faded swiftly; others that grew from a small spark of light. Each surrounded by its dim veil of darkness, yet flaming with light that could never be quenched. Coming and going like fireflies in springtime, filled they with space with Light and with Life.

Then spoke a voice, mighty and solemn, saying: 'These are lights that are souls among men, growing and fading, existing forever, changing yet living, through death into life. When they have bloomed into flower, reached the zenith of growth in their life, swiftly then send I my veil of darkness, shrouding and changing to new forms of life. Steadily upward throughout the ages, growing, expanding into yet another flame, lighting the darkness with yet greater power, quenched yet unquenched by the veil of the night.

So grows the soul of man ever upward, quenched yet unquenched by the darkness of night. I, Death, come, and yet I remain not, for life eternal exists in the ALL; only an obstacle, I in the pathway, quick to be conquered by the infinite light. Awaken, O flame that burns ever inward, flame forth and conquer the veil of the night.' Then in the midst of the flames in the darkness grew there one that drove forth the night, flaming, expanding, ever brighter, until at last was nothing but Light.

Then spoke my guide, the voice of the master: 'See your own soul as it grows in the light, free now forever from the Lord of the night.' Forward he led me through many great spaces filled with the mysteries of the Children of Light; mysteries that man may never yet know of until he, too, is a Sun of the Light. Backward then he led me into the Light of the hall of the Light. Knelt I then before the great Masters, Lords of ALL from the cycles above. Spoke he then with words of great power saying: 'Thou hast been made free of the Halls of Amenti. Choose thou thy work among the children of men.' Then spoke I: O, great master, let me be a teacher of men, leading them onward and upward until they, too, are lights among men; freed from the veil of the night that surrounds them, flaming with light that shall shine among men.

Spoke to me then the voice: 'Go, as ye will. So be it decreed. Master are ye of your destiny, free to take or reject at will. Take ye the power, take ye the wisdom. Shine as a light among the children of men.' Upward then, led me the Dweller; Dwelt I again among children of men, teaching and showing some of my wisdom; Sun of the Light, a fire among men. Now again I tread the path downward, seeking the light in the darkness of night. Bold ye and keep ye, preserve my record, guide shall it be to the children of men."

These tablets were written by Thoth somewhere between 30,000 and 36,000 BCE and translated by Dr. M. Doreal for the edification of modern man. I include the entire description because it provides a number of truths regarding the Halls of Amenti and in my previous book *Ultimate Truth: Book I*, I discussed how the human race was genetically modified by a highly advanced race of beings called the Nefilim. And while that is still my position, I have to add to the details in order to make it clearer. According to Drunvalo Melchizedek, there were seven of these beings which volunteered by forming a pattern of seven interlocking spheres much like the first stages of the "Flower of Life" (which we discussed in a previous chapter) which then created a white-blue flame of consciousness. This flame or "Halls of Amenti," was then placed in the womb or center of the Earth which is roughly a thousand miles under the surface of the Earth and is connected to the Great Pyramid through a fourth-dimensional passageway. This passageway is primarily used for the creation of new races or species. In the middle of the hall sits a cube with a five foot whitish blue flame that was created by the Nefilim. This whitish blue flame is considered to be pure consciousness which is the planetary "ovum" which was established for human beings to begin their evolutionary path.

In order for there to be life, there has to be both the male and female aspects. In the case of our genetic enhancement, it is believed the Nefilim served as the female aspect while a neighboring race from Sirius B served as the male counterpart. These were the sixth dimensional Sirians that took part in the original creation of humankind. As the story goes according to Drunvalo Melchizedek; there were 32 members of this race, 16 males and 16 females who were married into a single family. On Earth, marriages consist of one male and one female which serve as a reflection of our hydrogen Sun which has only one proton and one electron. Some planets have helium Suns with two protons, two electrons and two neutrons which requires two males and two females joining together in order to procreate. However, the Sun for Sirius B consists of the chemical element "germanium" (Ge) which has an atomic number of 32 thus requiring 16 males and 16 females to reproduce. These Sirians entered directly into the womb of the Halls of Amenti where they laid down facing upward with their heads towards the center of the flame. During this process, the Sirians "conceived" or merged with the flame or "ovum" of the Nefilim and they placed the resulting eggs into the wombs of seven Nefilim women from which the first Homo sapiens were eventually born. This process took approximately 2,000 years to complete at which time this genetically modified human being was born in Gondwanaland, off the western shore of southern Africa.

At first brush, this all seems a bit paranormal but upon further investigation; I discovered that much of this information has been supported by science. Eckar Ana-Shay Deane and Michael Deane discuss the morphogenetic field of our planet by stating how Earth received its field some 25 million years ago when the Halls of Amenti were first constructed. They describe how this pattern of energy/morphogenetic field had the appearance of a standing wave pattern, composed of fourth and fifth dimensional frequencies, and thus appearing as "blue" in color. This description is similar to Thoth's in the *Emerald Tablets* as well as that of Melchizedek in *The Ancient Secret of The Flower of Life: Volume 1*. The Deans describe the Halls of Amenti by saying; "Visually, this standing wave pattern looks like an electric blue flame with a pale shade of green, several inches in height. This "blue flame" is what constitutes Earth's morphogenetic field and it later became known as the "Staff of Amenti" which is the item referred to in the Bible as the "Staff of God," or the "Rod and the Staff." The "Rod" represents the standing wave pattern within Earth's core in dimensions 2, orange-gold in color, and composed of the frequency patterns of dimensions 1, 2 and 3. While the "Blue Flame" or "Staff of Amenti" is composed of frequency patterns of dimensions 4, 5 and 6. Human beings can ascend out of the incarnational cycles through the "Blue Flame" or fifth dimension and continue their evolution. So this Blue Flame represented as the Halls of Amenti is actually the key to our human lineage and the evolution of Earth.

Eckar Ana-Shay Deane and Michael Deane go on to describe how all forms are built upon unseen templates of light and sound called morphogenetic fields. These fields are composed of a set of electro-tonal standing wave patterns called "scalar waves" which are divided into grids and these planetary grids are what control the Interdimensional Stargates. They believe there were Geomantic Light-Code Seals (electromagnetic frequency seals) placed on them by the Ancient Priests of Ur and visiting Stellar Races. However, now is the time to begin releasing the Stargate seals which will prompt the opening of the Halls of Amenti. When a seal releases, its dormant standing scalar wave patterns come to life in the planetary shields. And since we are all connected to the planetary electromagnetic field, this release will correspond to the wave patterns of our bodies. Awakening the dormant wave patterns within the human body begins activation of the higher chakra centers, the *KA* and dormant DNA codes. We haven't been able to access this aspect of our being because an ancient soul group called the "Keepers of the Eternal Flame" was appointed by the Priests of Ur as Guardians of the Amenti Stargate Seals. This particular soul group reincarnates on Earth during time periods when the Stargates can be opened. Some believe the period between 2000-2017 is the first time the Stargates will fully open in over 200,000 years. The U.S. Government is aware of this time frame which is why now more than ever, they are seeking to locate this Stargate in order to harness its abilities.

Physicists have speculated that a Stargate may in fact be the only hope for intelligent life by allowing an escape into Hyperspace.

Hyperspace

Hyperspace is defined as space that has four or more dimensions. It is a space where the laws of physics are circumvented allowing "faster-than-light" travel or "time travel." In his book *Hyperspace: A Scientific Odyssey*, theoretical physicist Dr. Michio Kaku describes Hyperspace by other names to include; the "Kaluza-Klein" theory, "Super Gravity," and "Superstring Theory," which he believes can predict the actual number of dimensions within the Universe. Sound fictional? Think again. In a previous chapter I stated how there is often more truth in science-fiction than we are led to believe. As such, science-fiction is actually science-fact. In his book, Kaku illustrates this by mentioning how Nobel Prize winner Isidore I. Rabi admonished science-fiction writers for having done more to communicate the romance of science than physicists overall. Nobel Prize winner Steven Weinberg also stated that theoretical physics seems to be more like science-fiction.

For many years physicists have entertained the idea of time travel via "wormholes" linking different areas of space and time. Physicists at the California Institute of Technology have even proposed the possibility of building a time machine consisting of a wormhole that would support this theory. Hyperspace travel via higher dimensions is now being addressed in research laboratories around the world. The Institute for Advanced Study at Princeton is now one of the active centers of research on higher-dimensional space-time. Physicists now believe these higher dimensions may actually be the decisive step in creating a comprehensive theory that unites the laws of nature. In fact, cosmologists are even suggesting the possibility of parallel universes which are interlinked by these very wormholes. For centuries, Mystics and Philosophers have speculated about the existence of other universes and tunnels between them. It is only in recent times that science has begun to consider the possibility of parallel dimensions. Today, this type of thinking is no longer fictional. Such things as Stargates, wormholes, and time travel have all become legitimate fields of scientific research. Twenty-two years ago, physicist Kip Thorne along with his collaborators at the California Institute of Technology suggested that time-travel was not only possible but also probable under certain conditions.

In his theory on Hyperspace, Dr. Michio Kaku explains how prior to the Big Bang, our cosmos was actually a perfect ten-dimensional Universe, a world where interdimensional travel was in fact possible. However, this ten-dimensional Universe "cracked" in two, creating two separate universes: one consisting of four dimensions and another consisting of six. He says the Universe in which we now live, is the result of that cosmic cataclysm. According to Kaku, if this theory is correct, "It demonstrates that the rapid expansion of the Universe was just a rather minor aftershock of a much greater cataclysmic event, the cracking of space and time itself." This theory would imply that there are in fact other dimensions in which we have yet to experience. The problem with trying to understand this theory is that we lack the mathematical formulas and the technology necessary to prove it. According to this hypothesis, Dr. Kaku asserts that the manifold of ordinary three-dimensional space is curved in four or more "higher" spatial dimensions in which this curvature causes certain widely separated points in three-dimensional space to be run parallel to each other four-dimensionally. He believes by creating an opening in fourth dimensional space via a "wormhole," that this will allow instantaneous transit between the two locations. He uses the analogy of a folded piece of paper, where a hole punched through two folded sections is more direct than a line drawn between them on the sheet. Unfortunately, in the scientific world if it can't be proven mathematically, then it's nothing more than speculation or an unscientific hypothesis. Be that as it may, we know beyond the physical dimensions lie other facets of the Universe just waiting to be realized. Unfortunately, how can we prove the existence of something without the proper means of science? We're trying to substantiate a dimensional reality beyond that of the 3rd dimension without any higher forms of technology. We lack understanding when it comes to anything unsupported by our physical senses. In this regard, how can we become aware of a reality undetected by human faculties? The vibrations and frequencies on which these parallel dimensions and realties exist far exceed anything we are capable of sensing or becoming aware of. And for this reason, we relegate any possibility of their existence to science-fiction and we're only able to experience these types of realities in movies like; *Star Wars*, *Star Trek*, *Contact* or *Stargate Atlantis*.

Hypothetically, in order for a ship to enter Hyperspace, it would have to utilize "warp" speed which means it would have to travel faster than the speed of light. And since light travels roughly at 186,000 miles per second or 671 million miles per hour, anything traveling faster than this would definitely alter time. Often times in the movies whenever "warp" speed is engaged, the stars outside the vessel appear to be streams of light. Under normal circumstances, nothing travels faster than the speed of light. But, according to Dr. Kaku, Hyperspace actually utilizes another dimension to "sidestep," as it were, the light "speed limit." While others theorize that it phases matter directly into another Universe similar to "other-space" or "subspace," thus gaining superlight speeds. Upon entering this phase of travel, the vessel would then leave conventional existence, or "real-space" rendering conventional notions of velocity irrelevant because the speed of light in Hyperspace is not a barrier as it is in real space. Once the starship reaches the point in Hyperspace that corresponds to its destination in real space, it simply re-emerges.

One of the reasons why science will not support the existence of Hyperspace is because of the gravitational force or "G-force" which causes stresses and strains on an object during high speed travel. Because of these strains, large G-forces may be destructive to the human body. Again Dr. Kaku explains how Hyperspace is actually an alternate state of existence used by starships to achieve "faster-than-light" travel. He says it is a phenomenon not completely understood by scientists; and that it was alternately described as a parallel Universe, an extra dimension of space, an alternate mode of physical existence, or simply the Universe as viewed traveling faster than the speed of light. Under normal circumstances the idea of intelligent beings traversing the galaxies traveling hundreds, sometimes thousands of light years to get to Earth would seem incomprehensible, however Hyperspace would allow a starship to breach other dimensions where it can cover vast distances in an amount of time greatly reduced from the time it would take in "normal" space. This would circumvent the enormous amount of time it would take to get from galaxy to galaxy. So in reality, we're not talking about high speed travel at all but rather a crossing over into different dimensions via a breach in the fabric that separates time and space? This would be like the "rabbit hole" in *Alice and Wonderland* which would serve as a gateway into a very different reality.

If the theory of 10 dimensions postulated by Dr. Kaku is in fact precise, then there has to be other dimensions in which to experience. The question is; when and how will we be able to do this? What has to happen first is that we must broaden our scope of understanding to allow for a less conventional view. What may seem like fiction today will some day become commonplace. But we have to be courageous enough to let go of our conventional wisdom in order to foster a new paradigm of science. All technology at one time or another challenged the status quo but it wasn't until we were receptive enough to accept new ideas that we were able to forge ahead into the technological era that we're experiencing today. Many of the inventions of our time were met by criticisms and extreme resistance in the realms of religion and science. However, it wasn't long before society began to embrace change which allowed for the modern age to flourish. Where would we be technologically if we never accepted the theories of Newton or Einstein or even quantum mechanics simply because they seemed fictional or too far fetched? Everything we've been taught in the schools and throughout life has served as a barrier to change and any new forms of thought. It was Einstein who said education served as his greatest hindrance. Our greatest hindrance is our inability to stretch the imagination because we rely far too heavily only on what can be proven scientifically. Beyond the realm of science everything is simply imaginary or fictional. Until we let go of such rigid ways of thinking, technology will continue to grow at a "snail's pace." As long as we're resistant to ideas such as "time-travel" "wormholes" "hyperspace" and the like, we will forever be stagnated in our future growth. Although; "When the final chapter in this long saga is written by future historians of science, they may well record that the crucial breakthrough was the defeat of common-sense theories of three or four dimensions and the victory of the theory of Hyperspace."—Dr. Michio Kaku.

Antimatter

In October 1955 the *New York Times* reported: *"New Atom Particle Found; Termed a Negative Proton."* Practically thirty years prior to this, science fiction writers latched on to the concept of anti-worlds and anti-universes based on the work of theoretical physicist Paul Dirac. These writers postulated the possibility of using "antimatter" to power space vehicles beyond the speed of light. Although since then, antimatter has been relegated to the collective consciousness as only a fictional concept. However, based on recent breakthroughs in physics, antimatter could in theory power not only spacecraft but also our world in general.

So what exactly is this elusive antimatter and how did it come into being? Well, in order to understand antimatter, we first have to know what matter is. Matter, as we know, is the building blocks for every physical thing in existence. Anything you can touch is made up of matter including the human body. This matter itself is comprised of even smaller stuff which we call particles. The best example of this would be to imagine a huge building consisting of several bricks organized into one massive structure. Upon looking at the building we only see its immense size but in reality the building itself is actually comprised of much smaller bricks or building blocks strategically placed in order to give the building its form. But, upon closer observation, we will find that the bricks themselves are actually comprised of even smaller building blocks called particles and these particles themselves consist of even smaller building blocks called atoms. These atoms themselves consist of even smaller things called; protons, neutrons and electrons. All matter is nothing more than a sophisticated structure of fundamental balls of electrically charged energy and although physicists knew this during the late 1920s, they still couldn't quite figure out how electrons actually functioned. That is until 1928 when Paul Dirac determined that there was something extremely unusual about the properties of the electron. What he discovered was that there was such a thing as "twin" particles where protons, neutrons and electrons have their opposites as anti-protons, anti-neutrons and anti-electrons. Although he didn't actually call it "antimatter," he called it an "anti-electron" and it was later referred to as a "positron" since they are positively charged atoms. Dirac interpreted this to mean that for every particle that exists there is a corresponding antiparticle, exactly matching the particle but with an opposite charge. For the electron, for instance, there should be an "anti-electron" identical in every way but with a positive electric charge. His theory was derived from the moment of singularity where an explosion simultaneously created matter and its counterpart antimatter.

Accordingly, somewhere between 13 and 15 billion years ago depending on who you ask, the physical Universe spawned into existence through a colossal surge of energy known as the "Big Bang." In that instant, matter was formed but it is also believed that matter's opposite also formed as a type of antimatter. To better understand matter's opposite, let's say you have a sheet of paper and you use a hole-puncher to stamp out little circles. These little circles become physical matter while the hole left behind becomes its counterpart or opposite. It's the invisible aspect or the reverse of its original state. They both exist only in opposite form, one as the physical hole and the other as the non-physical hole. They become mirror images of one another and they have such an affinity for one another that they virtually explode and annihilate each other upon contact producing a tremendous amount of energy. In particle physics, antimatter is the extension of the concept of the antiparticle to matter, where antimatter is composed of antiparticles in the same way that normal matter is composed of particles. Furthermore, mixing matter and antimatter in what is called "fission" would lead to the annihilation of both in the same way that mixing antiparticles and particles does, thus giving rise to high-energy photons (gamma rays) or other particle—antiparticle pairs. But this poses an anomaly because if one was created as a result of the other then there has to be an equal amount of each right? Well, according to theory, there must have been one more particle of matter at the time which prevented the total and complete annihilation of all matter by its counter-part antimatter.

So without that tiny surplus of matter there would be no stars, no planets, and no humans. The Universe would consist only of light in an empty space. Many scientists believe that this preponderance of matter over antimatter (known as baryon asymmetry) is the result of an imbalance in the production of matter and antimatter particles in the early Universe, in a process called *baryogenesis*. And it is for this reason alone that the physical Universe exists. Needless to say, the apparent irregularity of matter and antimatter in the Universe is still one of the greatest unsolved problems in physics.

But for arguments sake, let's say that antimatter was not completely annihilated by matter, then there's a great possibility for the existence of antimatter stars, antimatter planets and antimatter universes in far away galaxies of which our science is too limited to understand. Perhaps more advanced races have already learned to harness the secrets of antimatter which allows them to utilize such things as "Hyperspace" travel. I find this to be highly probable considering how far along they are on the space-time continuum. At the point where humanity is in terms of harnessing such a power, it would be safe to say that we have quite a long ways to go before we are able to understand how to properly produce such energy.

The production of antimatter energy is extremely costly. In fact, it is the most costly substance in existence, with an estimated cost of $25 billion per gram for positrons, and $62.5 trillion per gram for anti-hydrogen. This is because only a few antiprotons are produced in reactions in particle accelerators and because there is a much higher demand for other uses of particle accelerators. According to the European Organization for Nuclear Research (CERN), it costs a few hundred million Swiss Francs to produce about 1 billionth of a gram (the amount used so far for particle/antiparticle collisions). Although once antimatter energy is produced it doesn't take much to provide us with tremendous amounts of power.

Antimatter has tremendous energy potential, if it can be harnessed. In July of 2002, a solar flare created about a pound of antimatter, or half a kilo, according to new NASA-led research. That's enough to power the entire United States for two days. In 1905, Albert Einstein wrote down the famous equation $E=mc^2$ which says that mass (m), is a very concentrated form of energy. Based on this equation, if we could convert all of the energy contained in 1 kg of sugar, or 1 kg of water, or 1 kg of any anything, we would be able to drive a car for about 100,000 years non-stop. 1 kg corresponds to 25,000,000,000 kWh of energy; 1 gr would be enough to supply energy to a medium-sized town for a whole day. This is a known fact and scientist are very aware of this although to introduce this type of technology would cut into the profits of power conglomerates and oil tycoons whose only wish is to continue billing us for archaic forms of fuel. Presently, people like Al Gore and other lobbyists are preaching about "Global Warming" and "Climate Change" which is nothing more than a hoax to bilk the people of the world out of their hard earned money. They are selling us the idea of the planet heating up when in truth it is actually cooling down. As a means to an end, we will be forced to pay higher rates for fuel, electricity and eventually carbon tax for what they consider to be over-consumption. But, there are far more ways to harness energy than fossil fuels. Just to give you an idea, the reaction of 1 kg of antimatter alone with 1 kg of matter would produce the rough equivalent of 43 megatons of TNT. By comparison, Tsar Bomba, the largest nuclear weapon ever detonated, reacted an estimated yield of 50 megatons of TNT, which required the use of hundreds of kilograms of fissile material like Uranium and Plutonium.

Antimatter transforms all its mass into pure energy and it is for this reason that the use of antimatter fuel has been proposed as fuel for interplanetary travel and possibly even interstellar travel. Star Trek's "faster-than-light" science-fiction spaceships use antimatter power, but research projects have seriously begun to investigate how they can use antimatter fuel for real. Although antimatter sounds like the stuff of science fiction, it's also very real. Antimatter is created and annihilated in stars every single day. In fact; "Antimatter is around us each day, although there isn't very much of it," says Gerald Share of the Naval Research Laboratory, ". . . it is not something that can be found by itself in a jar on a table." I believe the only real problem would be manufacturing a vessel capable of utilizing antimatter as a fuel. But, since the energy density of antimatter is vastly higher than conventional fuels, the thrust to weight equation for such a craft would be very different from conventional spacecraft thus eliminating some of the concerns we discussed in the previous chapter on Hyperspace travel. With our current interaction with highly technical off-world beings, I believe this type of technology is already being made available to us. But, left to our own devices, this possibility wouldn't become a reality until far into the distant future as antimatter production is scarce, so scarce that it has only grown in minute stages since the discovery of the first antiproton in 1955. As it stands, the current antimatter production rate is between 1 and 10 nano-grams per year, and this is expected to increase to between 3 and 30 nano-grams per year by 2015 or 2020 with new superconducting linear accelerator facilities at CERN and Fermilab. Many researches claim these new accelerators will make it possible to obtain antimatter for just $25 million per gram as opposed to the current rate of $25 billion by optimizing the collision and collection parameters.

Be that as it may, antimatter which is the energy produced by colliding atoms, is a very real source of energy. The process of colliding atoms to produce energy is nothing new just look at the A-Bomb and the tremendous amount of energy it was able to produce. If science is able to harness this type of energy to create weapons of mass destruction (WMD) then why can't they utilize this same technology for powering our homes, our vehicles and our world in general? Truth is, they can and at some point we will be able to experience this form of clean energy but much like everything else, the powers that be first have to make money before introducing something like this to the general public. Antimatter, nano-technology, Stargates, intergalactic travel and all sorts of space-age technologies are available to us at this very moment but it has to be implemented in stages according to global control. This type of technology has been in existence for centuries only they've been concealed and hidden by certain individuals until the time is right. All of our sciences and modern day advances have all been practiced and used by ancient civilizations during more enlightened periods on Earth. It is only now during what we consider to be "modern times" that we are slowly being [re]introduced to these technologies. Antimatter will become the modern day fuel just as it has been for off-planet beings for millennia. It's just a matter of time before we begin to see automobiles, space-craft and industry powered by this phenomenal source of energy. Warp-speed is not too far off. Within the next twenty years or so we will begin to see more and more technology based on science fiction. Within the last ten years we've advanced more technologically than we have over the past thousand years. As we continue to receive more and more technology from extraterrestrial beings that have taken an interest in our development, we will gradually begin to increase our understanding of what is possible and what is not and what might seem like fantasy today, will some day become reality. Everyday, we move closer and closer to a "Jetson" like existence with our cars being able to communicate with us, and people being able to actually see the person on the other end of the phone or the computer. The future is not too far off people. In fact, the future is now!

Conclusion

In closing, I would like to draw your attention to what is called "The Secret Covenant of the Reptilians" which was written by an unknown author on www.librarising.com:

[An] illusion it will be, so large, so vast it will escape their perception. Those who will see it will be thought of as insane. [Matrix]

We will create separate fronts to prevent them from seeing the connection between us.

We will behave as if we are not connected to keep the illusion alive. Our goal will be accomplished one drop at a time so as to never bring suspicion upon ourselves. This will also prevent them from seeing the changes as they occur.

We will always stand above the relative field of their experience for we know the secrets of the absolute. [4th Dimension]

We will work together always and will remain bound by blood and secrecy. Death will come to he who speaks. [Secret Societies]

We will keep their lifespan short and their minds weak while pretending to do the opposite. [Population Control]

We will use our knowledge of science and technology in subtle ways so they will never see what is happening. [Radio, Television, E.L.F.]

We will use soft metals, aging accelerators and sedatives in food and water, also in the air. [Fluoride/Aspartame]

They will be blanketed by poisons everywhere they turn. [Chemtrails]

The soft metals will cause them to lose their minds. We will promise to find a cure from our many fronts, yet we will feed them more poison. [Pharmaceuticals]

The poisons will be absorbed trough their skin and mouths, they will destroy their minds and reproductive systems. [Sterilization]

From all this, their children will be born dead, and we will conceal this information.

The poisons will be hidden in everything that surrounds them, in what they drink, eat, breathe and wear. [Chemical Warfare]

We must be ingenious in dispensing the poisons for they can see far.

We will teach them that the poisons are good, with fun images and musical tones.

Those they look up to will help. We will enlist them to push our poisons.

They will see our products being used in film and will grow accustomed to them and will never know their true effect. [Subliminal Messaging]

When they give birth, we will inject poisons into the blood of their children and convince them it's for their help. [Vaccines]

We will start early on, when their minds are young, we will target their children with what children love most, sweet things.

When their teeth decay we will fill them with metals that will kill their mind and steal their future. [Mercury]

When their ability to learn has been affected, we will create medicine that will make them sicker and cause other diseases for which we will create yet more medicine. [Prescription Drugs]

We will render them docile and weak before us by our power.

They will grow depressed, slow and obese, and when they come to us for help, we will give them more poison. [Anti-depressants]

We will focus their attention toward money and material goods so they may never connect with their inner self. We will distract them with fornication, external pleasures and games so they may never be one with the oneness of it all.

Their minds will belong to us and they will do as we say. If they refuse we shall find ways to implement mind-altering technology into their lives. [Mind Control]

We will use fear as our weapon. [Terrorism]

We will establish their governments and establish opposites within. We will own both sides.

We will always hide our objective but carry out our plan. [Shadow Government]

They will perform the labor for us and we shall prosper from their toil. [Slavery]

Our families will never mix with theirs. Our blood must be pure always, for it is the way. [Ruling Elite]

We will make them kill each other when it suits us. [Wars]

We will keep them separated from the oneness by dogma and religion. [Divide and Conquer]

We will control all aspects of their lives and tell them what to think and how. [Education and the Media]

We will guide them kindly and gently letting them think they are guiding themselves. [Covert Control]

We will foment animosity between them through our factions.

When a light shall shine among them, we shall extinguish it by ridicule, or death, whichever suits us best. [Assassination]

We will make them rip each other's hearts apart and kill their own children.

We will accomplish this by using hate as our ally, anger as our friend.

The hate will blind them totally, and never shall they see that from their conflicts we emerge as their rulers. They will be busy killing each other.

They will bathe in their own blood and kill their neighbors for as long as we see fit. [Ritualistic Offerings]

We will benefit greatly from this, for they will not see us, for they cannot see us.

We will continue to prosper from their wars and their deaths. [Blood Sacrifice]

We shall repeat this over and over until our ultimate goal is accomplished.

We will continue to make them live in fear and anger through images and sounds. [Holographic Matrix]

We will use all the tools we have to accomplish this. The tools will be provided by their labor.

We will make them hate themselves and their neighbors.

We will always hide the divine truth from them, that we are all One. This they must never know! [Religion]

They must never know that color is an illusion and they must always think they are not equal.

Drop by drop, drop by drop we will advance our goal. [Global Agenda]

We will take over their land, resources and wealth to exercise total control over them. [NAFTA, NAU, EU]

We will deceive them into accepting laws that will steal the little freedom they will have. [Patriot Act]

We will establish a money system that will imprison them forever, keeping them and their children in debt. [Federal Reserve System]

When they shall ban together, we shall accuse them of crimes and present a different story to the world for we shall own the media. [Slander]

We will use our media to control the flow of information and their sentiment in our favor. [Time Warner, CNN, NBC, CBS, ABC]

When they shall rise up against us we will crush them like insects, for they are less than that. [NATO]

They will be helpless to do anything for they will have no weapons. [Gun Control]

We will recruit some of their own to carry out our plans, we will promise them eternal life, but eternal life they will never have for they are not of us.

The recruits will be called "initiates" and will be indoctrinated to believe false rites of passage to higher realms. Members of these groups will think they are one with us never knowing the truth. They must never learn this truth for they will turn against us. [Masonic Order]

For their work they will be rewarded with earthly things and great titles, but never will they become immortal and join us, never will they receive the light and travel the stars. [Illuminati]

They will never reach the higher realms, for the killing of their own kind will prevent passage to the realm of enlightenment. This they will never know.

The truth will be hidden in their face, so close they will not be able to focus on it until it's too late. [Hidden Agenda]

Oh yes, so grand the illusion of freedom will be, that they will never know they are our slaves. [Mental Prison]

When all is in place, the reality we will have created for them will own them. This reality will be their prison. They will live in self-delusion.

When our goal is accomplished a new era of domination will begin. [New World Order]

Their minds will be bound by their beliefs, the beliefs we have established from time immemorial. [Doctrines/Dogmas]

But if they ever find out they are our equal, we shall perish then. THIS THEY MUST NEVER KNOW!

If they ever find out that together they can vanquish us, they will take action. [Mass Consciousness]

They must never, ever find out what we have done, for if they do, we shall have no place to run, for it will be easy to see who we are once the veil has fallen. Our actions will have revealed who we are and they will hunt us down and no person shall give us shelter. [Reckoning]

This is the secret covenant by which we shall live the rest of our present and future lives, for this reality will transcend many generations and life spans.

This covenant is sealed by blood, our blood; we the ones who from heaven to Earth came. [Annunaki]

This covenant must NEVER, EVER be known to exist. It must NEVER, EVER be written or spoken of for if it is, the consciousness it will spawn will release the fury of the PRIME CREATOR upon us and we shall be cast to the depths from whence we came and remain there until the end of time itself.

This is exactly what I've been trying to say throughout this entire book. I've presented various concepts and ideals that require us to "*think outside the box.*" The problem with many of us is that we're too afraid to venture outside the confines of traditional thinking for fear of being labeled weird or crazy. The mental constructs that are in place have served to keep us comfortably within our conformed ways of thinking. Traditional science, academia, the media, religion, culture, our parents, societies and many other forms that shape the way we think, have all served as deterrents to true consciousness and spiritual liberation. We are pure consciousness having an experience in what we call reality. Anything outside of this understanding is only part of the illusion and contrary to the truth. Everything we've been taught and programmed to believe has been cleverly designed to keep us confined to the mental aspects of being rather than the vastness of pure consciousness. As a result; what we know as truth has only been a distortion of facts presented to us by the real controllers of knowledge.

Since birth, most of us have been conditioned to believe in a false reality. This false reality is much like the matrix presented in the hit movie *The Matrix Trilogy*. It is nothing more than an electrical construct or prison designed to keep us from venturing out beyond the borders of an imposed reality. Anything outside of this manipulated version of reality is deemed fantasy and relegated to the areas of sheer imagination. In movies like *Star Wars*, *Star Trek*, *They Live*, *Avatar*, *The Matrix* and countless others, there seems to be a tremendous amount truth of which we are unwilling to accept as factual. This is the program design. Once we begin to question the way things are, the Universe will begin to nurture us into a broader perspective and the veils of mistruth will fall away. This new found vision allows us to see an entirely different reality; one where holograms are no longer reality but rather images projected onto our mental projectors. The whole truth is that, we've been lied to. We've been misled into believing in our limitedness when we are actually limitless beings experiencing this reality as infinite consciousness . . . nothing more. Everything else is merely false programming.

In this book, I attempt to shed light on much of what I consider to be the truth but as I stated earlier, "Truth-or pieces of truth revealed to any one of us are part of a larger mosaic, and thus it is up to each of us to arrive at our own conclusions concerning the truth that others have to share with us." It is not my job to try to convince anyone of what the truth is. We each have to discover the truth for ourselves. I can however, offer you new ways of viewing yourself but it is up to you to decide what is true for you. I'm only a means of expression, a messenger so-to-speak who is willing enough to speak the truth in spite of being labeled crazy or a conspiracy theorist both of which happen to be confirmation that I'm not plugged into the Matrix.

I've covered many topics in this book ranging from Hermetic Wisdom, Egyptian gods and religious archetypes, Ascended Masters, Extraterrestrials, to truth about a global cabal of Illuminati bloodlines seeking to form a fascist one world government. Although you may not agree with much of what I've postulated here, I'm almost certain that you've found most of this material interesting if not enlightening, in which case my job is done. The words utilized here are only meant to convey a message. They are only symbols of expression designed to awaken the dormant aspects of your being. Since we are all encoded with truth, we recognize it when we hear it. It seems to resonate with that which we already know but have never connected with. All truth is encoded in our human DNA it just needs to be reactivated by the vibration of these words or symbols. When that which is truth is uttered, consciousness receives it unto itself and a certain recognition takes place on the cellular level. When we hear or read information that we know to be true, even though we don't know how it is we know what we know, a certain thing happens. We think of what is being read as being "deep," which is exactly where it penetrates us . . . deep in the nucleus of our cells which is where all truth resides. Words alone don't have power, but rather it is the vibratory frequency of words that allows our spiritual selves to decode these vibrations into viable information.

There are those among us who would seek to deprive us of this knowledge. As such, they set up institutions to serve as barriers against human evolution. These institutions only serve to keep us docile and enslaved to the mainstream computer. Once we begin to wake-up and realize that everything we've been led to believe has all been distorted, we can finally begin to re-educate ourselves into what is real; not real according to the status quo, but real according to divine truth. Chances are, since you're reading this book, then you are already aware of the truths that I speak for were it not so; you wouldn't have attracted it into your awareness. Nothing comes to us until we're ready, it's a universal law; when the student is ready the teacher will appear. I can only lead you to the door of the Oracle but it is up to you to decide to go in. As a light-worker, this book is my attempt to shed light on what I believe to be true. It is my way of disseminating information to help enlighten the masses. So in the words of Neo from the *Matrix* I say to those that would seek to keep us enslaved, asleep, docile, indoctrinated, uninformed, unconscious and fearful: *". . . I'm going to show these people what you don't want them to see. I'm going to show them a world without you . . . a world without rules and controls, without borders . . . a world where anything is possible. Where we go from there is a choice I leave to you."* . . . . Namaste—Dr. Peter

Glossary

Akashic Record—Universal filing system. It has all knowledge, life records of all souls that have spent lifetimes in physical creation. It is an account of each event that occurred during all moments of every lifetime.

Alchemy—The science of understanding, deconstructing, and reconstructing matter, although it is often seen only as the pursuit of turning common metals into gold.

All That Is—This is a term used in place of "God" or the "Creator," because it includes the observer as part of the Creator.

Antimatter—The concept where antimatter is composed of antiparticles in the same way that normal matter is composed of particles.

Annunaki—Extraterrestrial astronauts of the planet Nibiru sent to Earth to mine for gold in Africa some 300,000 years ago.

Archetype—Model or first form; the original pattern after which a thing is made, or to which it corresponds.

Ascended Master—One who has succeeded in unifying the physical body with the light body; thereby transcending limitations of space, time, disease, aging and death.

Ascension—The process of raising the frequencies of the physical body so as to merge with its higher dimensional counterpart, the light body, thus transcending the ordinary limitations of a third dimensional body.

Astral Plane—The world of the planetary spheres, crossed by the soul in its astral body on the way to being born and after death, and generally said to be populated by angels, spirits or other immaterial beings.

Atlantis—A continent hosting an advanced race of humans that sank 12,000-13,000 years ago as a result of warring between the original Atlanteans and visiting off-planet beings utilizing misguided technology.

Atman—The Essential Self, the divinity within. It is the individualized aspect of Brahman.

Atom—The basic unit of ordinary matter, made up of a tiny nucleus (consisting of protons and neutrons) surrounded by orbiting electrons.

Avatar—Decent or reincarnation of the same soul in a different body, a human incarnation of the Divine.

Bilderberg Group—A Secret Government group founded by Prince Bernard of the Netherlands during WWII to help carry out the global agenda for the New World Order.

Blessing—An ancient verbal thought code offered to release the charged potential upon an emotion or event.

Brahman—The unified Consciousness of pure being that permeates the Universe. The term could be used interchangeably with God.

Central Race—Creators of all human races, planets and stars in the Universe.

CFR—Council on Foreign Relations, part of the Secret Government consisting of high-ranking officials, politicians and heads of states.

Chakra—Literally, "wheel" in Sanskrit. The *"Kundalini"* energy flows through these seven centers of energy along the spine, maintaining the life force of the body. When the chakras are dormant, one lives in separation consciousness, but when they are fully activated, one becomes enlightened.

Channeling—The process of receiving communication from an infinite number of dimensional realities through writing, verbal relay, artwork, music composition or any other form of creative expression.

Charge—A strong feeling as to the right, wrong or appropriateness of an outcome. It is the electrical potential surrounding an expectation, act or situation.

Christ Consciousness Grid—Higher octave of the planetary grid, holding the morphogenetic fields for a fourth dimensional, spiritually awakened planet.

Compassion—Thought without attachment to the outcome, feeling without the distortion of an individual's life bias and emotion without the charge of polarity.

Consciousness—The underlying binding force of all creation. It exists in infinite manifestations that defy definition.

Cosmic Mind—The all pervading intelligence of the Universe.

Cosmic Law—A Universal set of laws and principles that maintains order and governs all celestial bodies both great and small.

Cosmology—The study of the Universe as a whole.

Dimensions—A measure of vibrational frequency, or density. The third dimension is a level of extreme vibrational density and a duality between "good" and "evil."

DNA—Is the abbreviation for Deoxyribonucleic Acid which is a compound found in chromosomes and consists of a long chain molecule comprising many repeated and varied combinations of four nucleotides, one of which is the sugar deoxyribose; subdivisions of the molecule are believed to be the genes. It is the major repository of genetic information.

Draconians—Oldest reptilian hybrid race created by the Carians that are believed to feed off human children.

Duality—A correspondence between apparently two different parts or opposites. The term "dualism" was originally coined to denote co-eternal binary opposition.

Ego—The "I" or self as distinguished from the selves of others. It is the part of the psyche that is conscious in physical reality and acts as the mediator between inner and outer worlds.

Electromagnetic Force—The force that arises between particles with an electric charge; the second strongest of the four fundamental forces.

Electron—A particle with negative electric charge that orbits the nucleus of an atom.

Elohim—Chief inter-dimensional creator beings.

Enki—In Sumerian, Enki means "Lord of Earth" and is considered to be the one who imparts the knowledge of civilization to mankind. He was the god of wisdom and knowledge.

Enlightenment—A state of consciousness where the self, or ego, is recognized to be an illusion. When the self dissolves, a new identity emerges which is the "Higher Self."

Enlil—In Sumerian means "Lord of the Air" and was considered to be the chief of all lands. The Sumerians considered him to be supreme. He was the half brother and rival of Enki with each one claiming to be the firstborn or ruling deity.

Entrainment—The alignment of forces, or fields of energy, to allow maximum transfer of information or communication.

Etheric—Pertains to an environment that is not based on physical reality but still contains form. Many ideas or thought forms in the etheric may become manifest in the physical world.

Felines—Earth human ancestors from the Lyran Constellation and the first parent races in this Universe.

Final Frontier—The void that exists beyond any celestial body including the Earth.

Flower of Life—The modern name given to a geometrical figure composed of multiple evenly-spaced, overlapping circles. They are arranged to form a flower-like pattern with a six-fold symmetry, similar to a hexagon. The center of each circle is on the circumference of six surrounding circles of the same diameter.

Frequency—Frequency is the rate at which matter or consciousness vibrates. Matter is vibrating energy. Different vibratory rates denote the properties of matter.

Genetic Code—The set of rules by which information encoded in genetic material (DNA or mRNA sequences) is translated into proteins (amino acid sequences) by living cells.

Global Elite—A network of secret societies run by a race of interbreeding bloodlines originating in the Middle and Near East in the ancient world. They consist of The Illuminati, Round Table, Council on Foreign Relations (CFR), Trilateral Commission (TC), Bilderberg Group (BG), International Monetary Fund (IMF), United Nations (UN), Royal Institute of International Affairs (RIIA), or Chatham House, Federal Reserve, the media, military, science and religion. Just to name a few.

Global Mind—The morphogenetic field of a unified planet.

God—The matrix of intelligence underlying all creation and the vibratory template that represents all possibilities which expresses itself as both masculine and feminine expression.

Halls of Amenti—Our local Star Gate.

Hathor—An Ancient Egyptian goddess who personified the principles of love, motherhood and joy. This was also a race of beings from Venus with extremely advanced technologies that utilized sound vibrations to help build monoliths.

Hermetic Wisdom—This is the wisdom of Hermes the Greek incarnation of Thoth according to the Kybalion.

Hollow Earth—Earth along with other planets, has a hollow core and inner sun, resulting from its centrifugal motion as gases cooled and lava began to solidify. Civilizations exist within inner Earth, which can be accessed through openings at the North and South Poles.

Homo sapiens—The single surviving species of human evolutionary development, or modern man, belonging to the genus *"Homo"* and the primate family Hominidae.

Horus—Depicted as the Falcon god who was the patron deity of Nekhen in Upper Egypt and who is the first known national god. He was the son of Isis and Osiris. He served many functions in the Egyptian pantheon, most notably being the god of the Sky, god of War and god of Protection. He also served as the prototype for many of the savior god figures to include Jesus the Christ.

Human—The Earth human who is a subset of the larger humanoid family of the Lyran parent race.

Humanoid—Anyone of Lyran descent.

Hybrid—Anything derived from heterogeneous sources or composed of elements of different or incongruous kinds.

Hyper Space—Higher dimensional areas of space and time.

Illuminati—A secret group of members claiming to possess superior enlightenment and dominion over the Earth which controls the direction of the world from the lower 4th dimension. They are considered to be genetic hybrids which are the result of interbreeding between reptilians and humans many thousands of years ago that are still seeking to keep humans from their natural evolutionary processes.

Incarnate—The process whereby a soul will embody itself in a physical vehicle in a separate density such as the third or fourth. Upon incarnation, there is a memory loss of the greater identity of an individual consciousness.

Inner Earth Sun—This is a radiant Sun in the center of the Earth that serves as a source of light and warmth for civilizations on the inner surface of Earth.

Inner Guru—The concept of each person possessing a higher aspect of the self which serves as a guide or inner teacher for that individual.

Inner Technology—The intricate bio-electrical system of energy, waves, frequencies and vibrations that comprises the spiritual aspects of the multidimensional human being.

Isis—Wife/Sister of Osiris, sister of Nephthys, and mother of Horus. She is the goddess of immense magical powers and the archetypal maternal figure. She was the original virgin mother and the third member of the Trinity.

Jesus Christ—Mythological figure that serves as the foundational belief of Christianity but is actually based on the Sun or "Creator" and "Giver of Life" as it travels throughout the 12 zodiacal houses or constellations. This figure was derived from pagan Sun worship and previous deities all having the same attributes and characteristics.

Karma—The law of Universal action, which states that we reap what we sow. It is the means whereby a soul gathers experience through its journey of existence.

Kundalini—The life force energy that runs through channels or nadis, in the spine, known as the *"ida," "pingala,"* and *"sushumna."* It passes through the seven chakras, or centers in the body as it rises from its dormant position at the bottom of the spine up to the crown of the head, where it meets the descending cosmic energies activated by the *"deeksha,"* resulting in enlightenment.

Lemuria—A continent hosting a fourth dimensional civilization in an age prior to and also concurrent to Atlantis, which sank under the ocean tens of thousands of years ago. Remnants of the Lemurians are believed to still exist in certain underground locations one of which is *"Telos"* underneath Mount Shasta in Northern California.

Light Worker—An individual who has elected to share light and wisdom as a result of an awakening or spiritual enlightenment in an effort to help raise planetary awareness.

Logos—A highly evolved consciousness ensouling a planet (planetary logos), sun (solar logos), galaxy (galactic logos), or Universe (Universal logos).

Lyrans—Creators of Earth people from the Lyran Constellation.

Ma'at—The Ancient Egyptian concept of truth, balance, order, law, morality, and justice. She regulated the stars, seasons, and the actions of both mortals and the deities, who set the order of the Universe from chaos at the moment of creation.

Macrocosm—A large-scale model of a smaller unit. An example is the solar system representing the structure of atomic particles.

Maldek—A hypothetical planet posited to once have existed between the orbits of Mars and Jupiter whose destruction supposedly led to the formation of the asteroid belt.

Mass Consciousness—The singular identity of a group.

Matrix—A collection of grids, appearing as stacked upon one another which provide a structure for the gradual transition of energy-information from one zone of parameters to another.

Magnetosphere—A protective magnetic field around the Earth, generated by the spin velocity, and containing the "mind-field" of the planet, like the aura of the human body.

Merkabah—(*Mer* = Light, *Ka* = Spirit, *Ba* = Body) Also known as the "light body" or "vehicle of light," that holds the sacred geometries of higher dimensional consciousness.

Microcosm—Anything regarded as a world in miniature.

Maitreya—According to Ascended Master Teachings, Maitreya holds the position of World Teacher and Planetary Buddha or Cosmic Christ in their concept of a Spiritual Hierarchy.

Merovingians—French royal bloodline comprising the 13 ruling families, kingships, secret societies and many of the U.S. presidents, heads of states, bankers and politicians.

Multidimensional—Possessing many different dimensions.

Multiverse—All Universes together.

Nadis—The channels in the spine, and also throughout the body, which carry the "*Kundalini*" energy.

Neutron—An uncharged particle, very similar to the proton, which accounts for roughly half the particles in an atomic nucleus.

New World Order—"Global Dictatorship," A world with one central government, a central bank, a world army and one ruling elite class governing the masses.

Nibiru—12th planet of our solar system and home of Enki and brother Enlil. Nibiru is inhabited by a highly advanced race of beings commonly referred to as the Nephilim/Nefilim with a subservient group called the Annunaki. Nibiru orbits Earth every 3,600 years traveling between the Sirius System and the Solar System.

Octave—Is the integration of levels. It is a realm of existence that consciousness will move into after integrating the other densities.

Omniverse—Consists of our matter Universe as well as its anti-matter counterpart Universe and the 12 densities.

Osiris—One of the principle Egyptian gods of Osirian or extraterrestrial origins and son of Ra the Sun god. He is depicted as the prototype for many of the savior figures to include Jesus. At times, Horus and Osiris were interchangeable.

Over-lighting—The process whereby a high initiate may take over the incarnational stream of a lesser initiate for a specific period of time.

Oversoul—The Master identity that oversees its many subdivisions in many realities.

Panspermia—The hypothesis that life exists throughout the Universe and was distributed to various planets for seeding and evolutionary processes.

Photon—A quantum of light.

Photon Belt—Earths encounter with a band of high frequency photons every 13,000 years which results in either a cataclysmic destruction or a spiritual rebirth, or both.

Planetary Grid—A geometrical field around the Earth comprising the chakras and meridians of the Earth as a living body.

Platonic Solid—The surface delineating a very special, fully enclosed volume usually having the dimensions of each side equal.
Pleiadians—A race of beings that exists on the 5th and 7th levels of interdimensional reality. They serve as the Father principle of Earth Humans.

Polarity—The presence or manifestation of two opposites or contrasting principles or tendencies.

Polar Shift—Can be either a geographical pole shift, a magnetic pole shift or both which takes place every 13,000 years and is associated with cataclysmic changes on the Earth's surface.

Prana—The life-force energy equivalent to *"chi"* or *"mana."*

Precessional Year—The seeming movement of the constellations in the sky relative to us, based on the tilt of the Earths axis. The astrological world ages are computed according to a 26,000 year cycle.

Proton—A positively charged particle, very similar to the neutron, that accounts for roughly half the particles in the nucleus of most atoms.

Quanta—The vibratory patterns of light or *"pulsed waves"* created by discrete bursts of energy.

Ra—Ancient Egyptian Sun god and father to Isis, Osiris, Seth and Nephthys.

Reptilians—Highly technically advanced offspring of the Carians that are far less emotional than Humans with an advanced knowledge of Universal physics and laws. They represent the "dark" side of polarity while humans represent the" light."

Resonance—An exchange of energy between two or more systems of energy.

Sacred Geometry—The understanding of symbolic and sacred meanings and how they are ascribed to certain geometric shapes, and geometric proportions.

Sanat Kumara—Regent Lord of the World. Ascended Master and ancient teacher of light from Venus. Leader of the Orion Humans and head of the Christos Beings. Has assisted Earth and humanity for millions of years. One of the Seven holy Kumaras.

Satanic Grid—A grid composed of dissonant astral thought-forms and frequencies, which when linked with the chakras and meridians of the Earth, keeps it imprisoned in the third dimension.

Schumann Resonance—The "base frequency" of the Earth, measured at 7.83 hertz, or cycles per second which is rising towards 13 hertz which is the frequency of Ascension.

Seeding—The distribution and placement of biological and genetic materials on a given planetary surface.

Self—When this word is lowercase, it is the ego: an illusory center of identity, which is based in the concept of separation, of existence apart from the whole. When this word is uppercase, it usually refers to the *"Atman"* or Higher Self.

Set—The Egyptian god of chaotic forces and violence and prototype for the Christian *Satan*.

Shamballa—Secret city known as the "Hidden Kingdom," believed to be somewhere in the Himalayan mountains.

Shift of the Ages—The collective translation of our planet into an Age of Light, marked by higher vibrational fourth or fifth dimensional frequencies.

Sirians—4th and 5th dimensional beings that mostly exists in the light realms. They also ruled Egypt and the Roman Empire among other civilizations. They possess the most advanced technology in the Universe.

Soul—Also known as *"Atman," "Higher Self," "Antaryamin,"* or Essence which is the center of identity based in unity consciousness. It is a flow of consciousness revealed as the basis of human identity once the illusory self has been dissolved.

Soul Braiding—The merging of two souls or two parallel aspects of the same soul within one incarnation.

Stargate—An interdimensional "portal" or "wormhole," in the form of a device within the Universe that allows practical, rapid transfers of energy and information between two distant locations.

Starseeds—Galactic beings on Earth from Arcturus, Orion, Pleiades, Sirius and other distant galaxies.

Star Tetrahedron—The simplest of five regular polyhedral compounds.

Sumerians—One of Earths oldest civilizations located in southern Mesopotamia (Iraq/Iran). They were a non-Semitic people of unknown origin. Their foundation for civilization was given to them by the "DIN.GIR"—pure ones of the bright-pointed objects or "people of the fiery rockets"—or, extraterrestrials.

Telosians—Inhabitants believed to be living in the inner Earth beneath Mount Shasta in Northern California.

The Great Brotherhood of Light—A secret organization of enlightened mystics, and Ascended Masters, guiding the spiritual development of the Human race.

Thought—Energy of scalar potential which is the directional seed of an expression that can materialize as a real or vector event. It is the guidance system for where the energy of our attention may be directed.

Trilateral Commission—Secret Government committee not elected by the people from America, Europe and Japan.

Trinity—The doctrine which states that God is the Triune God, existing as three persons, but one being which was derived from ancient times rather than Christianity.

Universe—Ours is the 6th of 10 Universes which is a 21 trillion year old hologram. Our Universe has 6 sub planes (subdivisions), all below the astral plane while the astral plane itself has 150 sub planes, usually referred to as dimensions or densities. There are approximately 9 million different life forms in our Universe at this time. There are literally hundreds of thousands of races and sub races in the Universe. The Felines and Carians created the Reptilians and Humans in their image, thus becoming the first parent races in this Universe. Humans are the youngest of 4 primary races that were first created by the Felines on a planet in the Vega Star System of the Lyra Constellation.

Venus—Inhabited by 5th dimensional beings of which Sanat Kumara and Lady Venus are the hierarchy. It is considered to be the most advanced spiritual planet in the Universe. It is the base of the Christos Beings. Venusians are very highly evolved and they are considered to be one entire period of evolution in advance of Earth. It consists of two different life forms; one is physical and the other etheric.

Vesica Piscis—As two perfect spheres overlap one another by half, with each containing half the diameter of the other, a zone of commonality is created.

Walk-In—A soul exchange program performed by mutual agreement in which an incoming soul takes over a physical incarnation in place of the departing soul.

Zero Point—A shift associated with the raising of Earth's base frequency to 13 hertz, or the point of ascension and the collapsing of Earth's magnetic fields.

References and Suggested Reading

Abegg, Jr. Martin, Peter Flint, Eugene Ulrich 2002
The Dead Sea Scrolls Bible: The Oldest Known Bible Translated for the First Time into English [Publisher Unknown]

Adler, Margot 1979
Drawing down the Moon: Witches, Druids, Goddess-worshippers and Other Pagans in America Today, Beacon Press, MA

Albrecht, Katherine EdD., Liz McIntyre 2005
Spychips: How Major Corporations and Government Plan to Track Your Every Move with RFID, Nelson Current, Nashville TN

Aristotle
Metaphysics Book V Part 1 and *Posterior Analytics*, Book 2, Part 11. [Publisher and Publication date unknown]

Baigent, Michael, Richard Leigh, Henry Lincoln 1986
The Messianic Legacy, Delta Trade Paperbacks, NY

Barnhart, Daniel MFA. 2005
Reincarnation, University of Metaphysical Sciences, Arcata CA

Beckwith, Dr. Michael 2000
40 Day Mind Fast Soul Feast, Agape Publishing, CA

Blavatsky, Helena 1888
The Secret Doctrine, Theosophical University Press

Blessings, William L. 2008
Inner Earth People and Outer Space People, Inner Light Publications, NJ

Boulay, R.A. 1997
Flying Serpents and Dragons: The Story of Mankind's Reptilian Past, The Book Tree, CA

Braden, Gregg 1997
Walking Between The Worlds: The Science of Compassion, and *Awakening to Zero Point: The Collective Initiation*, Radio Bookstore Press, WA, *Fractal Time* (2009), Hay House, Inc, *The Divine Matrix* (2007), Hay House, Inc *The God Code* (2004), Hay House, Inc. *The Isaiah Effect* (2000), Three Rivers Press, NY

Bramley, William 1990
The Gods of Eden, Avon Books, NY

Brennan, J. H. 1996
Astral Doorways, Thoth Publications

Burns, Dr. Cathy 1998
Masonic and Occult Symbols Illustrated, Sharing Publishing PA

Bushby, Tony 2001
The Bible Fraud, The Pacific Blue Group, Inc. Hong Kong

Byrne, Rhonda 2006
The Secret, Beyond Words Publishing, OR

Bryson, Christopher 2004
The Fluoride Deception, Seven Stories Press, New York, NY

Callaghan, Teri MS, MFT 2005
UFO's & Extraterrestrial Intelligence, University of Metaphysical Sciences, CA

Campbell, Patrick 1965
The Mythical Jesus, Waverly Publications, NZ

Cannon, Dolores 1992
Jesus and the Essenes, Ozark Mountain Publishing, AR

Carey, Ken 1988
Return of the Bird Tribes, Harper Collins Publishers, NY

Carlson, Peter 2004
Ike and the Alien Ambassadors [Publisher Unknown]

Carrington, Dave 2000
Date Set For Desert Earth [Publisher Unknown]

Cayce, Edgar Evans 1968
Edgar Cayce on Atlantis, Warner Books Inc. NY

Chaline, Eric 2003
The Book of Zen: The Path to Inner Peace, Barron's Educational Series

Cockburn, Alexander [Publication date unknown]
Gem War: The US Record, Counter Punch, Petrolia CA.

Coelho, Paulo 1993
The Alchemist, Harper Collins, New York, NY

Collier, Robert 1926
The Secret of the Ages, Robert Collier Publishing, Inc, NY

Connell, R. W. 1995
Masculinities, Cambridge, Polity Press; Sydney, Allen & Unwin; Berkeley, University of California Press.

Cooper, J.C. 1978
An Illustrated Encyclopaedia of Traditional Symbols, Thames & Hudson Ltd London

Cooper, William 1991
Behold A Pale Horse, Light Technology Publishing, AZ

Crème, Benjamin 1980
The Reappearance of the Christ and the Masters of the Wisdom [Publisher Unknown]

Crowther, Patricia 1974
Witch Blood! The Diary of a Witch High Priestess! House of Collectibles, NY

Cunningham, Scott 1988
Wicca: A Guide for the Solitary Practitioner, Llewellyn Publications

B. Hunley and D. Cook 1996
Are you in your right mind? [Publisher Unknown]

Dale, Cyndi 2009
The Subtle Body: An Encyclopedia of Your Energetic Anatomy, Sounds True Inc. CO

Dalrymple, G.B. 1991
The Age of the Earth, Stanford University Press, CA

Dawkins, Richard 2006
The God Delusion [Publisher Unknown]

De Long, Douglas 2000
The Ancient Teachings for Beginners, Llewellyn Publications, MN

Derohan, Ceanne 1995
The Land Of Pan: *The Loss of Power and Magic On Earth, Original Cause: The Reflection Lost Will Has To Give* and *Original Cause: The Unseen Role of Denial* Four Winds Publications, NM.

Doane, Thomas William 1883
Bible Myths and Their Parallels in Other Religions, Published by Bouton, republished in 2009 by General Books.

Doherty, Earl 1999
The Jesus Puzzle: Did Christianity Begin With A Mythical Christ? Canadian Humanist Publication

Doreal, Dr. M., Ms.D. Psy.D 2002
The Emerald Tablets of Thoth-The Atlantean, Dog Ear Publishing, IN

Dougherty, Sarah B. 1979
"Thoughts in a Divine Mind," (Sunrise Magazine, Theosophical University Press)

Drosnin, Michael 1997
The Bible Code, Touchstone, NY

Dumoulin, Heinrich 2005
Zen Buddhism: A History Volume 1, India and China [Publisher Unknown]

Eisler, Riane 1988
The Chalice & The Blade: Our History, Our Future, Harper & Row, CA

Eker, T. Harv 2005
Secrets of the Millionaire Mind, Harper Collins Publisher Inc, NY

Epperson, A. Ralph 1985
The Unseen Hand: An Introduction to the Conspiratorial View of History, Publius Press, Tucson, AZ

Essene, Virginia, Sheldon Nidle 1994
You Are Becoming a Galactic Human, S.E.E. Publishing Company, CA

Farrar, Janet and Stewart Farrar 1989
The Witches' God: Lord of the Dance and Eight Sabbats for Witches (1992), London: Hale

Farrar, Janet; and Gavin Bone 2004
Progressive Witchcraft: Spirituality, Mysteries, and Training in Modern Wicca: New Age Books, NJ.

Ferguson, V.S. 1995
Inanna Returns, Dar Publishing Company, WA

Ferro, Robert and Michael Grumley 1970
Atlantis: the Autobiography of a Search [Publisher Unknown]

Frissell, Bob 2001
You Are A Spiritual Being Having A Human Experience, Something In This Book Is True . . . (1997) and *Nothing In This Book Is True, But It's Exactly How Things Are* (1994), Frog Ltd. CA

Freer, Neil 2000
Breaking the Godspell: The Politics of Our Evolution, The Book Tree, CA

Gallagher, Ann-Marie 2005
The Wicca Bible: the Definitive Guide to Magic and the Craft, Sterling Publishing, NY

Gardner, Gerald B 1988
The Meaning of Witchcraft, Copple House Books, GA and *Witchcraft Today* (1999), Mercury Publishing, NC

Gardner, Laurence 2002
Bloodline of the Holy Grail: The Hidden Lineage of Jesus Revealed, Element Books, London

Garrett, Stephanie 1992
Gender [Publisher Unknown]

Gawain, Shakti, and Laurel King 1998

Living In the Light: A Guide to Personal and Planetary Transformation, Nataraj Publishing, CA

Grabhorn, Lynn 1992
Beyond The Twelve Steps: Roadmap to a New Life. Hampton Roads Publishing, VA

Graham, Lloyd M. 1975
Deceptions and Myths of The Bible, A Citadel Press Book Published by Carol Communications, NY.

Gray, John 1992
Men Are from Mars, Women Are from Venus, Harper Collins, UK

Greenberg, Gary 2000
101 Myths of the Bible: How Ancient Scribes Invented Biblical History, Sourcebooks Inc., IL.

Haanell, Charles F. 1912
The Master Key System, Republished in 2006, *Master Key Arcana* (2004), Kallisti Publishing, Wilkes-Barre PA, *Mental Chemistry* (1922), *The New Psychology* (1924)

Hagensick, Cher-El. L
The Origin of the Trinity: from Paganism to Constantine [Publisher and Publication date unknown]

Hand Clow, Barbara 1995
The Pleiadian Agenda: A New Cosmology for the Age of Light, and *Catastrophobia: The Truth behind Earth Changes In the Coming Age of Light* (2001), Bear & Company Publishing, NM and *Alchemy of Nine Dimensions: The 2011/2012 Prophecies and Nine Dimensions of Consciousness* (revised and expanded edition), with Gerry Clow (2010) Hampton Roads Publishing, Inc. VA

Hancock, Graham 1995
Fingerprints of the Gods, Crown Trade Paperbacks, NY

Harrington, Daniel J. 1996
Wisdom Texts of Qumran, London Rutledge

Harrow, Judy 1985
Exegesis on the Rede Harvest [Publisher Unknown]

Hawking, Stephen 1988
A Brief History of Time, Bantam Books, NY

Henry, Todd J. *2006*
The One Hundred Nearest Star Systems [Publisher Unknown]

Henry, William 2003
Cloak of the Illuminati, Adventures Unlimited, IL

Heselton, Philip 2001
Wiccan Roots: Gerald Gardner and the Modern Witchcraft Revival. [Publisher Unknown]

Hicks, Esther and Jerry 2004
Ask and It Is Given: Learning to Manifest Your Desires, Hay House *The Vortex: Where the Law of Attraction Assembles All Cooperative Relationships,* (2009) Hay House

Hill, Napoleon 1960
Think & Grow Rich, Random House Publishing, NY

Hochheimer, Alex H
The Philadelphia Experiment from A-Z [Publisher and Publication date unknown]

Holmes, Ernest 1982
How to Change Your Life, Health Communications, Inc. FL

Hutton, Ronald, 2001
The Triumph of the Moon—A History of Modern Pagan Witchcraft [Publisher Unknown]

Hyena, Hank 1999
Pleiadian Warning: Evil Lizards and Sex Slaves! [Publisher Unknown]

Icke, David 1995
. . . And the Truth Shall Set You Free, The Biggest Secret (1999), *Children of The Matrix* (2001), *The David Icke Guide to the Global Conspiracy (and how to end it)* (2007), *Truth Vibrations* (1994), *The Robot's Rebellion* (1994), *Human Race Get Off Your Knees: The Lion Sleeps No More* (2010), David Icke Books. UK,

Irwin, William 2002
The Matrix and Philosophy: Welcome to the Desert of the Real, Open Court, IL

Jho, Zoev 1993
E.T. 101: THE COSMIC INSTRUCTION MANUAL, Intergalactic Council Publishing, Inc. CO.

Johnson, Raynor 1953
The Imprisoned Splendour: An Approach to Reality, Based Upon the Significance of Data Drawn from the Fields of Natural Science, Psychical Research and Mystical Experience, Hodder & Stoughton, London

Kaku, Dr. Michio 1995
Hyperspace: A Scientific Odyssey through Parallel Universes, Time Warps and the 10th Dimension, and *Parallel Worlds: A Journey Through Creation, Higher Dimensions and the Future of the Cosmos* (2006) Anchor Books, New York

Kay, Tom 1997
When the Comet Runs: Prophecies for the New Millennium, Hampton Roads Publishing Co. VA

Keyes, Ken Jr. 1975
Handbook to Higher Consciousness, Living Love Center

Laszlo, Ervin 2007
Science and the Akashic Field: An Integral Theory of Everything, Inner Traditions, VT

Leedom, Tim C. 2007
The Book Your Church Doesn't Want You to Read, Cambridge House Press, New York

Lembke, Karl 2002
The Threefold Law [Publisher Unknown]

Lipton, Bruce H. Ph.D 2005
The Biology of Belief, Hay House, NY

Lovecock, James E. 2000
Gaia: A New Look at Life on Earth [Publisher Unknown]

Mackey, Albert G. 2004
The Symbolism of Freemasonry, Cornerstone Book Publishers, LA

Manitara, Olivier
The Essenes: From Jesus to Our Time [Publisher and Publication date unknown]

Marciniak, Barbara 1995
EARTH: Pleiadian Keys To the Living Library and *Bringers of the Dawn: Teachings from the Pleiadians* (1992), Bear & Company Publishing, NM

Massey, Gerald [Publication date unknown]
The Historical Jesus and the Mythical Christ, Health Research

Maynard, Sharon 1995
The Ancient Ones: The Mission Remembered, Lemon Tree Press, WA

McKinsey, Dennis 1995
The Encyclopedia of Biblica Errancy, Prometheus Books, New York

McTaggart, Lynne 2008
The Field: The Quest for the Secret Force of the Universe, Harper Collins Publishers, NY

Mead, G.R.S. 1919
The Doctrine of the Subtle Body in Western Tradition [Publisher Unknown]

Melchizedek, Drunvalo 2000
The Ancient Secret of the Flower of Life: Volume 1&2, *Living In The Heart* (2003), Light Technology Publishing, AZ and *Serpent of Light: Beyond 2012*, (2007) Weiser Books, CA

Moosbrugger, Guido
And Still They Fly [Publisher and Publication date unknown]

Montgomery, Ruth 1976
The World Before and *Strangers among Us* (1979), Fawcett Crest, NY

Muhammad, Elijah 1965
Message to the Blackman in America, Secretarius MEMPS Ministries, AZ

Mulford, Prentice 1889
Thoughts are Thing, Republished in (2007) by Barnes & Noble, New York *The God in You,* (2007) Wilder Publication, VA

Nga Tama a Rangi 1849
Wī Maihi Te Rangikāheke [Publisher Unknown]

Narcotics Anonymous 1982
Basic Text, Narcotics Anonymous World Services, CA

Ousely, Rev. Gideon
The Gospel of the Holy Twelve [Publisher and Publication date unknown]

Paramahansa, Yogananda 1946
Autobiography of a Yogi, Self Realization Fellowship, CA

Pinkham, Mark Amaru 1997
The Return of the Serpents of Wisdom, Adventures Unlimited Press, IL

Piper, Otto A. 1958
The Book of Mysteries [Publisher Unknown]

Prophet, Elizabeth Clare with Patricia R. Spadaro and Murray L. Steinman 1997
KABBALAH: Key to Your Inner Power, Summit Publications Inc., MT

Redfield, James, and Carol Adrienne 1996
The Tenth Insight: Holding the Vision, an Experiential Guide, Warner Books, NY

Remsburg, John E 1909
The Christ: A Critical Review and Analysis of the Evidence of His Existence, The Truth Seeker Company, New York

Roberts, Jane 1995
The Seth Material, Buccaneer Books

Robbins, Dianne1996
TELOS: The Call Goes Out from the Hollow Earth and the Underground Cities, Spirit Passage Publishing, NM

Robinson, Lytle 1972
Edgar Cayce's Story of the Origin and Destiny of Man, Berkley Books, NY

Rogers, Dr. Peter C. D.D., Ph.D. 2009
Ultimate Truth: Book I, AuthorHouse Publishing, Bloomington, IN

Royal, Lyssa, Keith Priest 1989
The Prism of Lyra: An Exploration of Human Galactic Heritage, Royal Priest Research Press, AZ

Ruiz, Don Miguel 1997
The Four Agreements, Amber-Allen Publishing, CA

S, Acharya 1999
The Christ Conspiracy: The Greatest Story Ever Sold. Adventures Unlimited Press, IL

Schellhorn, G. Cope 1989
Extraterrestrials in Biblical Prophecy, Horus House Press, Inc. WI

Schlemmer, Phyllis V. 1993
The Only Planet of Choice: Essential Briefings from Deep Space, Gateway Books, Bath

Sharer, Robert J. 2006
The Ancient Maya [Publisher Unknown]

Sitchin, Zecharia 1990
> *Genesis Revisited,* Avon Books, NY, *The 12ᵀʰ Planet* (1976), *The Cosmic Code* (1998), Harper Collins, NY, *When Time Began* (1993), *The End of Days* (2007) and *The Lost Book of Enki* (2002), Bear & Company, VT

Sowa, John F.
> *Processes and Causality* [Publisher and Publication date unknown]

Spalding, Baird T 1964
> *Life and Teaching of the Masters of the Far East,* Devorss Publications, CA

Starbird, Margaret 1993
> *The Woman with the Alabaster Jar: Mary Magdalen and the Holy Grail,* Bear & Company, VT

Starr, Jelaila 1996
> *We Are the Nibiruans: Return of the 12ᵗʰ Planet; Book One and the Mission Remembered Book Two.* (2007), Published by the Nibiruan Council, KS

Stearn, William 1968
> *The Origin of the Male and Female Symbols of Biology* [Publisher Unknown]

Steiger, Brad and Sherry Hansen Steiger 1992
> *Star Born,* Berkley Books, NY

Steiner, Rudolf 1994
> *Theosophy: An Introduction to the Spiritual Processes in Human Life and In the Cosmos.* Anthroposophic Press, MA

Stone, Merlin 1976
> *When God Was a Woman,* Harvest/HBJ Books, NY

Swerdlow, Stewart A. 2002
BLUE BLOOD, TRUE BLOOD: Conflict & Creation, a Personal Story Expansions Publishing Company, Inc. MI. *The Healer's Handbook: A Journey into Hyperspace* (1999), Sky Books, NY and *Montauk: The Alien Connection* (2002)

Taylor, Richard P. 2000
Death and Afterlife: A Cultural Encyclopedia [Publisher Unknown]

Temple, Robert 1976
The Sirius Mystery, Destiny Books. VT

Three Initiates 1908
The Kybalion, Penguin Group, NY

Thurman, Robert A.F. 1994
The Tibetan Book of the Dead: Liberation through Understanding in the Between, Bantam Books, NY

Todeschi, Kevin J. 1998
Edgar Case on the Akashic Record, A.R.E. Press VA

Tolle, Eckhart 2005
A New Earth: Awakening To Your Life's Purpose. Penguin Group, NY, and *The Power of Now: A Guide to Spiritual Enlightenment.* New World Library, CA

Towne, Elizabeth 2007
Life Power and How to Use It, Wilder Publications, Radford VA

Trever, John C. 2003
The Dead Sea Scrolls [Publisher Unknown]

Trimarco, Genevieve, and Christene Breese, D.D., Ph.D 2005
World Religions; University of Metaphysical Sciences, CA

Valiente, Doreen 1973
An ABC of Witchcraft Past and Present, Hale.

Van Inwagen, Peter 1983
An Essay on Free Will, Oxford, Clarendon Press

Vanzant, Iyanla 1996
The Spirit of a Man: A Vision of Transformation for Black Men and the Women Who Love Them Harper Collins, NY

Velikovsky, Immanuel 1977
Peoples of The Sea, Doubleday & Company Inc. NY and *Worlds In Collision* (1950), Dell Publishing Co, Inc. NY

Von Daniken, Erich 1999
Chariots of the Gods, Berkley Books, NY and *History is Wrong* (2009) The Career Press, Inc. NJ

Waeber, Rolf 2005
An Overview of Extraterrestrial Races: Who is Who in the Greatest Game of History, Trafford Publishing, Canada

Walker, Brian Browne 1992
The I Ching or Book of Changes: A Guide to Life's Turning Points, St Martin's Press, NY

Walsch, Neale Donald 1995
Conversations with God: An Uncommon Dialogue, Book I, II, III G. P. Putnam's Sons New York

Wattles, D. Wallace 1910
The Science of Getting Rich [Publisher Unknown]

Wilde, Stuart 1996
Infinite Self: 33 Steps to Reclaiming Your Inner Power, *Whispering Winds of Change* (1993), *The Quickening* (1988), *The Art of Redemption* (2007), and *The Force* (1984), Hay House, CA

Williams, Paul 1973
  Das Energi, Entwhistle Books, CA

Williamson, George Hunt 1996
  Secret Places of the Lion, Destiny Books, VT

Windrider, Kiara 2002
  Doorway to Eternity: A Guide to Planetary Ascension.
  Heaven on Earth Project, CA and *DEEKSHA: The Fire from
  Heaven* (2006), Inner Ocean Publishing, HI

Websites:

http://www.enkispeaks.com
http://www.nibiruancouncil.com
http://www.paoweb.com
http://www.steelmarkonline.com
http://www.floweroflife.org
http://www.Jeddahmali.com
http://www.ascendedmaster.com
http://www.jeshua.net
http://www.earthrainbownetwork.com
http://ourstory-not-history.com
http://www.disclosureproject.org
http://www.thewatcherfiles.com
http://www.cosmologycorner.com
http://www.librarising.com
http://www.dontwatchthisfilm.com

Sources:

Good News Bible: Today's English Version
Bible: King James Version
Merriam-Webster Online Dictionary
Encyclopedia Britannica
Random House Unabridged Dictionary
Wikipedia-The On-Line Free Encyclopedia

Films/Documentaries:

Infinity: The Ultimate Trip Journey beyond Death, Sacred Mysteries Productions 2002

The Elegant Universe, WGBH Educational Foundation 2003

What The Bleep Do We Know? Captured Light Industries/Lord of the Wind Films 2004

America: Freedom or Fascism, produced by Aaron Russo/Richard Whitley 2006

How to Know God, by Deepak Chopra 2006

Conversations with God, Spiritual Cinema Circle 2006

The Secret, TS Production LLC 2006

Zeitgeist: Spirit of the Times, produced by Peter Joseph 2007

Zeitgeist: Addendum, produced by Peter Joseph 2007

The Seven Spiritual Laws of Success, by Deepak Chopra 2007

The Science of Miracles, Gregg Braden 2007

Pass it On, Produced by Scott Evans and Greg S. Reid 2007

Contact Has Begun: A True Story with James Gilliland, DCI Enterprise LLC 2007

Spirit Space: A Journey into Your Consciousness, WireWerks Films 2008

The fall of the Republic, produced by Alex Jones 2009

The Obama Deception, produced by Alex Jones 2009

Kymatica, produced by Benjamin and Daniel Stewart 2009

The Living Matrix, Becker Massey, LLC 2009

Invisible Empire, by Jason Bermas and Produced by Alex Jones 2010

End of Liberty, produced by Gerard Adams 2010